The
FINANCIAL TIMES
on
Management

The
FINANCIAL TIMES
on
Management
Grappling with Change
and Uncertainty

CHRISTOPHER LORENZ
and
NICHOLAS LESLIE

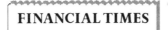

FINANCIAL TIMES

PITMAN PUBLISHING

To all our colleagues whose combined work has made this book possible

Pitman Publishing
128 Long Acre, London WC2E 9AN

A Division of Longman Group UK Limited

First published in 1992

© Christopher Lorenz and Nicholas Leslie, 1992

A CIP catalogue record for this book can be obtained from the British
Library.

ISBN 0 273 60006 0

Phototypeset in Linotron Times Roman
by Northern Phototypesetting Co. Ltd., Bolton
Printed and bound in Great Britain by
Biddles Ltd, Guildford and King's Lynn

CONTENTS

Part One

CHRISTOPHER LORENZ ON GRAPPLING WITH CHANGE AND UNCERTAINTY IN THE 1990s

Whoever desires constant success must change his conduct with the times

Niccolo Machiavelli, 1469–1527

Like potentates, politicians and civil servants, managers have always tended to complain about the accelerating pace of change. They have also deplored the rampant increase in uncertainty that often follows in its wake (though not always – change *can* sometimes be along entirely predictable lines).

Although unexpected change can be coped with, and even moulded, in various ways, there is a deep yearning within most of us for stability – or at least for predictability. The literature of most countries, and the folklore of many companies, is full of yearning for some past 'golden age' of calm and certainty.

Yet the reality is usually very different. Most social and economic historians would agree that periods of calm, predictability and certainty have been the exception rather than the rule, especially since the early 19th century. In the memory of the majority of people alive today, in most industrialised countries, it is only the quarter-century between 1946 and 1971 that could be described as calm and relatively certain – and then only in the fields of economics and business, with the 1960s the only really 'golden age'. In politics, the period was peppered by constant crises, wars in Korea, Vietnam and the Middle East, together with intermittent flare-ups in Eastern Europe. There was also the constant threat of nuclear conflagration, which came near to reality at least once, over the Cuba missiles crisis.

So it is not surprising that many people outside the business world belittle the widespread claims of business writers, gurus and consultants that things have never been so uncertain for companies and their managers as they are today.

Yet consider the realities of the business world since the late 1980s. As every month – almost every week – goes by, the landscape seems to change in some unexpected fashion. In politics, iron curtains and concrete walls come tumbling down, raising hopes of new business opportunities sky high – before they then recede into some uncertain future as one country after another is torn apart by strife, or hits economic problems that are even worse than expected. In areas of the world which seem cast-iron certainties for high and sustained economic growth, markets can prove surprisingly impenetrable to foreign companies – as they are finding to their cost in many Pacific Basin countries.

In economics, short-lived recessions turn all too easily into double-, or triple-, dip affairs, and even slumps whose ends are as unpredictable as the many false dawns which optimists detect along the way. Powerful countries which have always had low interest rates suddenly become afflicted, for political or other reasons, with mountainous public spending commitments. Their interest rates soar, cramping the ability of less mighty countries in their region to manage their own economies as they would have wished. Even in an era of tightly managed exchange rates, this can be a nightmare for the manager – as Britain's business leaders could be heard complaining loudly by the summer of 1992.

In the marketplace itself, consumers react to such changes in unpredictable ways, cutting their spending just when past experience (and the misguided forecasts of economic 'experts') lead the manager to expect it will rise. By the same token, sales of certain products can boom surprisingly in tough times: as was the case until well into the early 1990s with Anita Roddick's Body Shop lotions and potions. And whole categories of goods and services can become hotbeds of innovation – the food industry is an obvious example.

On the technological front, the speed and nature of change tends to be much more predictable than many managers realise. What is always uncertain is the relative ability of different companies to exploit it, and of consumers to embrace it. Japanese companies may be masters at the exploitation of technological change, but how many of them expected growing consumer resistance in the 1990s, even in gadget-mad Japan itself, to the needless increase in the complexity of many electronic products?

To one degree or another, all these external aspects of the business environment are ones over which only the mightiest company and its managers can hope to have much influence – the best the majority can do is observe outside events, analyse trends, and act (or react) as quickly and effectively as possible.

It is in the fields of corporate and business strategy, culture and structure, and all other aspects of organisation (including human relations) that the pace and direction of change has become so perplexing. All these fields are supposedly susceptible to managerial action, yet in unpredictable times they can be remarkably difficult to mould effectively. So, these days, can be one's own career. With organisations not only 'delayering' at an unprecedented rate, but also looking to subcontract (or 'outsource') more and more of their activities, it is hard for even the most successful managers to know whether their jobs will be part of their organisation's 'core' or its periphery a year or two from now – and therefore whether they will still be full-time employees. Hence, among other factors, the pressure among HR professionals and the more enlightened of their employers for managers constantly to learn new skills, and to take more control of their own continuing education and development.

It is the uncertainty in all these fields, external and internal, which has combined to produce an era which (to adulterate Harold Macmillan's famous phrase about the 1950s) really is worthy of the title 'You've never had it so uncertain'. Put more positively, it justifies the judgement that management has never been more demanding – nor more exciting – than it is in the 1990s. Not for nothing does one top European chief executive claim that 'modern management is one of the most challenging activities imaginable'.

Underlying the growing instability – and unsuitability – of so many companies' strategies and organisations is a set of much-discussed factors. Three are particularly significant: the globalisation of competition; the speed with which multinational companies now spread new technology, and new product and service concepts, from country to country; and (a closely associated trend), the ability of computer and communications technology to process vast amounts of information quickly and cheaply, and flash it to computer screens around the world.

In the United States and Britain, a further factor compressing managerial timescales is the pressure (actual or perceived) from stock markets for short term results. In the last few years this has increased, rather than eased, in spite of the attempts of a few financial institutions to foster a longer term view of major capital investment and research and development projects.

Tom Peters, the American guru who in the late 1980s popularised the phrase 'thriving on chaos', has now[1] coined the term 'Nanosecond Management' to describe the quick-response, fast-change strategies,

---

[1] See Tom Peters, *Liberation Management: Necessary Disorganization for the Nanosecond Nineties* (Knopf: 1992)

structures and processes which managers and their companies need to apply in today's ultra-competitive world.

In one sense, Peters' image is a highly appropriate one: the Boston Consulting Group, McKinsey & Company, the Harvard Business School and a few pioneering individuals – plus plenty of Japanese exemplars – have all taught managers aplenty since the late 1980s about the importance of 'competing against time': reducing the time it takes to accomplish every aspect of management from product and service development to manufacture, delivery and field service.

The readiness of companies to show much greater flexibility than in the past by changing their strategies or structures (or both) is illustrated repeatedly by those examined in this book. Obvious cases include the willingness of ICI to reorganise itself repeatedly, and then de-merge itself, and BP's dumping of its new chairman mainly on 'style' grounds barely two years after his taking office. Another example has been IBM's need (a more appropriate word than willingness) to make several attempts in quick succession to change not only its structure but – much more importantly – its culture.

The book dwells at particular length on IBM because the computer giant's recent experience epitomises so many of the book's central messages.

These are all drawn directly from a broad, international cross section of the managerial front line, almost in 'real time', just after the action has occurred (or has changed course yet again). This approach contrasts with that followed by so many books on management, which adopt an over-rationalised academic view of events several years or more after they have occurred.

One message, that the seeds of many companies' future failure are hidden in (and reinforced by) their current success, is found in IBM's precipitous fall from grace in the mid-1980s. The company's longstanding receipt of adulation reached its zenith in 1982 with its celebration by Tom Peters and Robert Waterman as a decidedly 'excellent' company. But by 1986 the culture of caution and centralisation which had bred IBM's organisational and strategic success in more stable times was clearly proving its undoing. Six years and two transformation attempts further on, the company's survival in anything like its present size and shape was still uncertain.

The reason for that is the book's second message: that corporate cultures are not only much more powerful than many managers realise, but also far harder to change. Only one of the three major cultural and organisational change processes examined in these pages, that of US General Electric, has unquestionably succeeded – and that after a full decade, the first half of which was truly traumatic for everyone in the company. The jury is still very much out on the other two companies, IBM and especially Philips.

One of the reasons for GE's ability to change successfully was that it – or, rather, its incoming chairman in 1981, Jack Welch – did not wait until the eleventh hour to recognise that its culture, though strong, was no longer appropriate to the changing business environment. Both IBM and Philips took far too long to come to the same conclusion about themselves, so their task became far harder.

Message three is the apparently paradoxical one arising from the work of the Boston Consulting Group et al, that even while the lengthy cycle of cultural change is under way, and far from complete, companies must start moving like lightning to respond to changes in their competitive and technological environment.[2]

This is not merely a matter of introducing just-in-time supply and manufacture, or of shortening the 'time-to-market' development cycle for new products and services. It is also a question of redefining markets and industries (as the Japanese have done so often in consumer electronics and elsewhere), of changing the whole logistics of an industry (as Canon did with copiers and Benetton with clothing), and of championing the globalisation of an industry (as Electrolux did with household appliances).

That ties in closely with message four: that 'Nanosecond Management', to repeat the Peters' phrase, is not just a responsive strategy of blowing with the wind as it changes direction but also a proactive one of moulding the environment before your competitors can (weaving ahead of the wind, if you like, or even redirecting it). Sony, Microsoft, Benetton and Body Shop are obvious examples of companies which have done just that.

The realisation that one's company or unit is not necessarily a helpless pawn of a mobile battery of hostile and unpredictable forces is the most important breakthrough that any manager can make in the strife and storm-torn 1990s. It helps one towards a series of vital islands of relative stability, on which one can construct one's future competitive success.

---

[2] Not for nothing does Professor Andrew Pettigrew, head of Warwick Business School's Centre For Corporate Strategy and Change, describe the change process as 'like juggling lots of balls in the air while the platform on which the juggler stands is moving all the time. Drop one of the balls, or forget to pick it up in the first place, and the effect will be critical'.

Hence messages five to twelve. If the first four were all about change, these provide a set of points on which to build. Some of them, though not all, are fixed.

The fifth may seem at first to be a cliché, but it is far more fundamental than that. It is that no manager, and no company, will survive for long – let alone prosper – by standing still. Instead, they must constantly update their skills, knowledge, attitudes and behaviour. This is not merely a matter of training, but of education and development in the fullest sense. Absolutely vital to this process is that, at and across all levels, the company becomes really open in its willingness to share information, and to absorb it from outside.

The modern manager and company must not only – in a set of newly-fashionable phrases – 'learn how to learn', or become 'learning organisations'. They must also be able to do what one school of Japanese academics calls 'unlearn the outdated lessons of the past'.

'Unlearning' is far from a grandiose way of saying that organisations must, like some misguided Western managers and companies, move on rapidly from one management fashion to the next, always dumping the previous one. One of the great Japanese 'secrets' of success is the way that they build layers of competitive advantage on each other, without expecting any individual one to provide a lasting key to competitive success. To cite just a few of the weapons they have mustered, in relatively quick succession have come low-cost competition, quality, product proliferation, just-in-time, and differentiation, flexibility and time compression on every dimension of management.

At the same time, many Japanese companies, and a few American and European ones, have found various ways of overcoming cultural barriers to change – which is an obviously crucial element of an organisation's 'learning' process. Sometimes they rely on putting entirely fresh people on a new project, rather than depend on experienced teams, sometimes they mix the two. But always, like Honda, 3M, and Hewlett-Packard, they promote an atmosphere of openness, self-questioning and change. They are not only what Richard Pascale of Stanford University calls 'engines of inquiry', but they translate that inquiry into cohesion and action.

They also – message six – rely, at almost all levels, on teams of people from different specialist disciplines, rather than on either individuals or single departments. This applies from the very top to the bottom of an organisation.

Just as closely associated with the idea of 'learning' is message seven:

that you must find those competitive strengths where you have something unique, relevant and potentially lasting to offer, and build on them as much as you can. Honda has done this with its engine technology, for instance, as has 3M with its adhesives, coatings and substrates.

This, in simple terms, is the doctrine of 'leveraging core competencies', popularised in particular by Professor C. K. Prahalad of Michigan University and Dr. Gary Hamel of London Business School (it has also been taken up by the Boston Consulting Group). It is a much more rigorous test than the conventional one of just assessing an organisation's 'strengths', regardless of the degree to which any of these actually provide a unique and sustainable competitive edge.

The core competence concept is having a powerful effect on the corporate world. In both Europe and the United States, companies are redefining and focusing their 'cores', investing more heavily in them, and exploiting them more. At the same time, they are disposing both of businesses and of activities in which they are not strong enough, or which are not sufficiently critical to their future.

Hence, in part, the early 1990s wave of divestments of past misguided diversification drives. As in the late 1980s, some companies are still prepared to sell businesses which, only a few months before, they were confused or cynical enough to dub 'core'. But this tendency is less common than it was. Hence also, in part, the fashion for 'outsourcing'.

In the degree of stability which it provides – always assuming that the organisation's analysis of its various competences is brutally accurate, rather than merely optimistic – the 'core competence' concept is a welcome antidote to the over-exposed idea that companies should aim, above all, to be 'chameleons' or even amoebae, which constantly change not only their colour but also their shape. This is an exaggerated interpretation of the very considerable need to be what consultants call 'change-based and adaptive' (see several of the messages above).

The need to defend, reinforce and leverage one's 'core competences' also provides (message eight) a very necessary counterbalance against the popular idea that, in order to share costs and gain access to technologies and markets, companies must be prepared to collaborate on almost every front. The notion of a 'boundary-less' company, making general or specific alliances with various of its competitors around the world, has considerable validity in certain industries, especially those which are particularly capital-intensive or fast moving, or both. But it has been overstated to a dangerous extent by many of its advocates, encouraging some companies unwittingly to give away (frequently for very little in return) valuable competences which their competitors certainly regard as 'core'.

In today's world of widely available capital, technology, and skills, alliance enthusiasts are obviously right that it is not just uneconomic, but dangerous, for a company to try to do everything itself, especially when markets are liable to sudden change. But this does not mean that companies can 'abandon fixed emplacements', and 'leave behind their skills of defence', as a report from Business International (*Building Flexible Companies*) claimed in 1991. Far from it.

Which brings us to message nine: the need to build what consultants and academics in the last few years have come to call 'organisational capability'.

A rather off-putting piece of jargon, this arose as a counterweight to the conventional wisdom of the 1970s and early 1980s, that a company's main weapon in the battle to create sustainable competitive advantage was so-called 'strategic capability'. After fifteen years or more of spending heavily on strategic analysis and advice, yet finding that new strategies often failed either to take root in the organisation or to work in the market place, everyone realised the obvious: that, in far too many cases, sophisticated strategies were being imposed on companies which did not possess the organisational ability to implement them. Hence the growing emphasis since the mid-1980s not only on the old chestnut of organisational structure, but also on informal organisation issues – especially culture.

At a pinch, the term 'organisational capability' can be taken to cover a host of issues and processes, many of which – in a company which still thinks in compartmentalised terms – would be considered as 'human relations' issues.

These include all the consequences of delayering: the need for companies to cease operating in time-honoured hierarchical fashion as they flatten their pyramids in order to cut costs, accelerate decision-making and become altogether more flexible and competitive.

Instead of a series of levels which 'command and control' the one immediately beneath them, power and responsibility on many issues must be delegated, decentralised and diffused. Trust must be established between bosses, peers and subordinates (to use conventional language – or 'colleagues', in the new). Individual effort within narrow departmental boundaries must be replaced by cross-functional teams. Instead of information being withheld at each successive level in the hierarchy, it must become shared – or, at least, accessible – through informal 'networking'.

All this implies fundamental changes in the way that leaders behave. Most notably, it requires them to change their own behaviour – on most, though not all, issues and occasions – from one of 'command and control' to one of empowerment, in which they really do allow their subordinates much more initiative and responsibility than in the past. A popular school of thought holds that the main responsibility of bosses nowadays is to provide essentially four things: vision; coaching; mentoring and support of their subordinates (or 'colleagues') in their everyday work; and development of leadership at all levels for the future. This is an extreme view; in today's testing times the leader must still intervene on a number of occasions to take tough decisions. Some of them may have to be unilateral, however much consultation has gone into them. But such top-level interventions must be very much the exception. If organisations really are to be able to become more flexible and sprightly, this means always taking decisions at the lowest level possible (the political principle of 'subsidiarity'). Wherever possible, top level interventions must be based, as in many Japanese companies, on two-way persuasion, not mere authority which derives from what academics call 'positional power'.

This can be a difficult enough process in a small, one-product company. It is infinitely harder in a large, diversified multinational which is trying to decentralise decision-making on various fronts as part of a process of what has become known as 'global localisation'. When, like Motorola, the American electronics multinational, a company starts talking of splitting global (not just regional) decision-making between half a dozen chief executives in various locations around the world, the process of taking decisions becomes very intricate indeed.

Motorola, along with General Electric, 3M and Hewlett-Packard, is one of just a handful of western multinationals which by their actions have managed to redefine 'excellence' from its early 1980s meaning of a collection of static attributes – which became rapidly out of line with the demands of the changing business environment.

Instead, such companies have recognised that excellence is all about learning and handling change. They have come to terms with the difficult realisation that the requisite balance between different criteria, such as control and entrepreneurship, direction and autonomy, centralisation and decentralisation, is always changing.

Everything comes back, it seems – message ten – to the principles of flexibility, 'ambiguity', and 'paradox' enunciated in the early 1980s by Peters and Waterman, but not fully developed by them and others until later in the decade.

The challenge which these principles represent for individual managers, and for the companies at which they work, has been expressed with admirable succinctness by Professor John Stopford of the London Business School.

Among a daunting list of other strategic and organisational requirements, he argues that companies need to learn how to reap the supposedly contradictory benefits of differentiation and low cost. They have to get the best out of co-ordination and decentralisation at the same time, in order to secure global integration while preserving national focus and responsiveness.

Companies also need to organise themselves to work in cross-functional teams, yet make some functions more international than others. As well as having to decide which activities to continue in-house, and which to either subcontract to suppliers or handle through alliances, successful global competitors need both strategic variety and geographic spread.

Managing the organisational ambiguity and complexity which all this involves is one of today's toughest challenges. Among other things, it makes it extraordinarily difficult for any company to try to 'parent' the sort of variety of businesses which many companies operated in the 1970s and 1980s. This is 'just not feasible', Stopford rightly warns. Hence much of the drive to divest many of the businesses which were acquired in the dangerous name of diversification.

Hence, also – message eleven – the importance of recognising that management style and 'organisational capability' must be just as much aspects of a company's core competences (see message seven) as are particular skills in strategy, marketing and technology.

In a sense – message twelve, and final – the principles of flexibility, ambiguity and paradox are intimately intertwined with the debate about corporate governance which gathered force on both sides of the Atlantic in 1992. In the UK there is a growing body of opinion, sparked especially by Professor Charles Handy, that a company will only prosper if it puts the interests of its customers and employees at least as high in its order of priorities as the more conventional objective of creating maximum shareholder value.

Handy's redefinition of corporate purpose – under the title of 'What is a Company For?' – has been decried in some quarters as intriguing yet insufficiently hard-edged. But in 1992 two Harvard professors produced a book[3] containing extensive empirical evidence that his case is indeed strong.

[3] John P. Kotter and James L. Heskett, *Corporate Culture and Performance* (Free Press: 1992)

Their prime conclusion, from a series of studies, was that a company will adapt appropriately to its environment – and, if possible, mould it – only if all its members really care deeply about, and pay constant attention to, what the academics call 'the three managerial constituencies': customers, stockholders and employees. As each constituency changes its preferences and priorities, the company anticipates or responds.

The Harvard pair puts the three constituences in a slightly different order from Professor Handy, but their message is essentially the same as his. And as powerful.

This introductory chapter has taken an intentionally mixed approach, combining the practical experience of companies, across a wide range of managerial issues, with a degree of theory which one hopes has not proved indigestible. The pages which follow are all very much down-to-earth, analysing events almost as they unfolded between 1990 and 1992, and setting them in context.

We chose to focus on nine broad subject headings. From the breadth and depth of coverage of the FT Management Page over that period, we could easily have trebled the number of chapters and articles – such is the output of one of the only Management Pages in the world's press which appears almost daily. But that would have produced a book which certainly would have been indigestible – the very antithesis of the FT Management Page. What follows is therefore a careful selection. It does not pretend to be comprehensive, merely to illuminate some of today's key management issues. To preserve the flavour of uncertainty and rapid change which pervades our times, updating has been kept to a minimum – as has post hoc rationalisation. Where events moved rapidly following publication of an initial article, or set of articles (as at IBM) this is self-evident.

What follows, we hope, is an entertaining, informative and stimulating picture of management changing times from where it matters – the sharp end.

London, Autumn 1992

Part Two

CORPORATE RENEWAL IN CHANGING TIMES

1 CRACKING THE CULTURAL MOULD

INTRODUCTION

Anyone with a reasonable knowledge of a company ought be able to provide a credible characterisation of its corporate culture. If asked to describe how it came by that culture and what were the most important influences, the task becomes very much harder. And if pressed to put together a programme to bring about a major cultural change, few are likely to be able to rise to the challenge.

Would that it were easier, because the significance of a company's culture to its well-being and its prospects for long-term survival has been highlighted time and again in recent years. It is significant not only to the achievement of success, but also to maintaining it. As a company grows and consolidates its position, its culture emerges more clearly. The quality of its products, its way of doing business, its innovatory strength, its flexibility, its ethical position, the personality of its chairman and/or chief executive – all combine to create the culture by which a company is identified.

Some of the strongest cultures tend to be identified with strong-minded, entrepreneurial individuals – Kenneth Olsen at Digital Equipment and Anita Roddick at Body Shop are examples. But that self-same culture can become a strait-jacket if it does not evolve. Olsen, founder and president of Digital, consolidated its culture and success around minicomputers and integrated computer systems. But shifts in technologies at a time of market slowdown left it living in the past and ill equipped to break out of its culture into a better future. Losses ensued, Olsen retired in disgruntled fashion, and the company was left struggling to confront the need to change the way it did business.

For Anita Roddick it was a different story, but the significance was similar. The company embraced environmental issues and the idea of 'natural' products, and steered clear of using any ingredients in its products that had been tested on animals. But this culture came under pressure when a more aware and informed world began to question the company's interpretation of its claims just at a time when its growth was being stepped up to expand its overseas markets. It confronted the problem, by essentially defending its culture, but acknowledging the need for more precision in explaining it.

Both of these are relatively new cultures, less entrenched and perhaps more easily modified to meet changing times. The more difficult challenge is to change those which have become entrenched over more than a generation. And this chapter therefore concentrates on just three examples of companies which became giants in their fields, but which eventually came to realise that they would have to change their culture if they were not to become stifled by it. They are General Electric, the large, highly diversified US group embracing aero-engine manufacture to financial services; Philips, the Dutch domestic, electrical and electronic products group; and International Business Machines. IBM, which the *Financial Times* has twice examined in recent years as it has struggled to confront a rapidly changing computer world, has been studied particularly comprehensively.

Martin Dickson's report on GE illustrates how even a company at the forefront of management thinking must sometimes crack its internal mould in order to change both its behaviour and its own employees' perceptions of their company. The chief actor here was Jack Welch, the charismatic Executive Chairman of GE. Welch is shown to be someone who feels that attitudes need to be changed constantly. His first strategy after taking over as chief executive in 1981 was to re-shape the group, slimming its management layers and selling businesses with the aim of making all parts of GE more global.

His more recent objective has been to achieve what so many of the biggest groups in both the US and UK have come to realise is necessary – greater flexibility and entrepreneurialism. Bureaucracy tends to grow in proportion to size and GE was no exception. Welch's plan was to break down the bureaucracy and thus the barriers that built up within and between components of the group. By encouraging more initiative at all levels, and greater communication across all parts of the group – for example, between scientists and product managers – he has sought to make the group boundaryless and able to bring new products to market more quickly.

Philips faced a similar prospect, but many would argue that it was far more hidebound by the traditions of its culture than most companies of comparable size. It had a paternalistic culture which rested on its past leadership of many of its markets, such as washing machines, audio equipment and lighting. It had a very large manufacturing base in the Netherlands and was exceedingly socially minded where its employees were concerned – redundancies being something that happened elsewhere.

Guy de Jonquieres describes Philips' awakening to the realities of its changing world and the enormous difficulty it faced in trying to change the attitudes among its employees.

IBM's problems, meanwhile, were definitely greater than it realised. Being so dominant in computers – its profits for years were bigger than the sales of its nearest rival – it woke up very late to the challenge that was being mounted to its pre-eminence. The *FT*'s first major look at IBM in early 1990 – by a team drawn from the east and west coast of America, as well as the UK and Japan – examined the threat that the computer giant faced and its plan to tackle the company's deeply conservative corporate culture. The core of the plan was to make IBM much more responsive to the needs of its customers.

The second visit to IBM was in late 1991 when the company, in the words of its chairman, John Akers, was setting out on a reorganisation that would lead to a 'fundamental redefinition of how IBM does business'. This was to break the group into independent, more accountable units which were to trade at arm's length with each other. Depending on performance, they might or might not be retained – or might be sold or made part of an alliance with another company.

The importance – and challenge – of trying to make such a shift in culture cannot be understated. For years IBM dictated the way business was done in the computer world, and its management and employees acted accordingly, believing IBM was correct and indomitable. Today, Big Blue, as it is often known, has come to realise that such an insular culture is out-dated and that it must now create something much more flexible, more entrepreneurial and more customer driven.

WHY GE ENCOURAGES LESE-MAJESTE

By Martin Dickson

First published 5 October 1990

Can this be for real? Some junior executive has just had the temerity to give Jack Welch a piece of advice on how to do his job better. And as chairman of General Electric, Welch is one of the most powerful and influential businessmen in the United States.

The advice was pretty cheeky, too. It was delivered after this junior executive went on one of the courses Welch addresses at GE's campus-like management training school in Crotonville, New York state. Welch helicopters in every few weeks from his headquarters in nearby Connecticut to give the troops his vision of the company's future.

Afterwards, the students fill in a questionnaire on their boss's performance. Though enthusing about Welch's message, our junior executive went on to advise his chairman that he could save company money if only he cared to walk the 200 yards from his helicopter to the centre, rather than tying up a chauffeur-driven car.

Although perhaps delivered tongue-in-cheek, it is the kind of lese-majeste which would have many company chairmen shaking with anger. But Welch seems to be delighted, for it is just this kind of constructive criticism that he is trying to encourage at GE. The aim, he says, is to create an atmosphere where 'it's acceptable to speak out, where telling the truth is rewarded and where bosses who yell at people for speaking up are not'.

The incident underlines a remarkable experiment in management techniques taking place at GE, one of the biggest and most diversified manufacturing companies in the US, with interests ranging from aircraft engine manufacturing to financial services.

Welch's goal is extremely ambitious: to inject right down the line the attitudes of a small, fast-moving entrepreneurial business and continuously to improve GE's productivity, so that it remains competitive in the intense global market place of the 1990s.

This means a frontal assault on bureaucracy, a vice to which Americans seem particularly prone. But it goes far beyond this in seeking much greater involvement of the group's workforce and customers in the way the business is run. Welch calls this process 'work-out'.

The experiment has a wider importance, for GE – founded over 100 years ago by Thomas Edison – has a long tradition of leading the US in new management techniques. In the 1950s, for example, it introduced the idea of separate profit centres, while in the 1960s and 1970s it set a trend (now reversed) of hiring legions of strategic planners.

Work-out is already having an influence elsewhere. For example, in the UK, British Petroleum is using elements of the scheme in its great management restructuring.

The company has already undergone one revolution, which radically changed its shape, since Welch took over as chief executive in 1981. He was a surprise choice to head the group, since he was only in his mid-40s and had a reputation for unorthodox ideas, albeit some which had proved very successful in building up GE's plastics business.

The maverick image was reinforced as he set about a wholesale reorganisation of a company which critics suggested did not need mending. He got rid of management layers. He scrapped his predecessor's division of the group into 350 strategic units. He sold businesses representing 25 per cent of GE's sales – ranging from the manufacture of semi-conductors, through houseware to mining – and cut more than 100,000 jobs through disposals, attrition and lay-offs.

But he also bought companies, notably RCA, bringing with it new defence electronics businesses and the NBC television network. He bought Kidder Peabody, the Wall Street securities house, a takeover which went sour almost immediately when one of its star deal-makers was accused of insider trading and the firm began to haemorrhage talent.

The aim of this controversial whirl of activity, says Welch, was to make sure that all GE's businesses were global in scope and either first or second in their sectors. 'When you hit a down draught and you're number four in a market, you get pneumonia,' he says. 'If you're one or two you get a little sniffle.' Being first or second in a market fulfils one of Welch's criteria for creating the 'ultimate' strong company. The other is to 'integrate diversity' – in other words, get ideas and people flowing across corporate boundaries, making the whole a great deal more than the sum of the parts.

'An integrated, diversified company can be a power-house, should be a power-house, if it is number one or two in its businesses and the integration is real,' he says, arguing that such a group offers investors less risk and greater consistency than single sector ones, since cyclical upturns in one part will offset downturns elsewhere.

Parts of this sound rather like a replay of the apologias put forward in the 1960s and 1970s to justify the creation of conglomerates, many of which were broken up again in the 1980s when fashion changed.

But Welch argues that a crucial difference between GE and a conglomerate is the degree of cross-fertilisation taking place between the group's divisions. Certainly, the company is putting immense effort into removing barriers both vertically – up and down the line – and horizontally – across divisions.

Integration involves exchanges of both people and ideas. Top executives are moved freely from one GE business to another where Welch thinks their particular mix of talents and experience will be useful. For example, the former head of GE Capital, the financial arm, was put in charge of NBC, while a new head for GE turbines has been plucked out of the aircraft engines division. Welch hopes that seven or so engineers will be 'stolen' from the aircraft side to give turbines a boost.

Exchanges of ideas take place at many levels and with varying degrees of formality. The most senior forum is the corporate executive council, which brings together the heads of GE's 14 businesses and a few top staff each quarter to swop views. Each individual business has its own miniversion of this institution.

Meanwhile, some 5,000 employees a year attend sessions at the Crotonville Management Development Institute – a long-time GE feature which had a lot of money spent on it in the 1980s. There they are exposed to new ideas in best business practices.

But exchanging information extends far beyond class-room theories. For example, scientists at the company's large research centre at Schenectady, in New York state, are encouraged to act like entrepreneurs, coming up with ideas and hawking them round the group, rather than waiting for product managers to come to them with ideas. The result, say analysts, is a much better record in transferring technology to the market place than have most other US companies. Welch says his aim is to create a 'boundaryless company', which he defines as meaning that 'between functions, between labour and management, between customers and GE, the lines arc blurred. We become one. We share'. This sounds horribly vague and well-meaning – the kind of remark that might come better from a minor Oriental mystic than a high priest of capitalism.

Yet the purpose is extremely down-to-earth: to improve productivity by getting everyone in the company – as well as customers – contributing ideas on the way work is organised.

Welch's key tool in this drive is the 'work-out' process. The idea was sown several years ago at Crotonville, after a number of junior executives had stood up in Welch's sessions and criticised aspects of their businesses.

He thought: 'Why can't we recreate these sessions in each business, where the person standing at the front of the room can do something about it?' Work-out involves a business leader talking to a small group of employees, drawn from all levels, and giving them his or her 'vision'. The employees go away, think about the ideas and about what bothers them about their jobs.

They then reconvene and discuss the issues.

The manager can accept or reject the ideas for improvements thrown up in the discussion, or can say he will think about them. But if his initial reply is 'maybe' he must report back to the group with a final decision within 30 days.

Cynics might argue that variations on this kind of operation have been tried at other western companies but almost always end in disillusion when management fails to deliver on its promises, or when staff become frightened of criticising their bosses.

But the GE operation is remarkable in that it is being applied rigorously across the company, and from top to bottom, and it is structured so that managers cannot get away with doing nothing.

This is because the company has hired independent experts from several universities to act as 'facilitators' – monitors who sit in on the sessions, make sure managers do not bully those who speak their minds, and check that they are sticking to their promises.

Work-out has only been operating since early last year and Welch says that so far about 90 per cent of the recommendations coming out of the sessions have been acted on.

This is because initially they have been very simple – amounting to getting rid of much of the unnecessary bureaucracy and administrative trivia which had piled up over 100 years.

At first ideas come hesitantly, but Welch says that once people see their suggestions being acted on, the trickle turns into a flood. 'It gives people self-confidence. They think: "Look, what I say is important. People act, people respond to it".' Work-out is now entering a more difficult area – improving the production process – but Welch says it is already producing results.

'Do you realise how silly it is for managers in an office to be fixing some of these flow things that people deal with every day?' he asks, adding that an ergonomics work-out at a plant in Louisville, Kentucky, 'made more progress than paying consultants for a decade, because the people on that floor knew it (the job) was breaking their backs more than those people coming in with pads of paper.' But these changes – which could yet lose momentum over the long term – have some powerful implications for traditional corporate roles, blurring the distinction between manager and managed, executive and blue-collar worker, and GE and its customers.

It demands more from workers, who are given greater responsibility, and much, much more from managers, who must still lead, yet be flexible and willing to accept criticism. That in turn requires a particular combination of self-confidence and sensitivity.

Welch says GE has had to remove some business leaders because they were not 'candid, and couldn't face reality'; he adds that 'we will undoubtedly have to lose some key managers in the 1990s who won't embrace the concept of "boundaryless", who won't be self-confident and simple'. Welch is not without critics. Some have accused him of merely replacing one hotchpotch of companies with another. Some argue that his delayering of the corporate bureaucracy in the 1980s left middle managers too stressed and too overworked; some complain that his job cuts, and the ejection of managers who cannot adapt to the demanding new regime, have hit company morale. Not for nothing has he been called Neutron Jack.

And while 'work-out' has been widely welcomed as an imaginative move forward, detractors argue that it would have been better if such a programme had been introduced several years earlier. In other words, Welch should have set about the group's human, or 'software problems', at the same time as remaking its 'hardware', rather than leaving the job until later.

Still, the acid test of any management theory has to be whether it actually produces results and in GE's case it has done so impressively, with the company recording double digit earnings growth for the past 15 quarters.

With the US teetering towards a recession in the wake of the Gulf crisis, analysts expect a substantial slow-down in that pace next year, and point in particular to the slump in US defence spending and the weakness of the financial services sector, where GE Capital is one of the largest players.

Nevertheless, the company seems to be in a much better position to withstand an economic downturn than it was in the 1981–82 recession. Whether GE's latest management techniques could be transferred to other companies is debatable, for much of the drive behind 'work-out' comes from the personality of Welch himself, who has shown a remarkable ability to adapt his management theories to suit the company's changing needs, particularly his new emphasis on the human dimension. The only child of a Massachusetts railway conductor, he is a slim man of middle height with bright, piercing eyes and immense bubbling enthusiasm. He is given to tapping you lightly on the arm to emphasise a point and to rushes of rhetorical questions. 'How real is our integration?' he says. 'It's a lot more real than it's ever been. Is it the ultimate? No. Are we working on it every day? Yes.' At times like these he sounds a little like a hot gospeller. Yet he is anxious to stress that he has not yet found the corporate holy grail.

'We are on a crusade,' he says. 'But we are only just beginning. We are two to three years into it. This is a long journey. We don't have all the answers.'

PHILIPS IN CRISIS

By Guy de Jonquieres

First published 25 May 1990

In happier days Cor van der Klugt, outgoing president of Philips, used to liken his struggle for improved international competitiveness to bringing about 'a change of religion' in the sprawling Dutch electronics and lighting manufacturer and its 300,000 employees worldwide.

That was before this year's disastrous first quarter results plunged the company into crisis, precipitating van der Klugt's early retirement and unleashing a desperate search for remedial actions to restore investors' shattered confidence.

It is a measure of the task ahead that Philips had only just emerged from an extensive shake-up intended to sharpen its performance. In the past four years, van der Klugt has closed some 70 factories, shed many peripheral businesses and imposed the authority of central product divisions on the company's once largely autonomous national subsidiaries.

However, as many large companies have discovered, it is one thing to re-shape an organisation and quite another to get the people in it to behave differently. All the more so when, as in Philips' case, it means changing attitudes, practices and beliefs which have become second nature over a period of a century.

Rapid-fire restructuring may have complicated matters by confusing some managers, rather than motivating them to perform better. As van der Klugt put it in an interview two years ago: 'You have a lot of well-drilled regiments and all of a sudden you say you want commandos. You can give them a different cap and uniform and they don't know what to do.' Ironically, Philips' corporate culture embraces many values and principles similar to those of the Japanese electronics companies which are its fiercest competitors. It has long prided itself on taking decisions by consensus and sticking to them over the long term. It is also renowned as a jobs-for-life employer, which provides generous welfare benefits to its staff.

But while these qualities have helped Japanese companies take world markets by storm, at Philips they have frequently been blamed for engendering complacency and feather-bedding. Critics, in the company as well as outside it, argue that the consequence has been to make it too inward-looking, risk-averse and bureaucratic.

Jan Timmer, who takes over as president in July, has already won praise for his efforts to break the mould. As head of consumer electronics, he split the monolithic division into separate units, increased the authority and accountability of line managers and made them immerse themselves much more closely in the day-to-day running of their businesses.

One of Timmer's priorities has been to give more emphasis to product design and marketing, which Philips has been widely accused of neglecting. In an attempt to catch up, it recently purchased 25 per cent of Bang & Olufsen, saying it wanted to tap the Danish consumer electronics manufacturer's design and marketing skills.

Philips has always been strong in research and development and has spawned a stream of innovations including videorecorders and compact disc players.

However, it took a long time to realise that consumer electronics markets were driven more by fashion than by technology, and that products which it had pioneered could be easily copied and improved upon by nimble Asian competitors.

Adjustment was made harder by the long-standing segregation of Philips' management into technical and commercial directorates. Though the two sides of the business have been brought together, technical functions have continued to command greater kudos – and to attract better-qualified recruits – than commercial jobs.

Many critics argue, though, that the source of Philips' biggest handicap is to be found at its headquarters in the sleepy market town of Eindhoven.

Remote from Europe's main business hubs, the town seems an improbable nerve-centre for a company which has operations in more than 60 countries and makes much of its global ambitions.

Eindhoven is not only geographically isolated. It is also dominated by Philips, much as renaissance princelings dominated city-states. Home to more than 30,000 of the company's staff – the only other large local employer is a DAF truck plant – its streets are lined with Philips office buildings and factories.

Even the main hotel is company property.

One former executive argues that the headquarters bureaucracy has escaped drastic pruning because the axe would fall so close to home. 'It would mean that top managers would have to drive through the town every day, passing people on the street whom they had made redundant,' he says. 'The only solution would be to move the headquarters to somewhere like Amsterdam or Brussels.' This cosy environment has been blamed for giving top management an in-grown and parochial perspective. All the more so because Philips' top brass is still composed overwhelmingly of Dutchmen who have spent their entire careers with the company.

'Many of them have worked abroad,' says one frequent visitor to Eindhoven. 'But a surprising number of those who have got to the top have spent their formative years in developing countries. The experience seems to have bred a rather colonial outlook.' Some of Philips' foreign managers say they turned down offers of promotion to headquarters because they feared they could never break into the tightly-knit 'Eindhoven establishment', with its clique-ish rules and conventions. Significantly, Timmer is considered an outsider from the club.

Until now, external pressures on Philips to change its ways have been slight. Unlike West German companies, it has no powerful bank shareholder keeping tabs on its performance, and it is insulated against the threat of a hostile bid by a formidable barricade of takeover defences.

Hence Jan Timmer's hopes of overhauling Philips, and of making it more responsive to the outside world, are likely to depend heavily on how far he can impose his will on the company. 'Timmer will succeed only if he can break through the Philips culture,' says a former executive. 'And the only way to do that may be to destroy it.'

SMALL EARTHQUAKE – IBM SLIGHTLY HURT

By Alan Cane, Louise Kehoe, Roderick Oram
and Ian Rodger

First published 4–27 April 1990

The painful process of restructuring

The sleepy hamlet of Armonk in upstate New York is the unlikely home of International Business Machines, 'Big Blue', the world's largest computer manufacturer. Situated on the crest of a low hill, the modest, three storied building hardly lives up to the name 'Galactic Headquarters' by which it is known to IBM watchers around the world.

Yet Armonk is the epicentre of a corporate earthquake shaking up the way IBM does business and challenging the assumptions of IBM staff in every one of the more than 130 countries where the company operates.

For several years IBM's corporate well-being has been in need of both self-examination and radical surgery. This had been precipitated by the feeling that the world's most self-sufficient company had become bloated, bureaucratic and arrogant. Add to that IBM's disappointing results over the past four years, and the task facing Mr John Akers, the company's chairman and chief executive, when he assumed control in 1985, was vast.

The Akers initiative involved five restructuring measures, each of which has resulted in upheaval and trauma. They are: cutting total staff without redundancy; eliminating bureaucracy; world-wide decentralisation; more collaboration with software companies, systems houses and customers in solving business problems; concentrating on particular market specialisations.

This year, IBM's top executives are hoping to see the first real signs of healing, a process which has involved tackling the company's deeply conservative corporate culture and ultimately making it more responsive to its customers and the market.

The early indications are encouraging: worldwide revenue for the first quarter of this year totalled $14.2bn, up 11.4 per cent on the same period last year, while pre-tax earnings were $1.827bn, up 12.4 per cent on the first quarter of 1989. Mr Akers remains cautiously optimistic: 'Our strategy of listening to our customers and improving the competitiveness of our products and services is working.' This minor upturn must be set against the disappointing performance of the previous four years. In 1989, sales growth was a mere 5 per cent, for example, about half the industry average, compared with 28 per cent between 1983 and 1984. Earnings per share in 1984 totalled $10.77 last year, the figure was $6.47. This was a far cry from the heady early 1980s, when Mr Akers' predecessor, Mr John Opel, vowed that the company would grow at the same rate as the industry in every sector in which it had competition, and that it should aim to become a $100bn company by 1990.

IBM's poor record between 1986 and 1990 must also be judged in the context of an industry undergoing structural changes more profound than any since its emergence in the 1950s. All traditional mainframe and minicomputer manufacturers have seen their margins eroded by technological advances which are changing the cost structure of the industry. Wang of the US, Nixdorf of West Germany and Norsk Data of Norway are the best known victims.

It has been left to young and nimble companies, such as workstation manufacturer Sun Microsystems or software publisher Oracle Corporation, to exploit the latest advances and show that high technology can still mean high growth and profitability.

Yet in some ways, IBM's problems are unique. Its revenues from information technology last year topped $60bn, almost $50bn more than its nearest competitor. Its pretax profits at $6.6bn, down 26 per cent on the previous year, were still greater than Apple Computer's sales for the year.

So is IBM just a giant among computer makers, but an increasingly slow moving one? The implications of IBM's lacklustre performance go well beyond the fate of just one company, however large the measures it is taking have a significance well beyond a business school study of a turnaround strategy.

Its personal drama is being played out against a backdrop of globalisation of trade, deregulation and the continued rise of the industrial powers of the Pacific Rim.

IBM has been the bell-wether of the US computer industry, its success tied to its well-honed ability to dictate the terms and conditions on which the data processing market operates world-wide. Now that omniscience is under threat from three directions.

First, the traditionally homogeneous computer market is fragmenting into a series of niche markets each with its own market leader.

Second, the Japanese drive into computers is continuing to eat into IBM's market share in mainframe systems and undermine its credibility as market leader. The Japanese understand well that computers and semiconductors are not only important as industries in their own right, but as the driving force behind the technical growth of many other industries. That is why excellence in information technology is one of their principal industrial targets. IBM has been the US information technology industry's chief bulwark against Japanese computer manufacturers' increasingly powerful penetration.

In 1971, Japanese manufacturers held less than 4 per cent of the world computer market. Today, Japanese companies occupy third, fourth and sixth positions in the world league.

Third and most important, the customer has changed irrevocably. Much of IBM's success in the past has been due to the close ties it built with company data processing managers, individuals whose career advancement often depended on IBM's approval and who were thus in thrall to Big Blue.

With the emergence of departmental computing and personal computers, data processing has become a business tool, an opportunity for competitive advantage, as much as a utility. A consequence has been that decisions about data processing investment are examined much more closely by company boards whose members owe no allegiance to IBM.

IBM's response to this challenge has been to attempt to turn itself from a blue whale into a lean but friendly octopus, with the Armonk headquarters at the centre of a complex network of relationships with customers, software and services companies – and even with competitors.

It has implemented over the past four years a programme of reform and reorientation that goes far beyond conventional business turnround strategies in the process it has changed the company from a technology-driven to a customer-driven orientation.

This has involved some changes of perception that would have been unthinkable a decade ago. In short, IBM, more used to setting the pace than following the herd, is telling its staff that it may be the biggest computer company in the world, but that it is not the best and that many of its products and services are mediocre. Most unsettling of all, staff are being asked to come to terms with the notion that IBM, virtually a byword for discretion and self-sufficiency in the past, now needs not only to create synergy through partnerships and associations with other companies but welcomes the opportunity to communicate with the non-blue world.

Thus, Mr Jack Kuehler, IBM President, says: 'We are trying to take advantage of other people's ideas in a way we have never done before.' IBM's reluctance to listen to outside ideas had been reinforced in the early 1980s by years of record sales and profits. IBM, for instance, had been benefiting from its entry into the personal computer business where it quickly became market leader, solid growth in revenues from software and services, and a policy of persuading customers to buy rather than lease their computers.

When Mr Akers took over as chairman, in 1985, it quickly became apparent that 'things were going south', as Mr Douglas Sweeney, IBM's chief corporate strategist put it. When the conventional response of corporate belt-tightening proved inadequate, Mr Akers began the larger job of restructuring the company for the 1990s.

Understanding what had gone wrong involved a prolonged period of analysis in which IBM asked its own staff, outside consultants and its larger customers to tell it where it was failing.

The analysis made sobering reading. Applications software, software to solve business problems, was in poor supply, methods for automating the development of application software were inadequate, computers were proving difficult to connect or integrate and systems were hard to use. Most significant, customers were finding it hard to justify their investment in information technology.

Introspection came to an end abruptly on 31 December 1987 when Mr Akers apparently told his colleagues: 'No more diagnoses. Now let us focus on execution.' His initiative involved several measures designed to restructure IBM from top to bottom.

First, IBM is reducing its workforce gradually from 407,000 in April 1986 to a planned 373,000 by the middle of this year. It will achieve this through a combination of attrition and incentives to encourage early retirement. Some 53,000 administrative jobs have been eliminated as a result of the retirement programmes and the redeployment of administrative officers into line jobs, IBM says.

Second, it is creating a line-of-business (LOB) structure within the organisation under a new division, IBM United States, aimed at eliminating bureaucracy and to provide logical groupings for IBM's huge range of products.

Third, IBM is devolving power away from Armonk. IBM branch managers have been given a new and unfamiliar responsibility for dealing with customers and setting prices. IBM Europe, which has been devolving power to individual countries, provided the model IBM Italy, the working example. Mr Sweeney says: 'In Mr Ennio Presutti who runs IBM Italy you will find somebody measured on his revenue and profit performance. He has been in the job 10 or 12 years and that brings continuity and perspective.' IBM managers used to joke that the company's initials stood for 'I've Been Moved'.

Fourth, it has launched a broad-based campaign to collaborate with software companies, systems houses and customers to help them develop applications software to solve business problems. The partnerships involve a range of commitments from equity stakes (for instance in Intel which builds the main microprocessor in its personal computers) through to providing facilities to test their products.

Finally, IBM has introduced a policy of concentrating on particular market specialisations. It has established a SMALL working group to identify and help finance projects which offer outstanding commercial potential. One example is a retail banking system which IBM is building in collaboration with National Westminster Bank involving IBM's new proprietary database system DB2.

To date, competitors, never short of respect for IBM's marketing muscle, say they have noticed little change apart from heavy pressure on margins as IBM salesmen – freed from control from Galactic Headquarters – discount heavily to win business. Some are openly doubtful of IBM's ability to take on, say, Andersen Consulting or Electronic Data Systems, as a 'integrator', putting together hardware and software from different manufacturers to meet their customers' requirements.

But the Blue Whale has begun its metamorphosis. Mr Pierre Hessler, director of marketing and services, says three serious questions remain: 'The first is, how well are we going to do what we have set out to do. The second is how we compete with the Japanese manufacturers. And the third is how we position ourselves in professional services and our relationships with the big consultants.' IBM's competitors will be watching the struggle anxiously but with some resignation: Mr Vittorio Cassoni, managing director of Olivetti of Italy and once an IBM executive, points out that the problems in the industry are the same for all the big computer companies: 'The difference between IBM and the rest of us is that IBM has more time to resolve the problems from which we are all suffering.'

The cost of commitment

The phrase 'We're the shoemaker's children', is heard from coast to coast among US employees of International Business Machines. When it comes to getting new equipment, the customer always comes first.

Up at world headquarters in Armonk, north of New York, clunky old PC-XTs, IBM's long-outdated desk-top computers, still far outnumber state-of-the-art PS/2s.

Down at a New York City branch, many staff selling to the world's most sophisticated financial institutions do their work on old PCs. Until a year ago, some had to make do with 'dumb' terminals, that is those with no local processing capacity. Customers trying to send the branch a fax were often thwarted by its inadequate IBM-made machine.

Senior executives say the plethora of PCs is good news. Customer demand is so strong for the PS/2 that staff have had to wait at the back of the line.

But customers and competitors say this altruism is a sign of a crucial IBM weakness: the company that taught the world how to use computers is now less adept at using them than some of its customers.

Minute by minute around the globe hundreds of IBM plants and offices are pumping out vast volumes of data. The information is widely used around the company, but as yet IBM has failed fully to use it as a strategic tool. It must learn these skills if the current radical re-making of the company is to pay off. If it does not, the bureaucratic stagnation it suffered in the mid-1980s could turn into a management debacle in the 1990s.

IBM's present management information systems 'are adequate as opposed to Leading Edge', says Doug Sweeny, the company's director of business strategy and a close aide to John Akers, IBM's chairman who has inspired and led the companys transformation over the past five years.

The systems place IBM 'in the top 50 to 100 large companies. But they don't put us on the cutting edge', adds Stephan Haeckel, corporate director of marketing development.

Ford Motor has first-hand experience of the short-comings from buying 35,000 personal computers from IBM over the past three years.

'IBM's order entry and tracking system for personal computers isn't what it should be,' says Si Gilman, Ford's executive director of information systems. 'Under our suggestions they are making some changes. Five years ago they would have told us to get lost,' a sign that IBM is now making itself far more responsive to its customers.

Inadequate internal information systems have hurt other computer companies, notably Unisys and Sun Microsystems last year. But the weakness cost IBM much more earlier in the 1980s. As long ago as 1979–80 it identified weaknesses in its structure, culture, products and business strategy.

Executives confess they largely ignored them, though, because IBM was on a roll. Revenues and profits were booming as customers snapped up the first PCs. But some growth was illusory. Sales were inflated by, for example, many mainframe customers switching to buying equipment, rather than leasing which in the past had generated long-term income for IBM.

'I would hate to tell you the number of different customer master records IBM has and the number of different views of revenues they give,' one of the company's senior information systems specialists says.

By the time Akers took over as chairman in 1985, IBM revenues were stagnating. But the company assumed it was caught in a cyclical downturn, so took only minor belt-tightening actions. A year later, realising its problems were systemic, it plunged into a painful era of self-examination and reconstruction. For the first time in its long and illustrious history, IBM took to heart what customers were telling it. 'They were brutally frank and honest with us,' says Sweeny.

They were told that many IBM products lagged behind those of their competitors and were grouped in families which could not connect to each other the company was arrogant to the point of being blind sometimes to its customers needs sales people pushed products rather than unified hardware and software solutions to customers' computing requirements labyrinthian bureaucracy stifled creativity, enterprise and responsiveness and ran up IBM's costs.

'You had to be deaf or incredibly tenacious to get anything through the bureaucracy,' says the manager of a big IBM sales branch. 'There were more tree-huggers than maze-runners.' In the Fortune magazine ranking of the best-managed companies in the US, IBM plummeted from first in 1986 to 45th in 1989.

Akers, one of the all-time great IBM salesmen, decreed the company must become 'market-driven'. To that end, it began a drastic overhaul of its structure. It took some organisational ideas from a few customers it deeply admired, but ironically most ideas have come from within its empire. IBM Italy, for example, is considered a model for good customer relations.

We spent two-and-a-half to three years trying to figure out what was wrong, says Sweeny. We spent a year structuring and positioning ourselves. And now we've got a four or five year implementation programme.

At the very heart of the new IBM is the devolution of power and responsibility. The change flows down right from the top, from the senior management committee. 'We spend far less time on operational decisions, far more on strategic decisions and also on measuring our progress,' says Jack Kuehler, IBM's president.

Out in the field, IBM's perestroika has transformed the way employees do their jobs. 'We've got rid of a lot of pent-up frustration, eliminated a lot of silly bureaucracy,' said Jim Steele, manager of a New York City branch that boosted its revenues 52 per cent last year. Now if he feels harassed by the paper pushers, he reaches for a big rubber stamp: 'Cut Paperwork. Is this really necessary?' In the old days, people further up the organisation ran herd on each of the 360 lines of his branch budget. Now he is given revenue and cost targets and rewarded with a bonus if he meets them. Off his own bat, he decided to buy non-IBM fax machines. In-coming messages increased four-fold.

The branch's roster has shrunk from 180 to just over 160 in the past two years, but the simplified bureaucracy has allowed Steele to put more people out with the customers. On many large accounts, they have moved into the customers' own premises. Sales and service people are typically spending half their time with their customers, up from 25 per cent or so a few years ago.

They have far more freedom to set prices and devise complete solutions to customer needs, even if that means incorporating some non-IBM products in the package. In the past, says Steele, '90 per cent of our selling effort' was to people higher up IBM to get approval for such decisions on pricing and third-party products.

The prize for the big computer company considered most responsive to customers used to go to Digital Equipment, the world's second largest manufacturer after IBM. 'My big customers have told me that in the past year we've blown completely by DEC,' Steele says.

IBM's customers are quick to compliment it for its new helpfulness. 'They've lost a lot of their arrogance . . . like us, they realise they don't control the world,' says Gilman of Ford. 'This is shocking to old-timers in IBM. We're getting access to labs and technical expertise that used to be given very grudgingly.'

Max Hopper, senior vice president of information systems at American Airlines and a key customer adviser to IBM, says: 'I'm pleased in terms of the change in attitude I see. I see it turning but I think they still have a long way to go.' Another IBM sales veteran says: 'I think the strategy is very good, but it's going to take a long time to work out.

'It's hard for a lot of people who are used to the Big Blue blanket keeping them warm,' he added.

'We've worked hard to come out of our igloo,' says Kuehler. The demands the company is now making on its employees are quite different from the past.

Out in the field, 'you'll find some that are scared to death and you'll find others who are really fascinated and intrigued.' Adapting to the new business style can be equally challenging for managers.

'Some executives are scared to death,' says a senior east coast field manager. 'These say: "There's no way those hooligans out there in the field can handle being this close to the customers. They'll give away the store." ' At heart, the IBM culture has not changed, says Walt Burdick, senior vice president personnel. 'Our basic beliefs remain constant.' Respect for the individual, meritocracy and a 50-year-old policy of no layoffs are the foundations. IBM is spending $1.2bn a year educating and training its workforce for their newly re-focused mission. Nobody is moved from back office to front line against their will. Anyone fired can appeal directly to Akers, and some 700 do so each year.

Some things seem timeless. Walking the bright orange carpeted corridors of the Armonk headquarters is like stepping into a 1960s Life magazine picture spread. The loudest noise at 10.30am is the clonk, clonk of the 19-year-old escalators. Absent is the bustle and energy found among California's leading computer makers.

IBM facilities dotted across wooded hill tops north of New York seem isolated. In contrast, Silicon Valley competitors, such as Hewlett-Packard, Apple Computer and Sun Microsystems live on each others' doorsteps. Intelligence passes quickly from one to another.

The 'open door policy' senior IBM executives espouse is often frustrated by the formality of their offices and a cadre of administrators. The reverent hush hanging over the corridors seems to discourage the casual interaction which many entrepreneurial companies find a well-spring of ideas and motivation.

At Hewlett-Packard, another leading US computer company, for example, only chief executive John Young has a walled office – and even then they are made of glass. Everyone else has open plan offices.

IBM has simplified its corporate structure a lot, but it remains a behemoth with interlocking committees to co-ordinate its activities worldwide. Some customers and competitors wonder if a company of its size can ever become as sprightly as many of its far smaller competitors.

'IBM has still got the infrastructure, the processes and the measurement systems that came from our tradition of success,' says a senior executive.

'We are re-inventing those processes right now, but the organism has still got the cardiovascular and neurological network associated with its old form.' Only last October did IBM grasp that nettle when the annual strategic planning conference focussed in earnest on the company's own management information systems. Reports and proposals from around the world are due in Armonk this month. Building state-of-the art internal information systems is 'a major undertaking . . . but we will have operational benefits from this within a year or two, the executive adds.

Until that is accomplished, IBM could find it hard to control the entrepreneurial forces it has let loose, or to accurately measure their success, some people both inside and outside the company worry.

IBM has seen only marginal payoff so far from devoting more people and resources to the field. Sales, administration and general expenses have risen 29 per cent over the past two years. Its revenues have risen 24 per cent over the past four years, but annual sales per employee have risen only slightly faster, by 31 per cent to $163,600.

Akers told the annual senior management meeting in January that he was unhappy with the pace of change. 'We need to have a greater sense of urgency,' was his message, a senior strategist says.

One further danger lurks. IBM has chosen to emulate some companies others in the computer industry were touting five years ago for their organisational and management techniques. By the time IBM has completed its mighty transformation around 1994, it could be the very model of a mid-1980s company.

The best 1990s companies, though, will have learnt even quicker responses to the accelerating rate of change in their industry. To keep up with them, IBM has to learn much more about using its might more effectively and speedily.

Many of its executives acknowledge still more change is needed to bring IBM to the forefront of the industry. Says one: 'Has the last shoe fallen from this centipede? No way.'

Adopting market-driven policies

International Business Machines has a new plan of attack. As the $63bn computer giant attempts to transform itself into a more agile competitor in the 1990s, 'Big Blue' is setting new goals and adopting new credos.

'The new IBM is market driven,' declares Jack Kuehler, IBM president. What this means, he and other IBM executives claim, is that the company's future direction will be set by the needs of its customers, rather than by the advance of computer technology.

Prodded by customers who feel increasingly burdened by the tasks of applying computer technology to their businesses and who demonstrate a declining interest in 'what goes on under the hood' of a computer, as Kuehler puts it, IBM aims to offer 'information technology solutions'. The change is not altruistic. IBM is increasingly challenged by nimble competitors in the fastest growing segments of the computer market and threatened by the growing strength of Japan's largest electronics manufacturers in its staple mainframe computer market.

IBM aims to gain a new competitive edge, therefore, by greatly expanding its software and services revenues and becoming far less dependent upon computer hardware sales.

IBM will bundle computer hardware, software and support services to provide turn-key systems designed to meet the specific needs of individual customers and industry sectors. It will offer extensive professional services ranging from support in integrating new hardware and software into a corporate data processing system, to taking over total responsibility for a company's information management systems.

The shift to a 'market driven direction' represents a 180 degree turn for IBM which, throughout the 1970s and 1980s, focused almost exclusively upon technology as a market driver.

Although IBM has long offered extensive support services to its largest customers, the company provided these more as a means of encouraging hardware sales than as a significant source of revenues and profit.

Ironically, the 'new' IBM is returning to the company's roots. Back in the 1950s, when it was entering the computer market as a challenger to Remington Rand, IBM emphasised customer relations and marketing over technology.

In his book, *A Business and its Beliefs*, Thomas Watson Jr, former IBM chairman and son of the company's founder, explaining how IBM was able to recover from its slow start, recalls: '. . . we had a salesforce whose knowledge of the market enabled us to tailor our machines very closely to the needs (of customers).' John Akers, current chairman of IBM, would undoubtedly like to be able to make the same claim. Over the past three decades, however, the scope of businesses that his company serves, and the role computers play in those businesses has vastly expanded.

It used to be enough for IBM to be the master of the data centre. Today, the computer vendor must also have an intimate understanding of how customers' businesses operate. And while IBM's 'customer' used to be the data processing manager, today it is likely to be the board of directors.

Today: 'We cannot do everything alone,' Kuehler acknowledges. In order to provide complete 'solutions' to its customers, IBM must offer specialised applications programs that detail a computer's tasks as well as the hardware and systems software that are its areas of expertise.

'IBM has not made major investments in applications software in recent years,' says Marvin Mann, president of the services industries sector of IBM's Application Solutions division, an organisation formed in 1988 to address the new challenge.

To fill the gaps, IBM has turned to third party software developers, offering them incentives to create application programs to run on its computers. Over the past two years, IBM has formed hundreds of 'business partnerships'. These range from straightforward marketing deals with specialist companies, to equity investments in promising software development companies. There are also joint technology development agreements with major customers that develop industry-specific application programs which IBM can then offer to others.

For IBM, dependence upon outsiders for products that represent a critical factor in its strategic plans goes against the grain and the company's longterm goal is to increase 'IBM ownership' of key applications.

In the meantime, however, IBM is learning valuable lessons. 'Selling solutions is a different business, we have learned that,' says Mark Mauriello, manager of operations for IBM's financial services sector marketing organisation, one of the speciality markets IBM is targeting as a priority.

IBM now recognises that its field sales force is ill-equipped for the new mission of 'solution selling'. Says Mauriell: 'We still need them, but we also need specialists.

'To sell applications you have to be very narrow and deep. When customers buy software and integration services they want to deal with specialists who understand all of the details of the product.' In contrast, IBM's salesforce, which is charged with selling the company's entire product line, is 'broad and shallow'. IBM is also learning how to form partnerships with software firms that are often very small and entrepreneurial.

Gene Bedell, president of Seer Technologies, a newly-formed software company jointly owned by IBM, First Boston and the 70 employees of the start-up, says that he chose IBM as an investment partner despite 'very negative' reports from others who had formed partnerships with IBM.

'IBM has been very sensitive,' says Bedell. He and other employees of Seers formerly worked for First Boston where they developed trading management and risk management application programs that they will now develop into products for the investment banking industry. 'This is a very creative group. They do not wear dark suits and white shirts in the IBM style,' says Bedell, 'but IBM appreciates that if they try to change it, they will loose it. They assured me that they have learned from their previous mistakes.' IBM's business partnerships, and its investments in companies such as Seer, are aimed at putting IBM in closer touch with its customers.

'Our objective is to be close to the customer, to understand his requirements and to be much more responsive to them in terms of meeting those requirements – industry by industry and application by application,' says Mann.

To meet customer demands, IBM has also become more open to integrating computer equipment from other manufacturer's with its own.

With the recent introduction of a powerful new computer workstation that runs a version of ATT's UNIX operating system, IBM has also endorsed the 'open systems' trend toward industry-wide software standards that allow computers from different manufacturers to share software and data.

IBM's primary focus, none the less, remains its proprietary systems and software.

The company's lack of objectivity may, however, prove to be a barrier to its success in systems integration, a service market currently dominated by independent consultants.

'Most users are sceptical about IBM being a hardware neutral systems integrator,' says Joe Jennette, vice president systems group, at Computer Sciences, a major independent systems integrator.

Andersen Consulting, which has a systems integration group, long viewed as an IBM 'shop', also has reservations.

'Our relationship with IBM has changed significantly over the past couple of years,' says George Shaheen, chief executive. Despite years of close collaboration with IBM, Andersen now finds itself being kept 'at arm's length. They have told us that they now view us as a competitor.' IBM has three of the five major attributes needed to be a successful systems integrator, says Shaheen. 'They obviously have credibility and financial resources. Their technical prowess is also well recognised. IBM is weaker in "business acumen" or understanding the needs of the customer, and in "delivery capability, or the ability to implement integrated systems",' he suggests.

Indeed, IBM's record is not unblemished. The company has had mixed results in some of the major systems integration projects that it has undertaken for customers.

At Ford Motor Company, for example, IBM's efforts to build a computer network linking the automobile manufacturer's US dealers proved disastrous.

The project was abandoned.

Still, most of IBM's major customers welcome its move into solution selling.

'The real costs of computing are in software development, installation and maintenance, rather than hardware,' says Richard Griffiths, executive vice president of Bank of America.

'I can buy MIPs (speedy computer processor hardware) from anyone, but what I want are solutions to business problems. Applications are driving hardware purchases today.

'If you can't solve business problems, you cannot sell technology today. The more problems IBM can solve, the better, and the more I will buy!'

In a precedent-setting deal signed last July, Eastman Kodak handed over the keys to its corporate data centres to IBM. The computer company agreed to build, equip and operate an IBM-owned data centre to serve Kodak's needs.

Such endorsements provide IBM with confirmation that it is moving in the right direction – however even its staunchest allies warn that IBM still has a long way to go.

IBM is hardly alone in recognising the growing demand for computer systems that deliver on the promise of increased productivity. To remain a leader in the 1990s, IBM must pick up the pace of its transformation into a 'solution seller'.

A BIGGER SHOCK – IBM UNVEILS RADICAL REORGANISATION PLANS

By Louise Kehoe

First published in November and December 1991

27 November 1991

International Business Machines yesterday announced radical plans to reshape its worldwide operations by splitting the world's largest computer company into a band of increasingly independent companies and business units.

IBM could then assess each unit's performance and decide to sell off a stake, or the entire unit, or retain sole ownership.

The reorganisation 'will lead over time to a fundamental redefinition of how IBM does business', said Mr John Akers, chairman.

Each unit within the company will be required to meet specific financial goals and will report its financial results individually. The compensation of executives from each business unit will be tied to its financial performance.

'This will give IBM maximum flexibility to decide on the level of investment that it wishes to make in each segment of the business,' Mr Akers said. IBM may also create new ventures or acquire existing businesses.

The changes, expected over a period of years, will affect IBM's geographical units, which are responsible for marketing and services in each country, as well as product manufacturing and development business units.

IBM's marketing and service companies will focus on segments of the computer market, with each region determining for itself the best market opportunities.

The company's goal is to hone its competitive edge by creating business units that focus more sharply upon specific segments of the computer market.

The computer giant has been losing market share in several important sectors where it faces intense competition from smaller, specialised computer companies.

While the reorganisation will address long-term issues, IBM also announced cost-cutting measures aimed at boosting its financial performance next year.

The company plans to reduce its workforce by 20,000 people over the next 12 months to about 330,000.

IBM said that it will take a $3bn restructuring charge against fourth-quarter earnings to cover the costs of voluntary severance programmes, some consolidation of manufacturing operations and revaluation of assets.

The restructuring will result in cost savings of about $1bn in 1992 and about $2bn each year thereafter, the company said.

28 November 1991

The giant has stirred. International Business Machines, the world's largest computer company, aims to transform itself into a corporate federation of independent business units, each held accountable for its own financial performance and charged to become the best in its class.

Mr John Akers, IBM chairman, this week unveiled plans to banish corporate bureaucracy, improve efficiency and increase autonomy among the company's many business sectors. The restructuring plan, he said, 'will lead to a fundamental redefinition of how IBM does business'.

With 1990 revenues of $69bn, IBM ranks as one of the largest manufacturing companies in the world. The restructuring may be one of the most complex not forced by merger or regulatory demands.

Change will be gradual. It will take 'years' for IBM to liberate its business units and dismantle the intricate matrix management structure on which its business empire has been built.

The greatest impact will be among the company's 350,000 employees, who all face uncertainty about how their jobs will be affected.

IBM's reorganisation will also have an impact on the world computer industry. Instead of the monolithic Big Blue, IBM will become the name of a group of companies. Managers of these units will, for the first time, have their compensation tied directly to financial performance.

Each company will be measured against rigorous financial criteria and failure to meet these goals will directly influence IBM's corporate investment decisions.

Mr Akers said that an individual unit's performance would enable IBM to decide whether to retain sole ownership, sell a stake in the operation or completely divest it. 'This will give IBM maximum flexibility to decide on the level of investment that it wishes to make in each segment of the business.' IBM's corporate executives will divorce themselves from operating issues to focus on managing the company's investment strategy. By eliminating layers of management, IBM hopes to speed decision-making, shorten product development cycles and concentrate each product group's energies on becoming the 'lowest cost manufacturer of state-of-the-art information systems'. The hope is that product managers, freed of internal politics and bureaucracy, will be able to focus energy on beating the competition.

The success of IBM's plans will depend heavily upon the ability of individual managers to make the cultural adjustment from the protected corporate womb to the harsh realities of a profit-driven environment.

Moreover, many questions remain about IBM's plan for greater autonomy.

Business unit managers, given responsibility for financial performance, will inevitably need to have greater sway over marketing and sales.

However, these activities will remain the primary responsibility of IBM's geographically organised marketing and service companies, such as IBM Japan or IBM UK.

The product groups' relationships with these sales organisations may become akin to those between manufacturers and independent sellers.

Mr Akers offers the example of IBM Australia, which has focused its sales efforts on IBM's workstation products to the detriment of its mid-range computer line. In this instance, Mr Akers suggests, IBM's mid-range computer group might seek an alternative channel of distribution.

Still unclear, however, is how IBM's product groups will relate to internal suppliers such as IBM's disc-drive manufacturing operations or its huge semiconductor factories. In theory, IBM product groups will no longer be required to buy components internally but will have the right to choose the lowest-cost supplier.

There are also areas of potential conflict among newly autonomous IBM business units. Already, for example, high-performance workstations compete to some extent with mid-range minicomputer products. Similarly, adjacent geographic sales and marketing units which liaise on issues such as pricing and distribution could run into conflict if they do not continue to collaborate.

All of these issues will be worked out 'over time', IBM says. Within the next few weeks, however, IBM plans to disclose specific reorganisation plans for some of its business units.

'Because each business is different, the degrees of independence will range across a spectrum,' Mr Akers said. He explained that IBM's mainframe computer systems, for example, would require continuing matrix management to ensure co-ordination among related product groups. In contrast, IBM's mid-range AS/400 product group would have greater autonomy.

IBM's marketing and service companies will in future focus on segments of the computer market, with each region determining for itself the best market opportunities. Individual IBM sales organisations will also have the right to combine IBM products and services with offerings from other companies, to provide customers with 'total solutions tailored to their needs'.

Although many of the changes are continuations of trends of the past few years, IBM's corporate managers now appear ready to take a leap forward by relinquishing control over operational aspects of IBM's business.

18 December 1991

Ray AbuZayyad represents the new face of IBM. As general manager of IBM's newly-formed data storage products business group, he is in the forefront of the computer giant's plans to transform itself into a 'commonwealth' of increasingly independent business units.

Earlier this month, AbuZayyad was handed world-wide responsibility for IBM's $11bn disk drive, tape and optical data storage product business.

He is charged with shaping this technology development and manufacturing division into a company that can compete with any other disk drive maker.

That will entail speeding up product development and expanding market opportunities, as well as ensuring that Big Blue remains ahead in data storage technology.

The IBM storage products group is a microcosm of the changes that have been set in motion throughout the giant computer company.

The data storage products group is on a fast track. It is leading IBM's charge toward decentralised management for two reasons. Data storage is an easily defined segment of the computer systems market, with technologies that span a wide range of products – from miniature disk drives for portable personal computers to high capacity data storage for mainframes. More important, however, is the independent spirit of this West Coast group.

The disk drive operation 'has long had a strong-minded, entrepreneurial bent', says Jack Kuehler, IBM president, who himself began his IBM career at the company's disk drive development and manufacturing facility in San Jose.

'They are less willing to accept top down management' than other parts of the company, Kuehler says, acknowledging that not all of IBM's corporate executives at its distant Armonk, New York, headquarters have appreciated the independent spirit of the Californian group in the past.

Recently, for example, the data storage products group has led IBM's efforts to expand its third-party OEM (original equipment manufacturer) sales. As well as supplying each of IBM's computer product groups with disk drives, the group last year rang up about $200m in non-IBM sales.

With his new found freedom, AbuZayyad aims to expand aggressively these 'outside' sales to $1bn by 1993, or one third of IBM's total projected sales. In the past, however, IBM's mainframe computer systems group has frowned upon sales to competitors.

'Now we have declared to IBM and to the world that we are ready to do business as a company serving IBM systems platforms and also those outside IBM,' says AbuZayyad. That may well involve selling disk drives to IBM competitors, he acknowledges.

Readiness to seize new opportunities, even if it means 'rocking the boat', is hardly typical of IBM managers. In the past, IBM's culture has encouraged uniformity, hence the myth that IBMers always wear dark suits and white shirts.

Although IBM has long recognised the need to give its technology development groups some creative freedom, the scope for individual initiative has traditionally been much narrower in other parts of the company.

Other segments of IBM have been slower to embrace prior moves toward devolving decision-making. Within the storage products division, however, AbuZayyad has created specialist groups – each responsible for a different aspect of data storage technology and product development. They are 'a group of technology specialists eager to demonstrate that they can also become businessmen', he says.

The formation of the storage products business unit clearly illustrates the changing relationships among IBM's product groups, but it also highlights the potential for conflicts.

Product group managers will now be required to make their own decisions on issues such as product development and manufacturing priorities and pricing.

No longer will development of a new disk drive be delayed if one of IBM's computer product groups is running behind schedule. 'If they are not ready then I will sell to somebody else first,' says AbuZayyad.

Another element of the IBM reorganisation that could be the cause of resentment is the realignment of management responsibility for many of the company's plants outside the US. AbuZayyad and his team in San Jose are now responsible, for example, for data storage product factories and development facilities in Britain, Japan, Germany, Thailand and Argentina.

AbuZayyad is confident that he will continue to have good relations with country managers.

Organisations will 'buy' products from the development and manufacturing units. Like the product groups, the sales organisations will be measured in terms of their financial performance.

Country managers will also have greater say in future on how they market IBM products. These marketing and service groups will now focus on market segments based on 'their own judgments of opportunities', IBM says.

'We are embarking upon creating a very different IBM company,' says John Akers, IBM's chairman. IBM's corporate executives intend to withdraw from the operational aspects of management as rapidly as possible, he emphasises.

'We are going to require of management and individuals increased entrepreneurial activity and decision making and accountability,' he says, adding that 'some people (within IBM) will not take to this.'

In parts of the business where we do not have the prerequisite skills, IBM is 'aggressively considering' hiring outsiders for senior management posts.

That would be another big change for Big Blue.

2 WRESTLING WITH REORGANISATION

INTRODUCTION

When David Dworkin emerged in May 1992 as the new chief executive-designate of Storehouse Group – taking over from Michael Julien who retired for health reasons – it was perhaps not so great a surprise to readers of the *Financial Times* Management Page. For Dworkin's abilities had been analysed closely in April 1990 when, just five months after taking the helm of BhS, the chain store group within Storehouse, he had already engineered a significant sales boost, despite the worsening retail climate in the UK. His methods were not always conventional, particularly those which introduced an element of fire-fighting to the company's retailing approach. But it was clear then that, in a group which was crying out for effective reorganisation, Dworkin was beginning to produce results. Indeed, within a month of his being designated chief executive, a radical re-shaping of Storehouse's senior management was taking place, with head office numbers being halved.

Recession is always a catalyst for reorganisation. In the early 1980s UK industry set a pace which had as its central objective the creation of leaner and meaner businesses. Greater productivity was the name of the game, with frontline workforces being cut back, often heavily, and the remaining workers boosting output significantly. In the early 1990s there has been more de-layering of management and other white collar staff. At shop floor level, however, there has not been the scope for boosting efficiency through lower manning, at least at shop floor level, and it has been better management of already trimmed down resources that has been more often the main means to more efficient and competitive ends.

This chapter highlights a real cross-section of types and styles of reorganisation. For Edwards High Vacuum – part of BOC, the UK-based industrial gases group, and a manufacturer of industrial vacuums – the spur to reorganise was losses. Simon Holberton relates how at the heart of the company's bid to stage a recovery was attention to its structure and management style. Edwards emerged as an exponent of matrix management, a much discussed system which has champions and detractors in almost equal measure. It certainly works only if there is especially good communication and trust between senior management. That, Edwards believed, meant introducing a communications system of such sophistication that it eventually touched all elements of activity and enabled the company, among other things, to introduce just-in-time manufacturing.

BhS's reorganisation was different altogether. Here was a company which also had considerable strengths – a solid network of well-located outlets and a sound reputation – but the weaknesses of a retailer which had somewhat lost its way in a changing market that was moving heavily into recession. Short-term measures were set in train aimed at instantly boosting sales; in the process traditional retailing tenets were abandoned in order to shift slow moving stock and to bring in new lines more quickly. A more cohesive image was created by offloading peripheral activities and, overall, a more aggressive and considered use of available space was set in train.

In stark contrast, a reorganisation of the large US company, Tenneco, was prompted by threat of a takeover and subsequent break-up. Here, the reorganisation was both strategic and fundamentally structural. Indeed, so radical was the new strategy that the business on which the company was founded – oil – was sold off, leaving Tenneco with chemicals, packaging and manufacturing interests, most notably an agricultural machinery division centred round J I Case and International Harvester. The logic was based on which activities would command a more realistic price when sold to leave a rump with sufficient resources to secure a sound future. This was very much a deal inspired by opposing schools of strategic thought at that time: those who believed that, despite the group's high gearing, its long term industrial interests would be best served by keeping the group intact; and those who felt the short term financial interests of shareholders would be best served by securing a break-up value they believed to be far greater than its existing value. But that was in the era when highly leveraged deals were still possible, even if past the nadir of their popularity.

What the reorganisation was designed to do was give management the chance to exploit the remaining non-oil interests without so great a burden of debt. In common with Edwards High Vacuum – and, indeed, ICI in Europe, examined later in the chapter – one of Tenneco's objectives was not only to cut costs but to improve after-sales service and reliability.

The interface with the customer is a common thread among most of the examples discussed here. With so much of corporate reorganisation in the early 1980s having concentrated on the internals, quality of product and service has since become a significant competitive component. For ICI – by late 1992 in the throes of an even more fundamental reorganisation involving a demerger of its chemical and other activities – the creation of a cohesive European service and support operation at the end of 1990 was the culmination of a buying spree and organic growth over many years which had left it with a proliferation of activities with overlapping interests and resources.

Bringing them together, within the context of a shift in power from the geographic to the divisional side of its matrix, was designed not only to improve efficiency. It was also intended to make it easier for customers – used to dealing with a whole host of different ICI personnel – to interact with the company.

However, little more than a year later, under threat of a takeover and possible break-up by Hanson, it unwound much of the new operation and divided responsibility between its various divisions, In the uncertain 1990s even the best laid plans often have to be re-thought remarkably quickly.

Of a more purely internal, though equally radical, nature was the reorganisation by Hoover, the domestic appliance company, at its Merthyr Tydfil factory in Wales. Its dilemma was becoming common among manufacturing companies where working practices and manufacturing processes had been changing from the strictly segmented to the flexible – too many 'management' layers.

In Hoover's case the problem involved foremen. The company believed their role was becoming redundant as traditional lines of demarcation were broken down; it was clear that activities traditionally carried out by foremen would be better executed by supervisors. In opting for this approach, Hoover also removed an ambiguity that existed as to which side of the management/worker dividing line the foremen stood. They were to be management. This simplification of management hierarchy went hand in hand with moves to simplify manufacturing procedures which management felt had become equally bogged down because of a desire to produce a whole range of product variations that did not make economic sense. Better to concentrate efforts on making a smaller range of products of higher quality with better customer service.

THE REJUVENATION OF
EDWARDS HIGH VACUUM

By Simon Holberton

First published 14 May 1990

'Every other guy they had put in here was either sacked or became ill,' says Danny Rosenkranz.

Today Rosenkranz, at the age of 44, is in rude health and is his company's longest serving managing director. Far from being sacked, the 'they', or more particularly, Richard Giordano, executive chairman of BOC, the diversified gases business, has just promoted him to chief executive of one of BOC's three divisions.

The 1980s have been good to Rosenkranz but that is because Rosenkranz has been good for Edwards High Vacuum International – a BOC subsidiary which, under his tutelage, has come to a position of market leadership in the application of vacuums in industries as diverse as pharmaceuticals and semiconductors.

In late 1982, when Rosenkranz was forced to consider the fate of his predecessors in the light of the offer BOC had just made him, Edwards was a loss-maker. That year it produced a turnover of around £20m; today it earns a return on capital of between 20 and 25 per cent and will have sales this year of about £140m.

The story of Edwards in the 1980s is one of remarkable corporate rejuvenation. So remarkable, in fact, that the London Business School uses it as a case study for its MBA programme.

'The human side – what they do to make their version of matrix management work – is important,' says John Stopford of the LBS. 'They have built a team of people that are more interchangeable than most in British industry. There is real team-building at Edwards; many companies talk about it but few achieve it.' Remarkable as Edwards' rejuvenation was, building on past successes and maintaining the momentum is vital to the company's continued growth and development. Edwards' success has bred problems – essentially of size – which have forced it to change.

Size has forced Rosenkranz to think of how best to structure the company for the 1990s and late last year he restructured management completely.

Size has also exacerbated Edwards' most pressing financial problem: controlling its level of stocks. The solution currently being planned for stock control will also help it face tough international competition in the

US, Europe and Japan by improving the time it takes to manufacture and deliver its products.

For Rosenkranz the reorganisation of management that occurred towards the end of 1989 is fundamental to the company's continued growth. Like many managers of successful companies contemplating reorganisation he had to work out how to structure the business without risking the creation of unnecessary bureaucracy.

'It needed to be zoned, but how? By geographic region, by business sector, by two, by three? We decided to zone it vertically and take three (geographical) slices out of it. If we can get the people to work together it should work. We'll give it a go.' The restructuring represented a further evolution in Rosenkranz's approach to matrix management. He divided Edwards' sales and marketing into two units: systems and components. (Systems are complete solutions to a problem, such as a freeze-drying plant with all its ancillary support equipment, while components are things like vacuum pumps which may augment a system or be used on its own.) Both divisions are headed by a director who sits on the management committee. The world has been split into three regions – Europe, the US and Pacific – where the two directors are responsible for deploying their staff resources. Along with this head office reorganisation, the sales and marketing effort has also been revamped in those regions.

Dave Ringland, director of components, says the reorganisation of sales and marketing in the US is designed to make the UK manufacturing base more responsive to the market. 'We want them to tell us what the market needs in terms of products and specifications also of niches and opportunities. If we get that right, then we have got it right for at least 40 per cent of the world market.'

People from both sales and marketing teams are expected to be on the look-out for opportunities for each other. Says Alex Mudge, director of systems: 'Dave and I act as a service to both sides of the business. We don't want both sides of the business going in opposite directions.' This, along with their willingness to make statements about the other's area of responsibility, underlines the identity of purpose which seems to pervade Edwards. Senior management across the whole of the company's business – manufacturing, technical services, sales and marketing, corporate services or personnel – appears to understand where Edwards is and what it needs to get better.

Rosenkranz says that decisions are never taken at the company's monthly management committee meeting, formerly its board meeting – it just reviews what has happened. 'If something needs to be done, the relevant group will report and if it's approved, it's a decision,' he says.

He likes his people to work in groups. They congregate at all levels of the company and the meetings are inter-disciplinary. At sub-director level, teams look at things Edwards should be doing over the next few years. According to Rosenkranz, they tend to produce 'wish for' and 'wish not for' lists, but, he says, they are a way of getting people involved. 'We don't want to end up with departments not understanding each other.' But putting people into groups, which help make them understand the problems of others in the company, is half of the explanation of the apparent esprit de corps at Edwards.

The other half of making what Stopford calls 'the human side' work is information. On all senior managers' desks is a networked computer and the information it contains is the life-blood at Edwards.

At the heart of this system is Keith Pointon, Edwards' quietly-spoken commercial director. For Pointon, a matrix management system needs a clever information system to make it work. 'It helps keep conflict between senior management to a minimum, because it helps issues to be seen in a clear way and discussed unemotionally,' he says. 'Information has enabled us to keep abreast of change – it has helped us get beyond the obvious to get to total costs.' The latest venture in the application of information, which will be tested towards the end of the year, is an extension of Edwards' use of information.

Pointon and K Rajagopal, manufacturing director, are currently working on a system which, if successful, will revolutionise manufacturing and distribution, and, in Pointon's words, 'dynamically link the factory with the customer'. Edwards' UK and international operations will be linked by a computer network. Into this, sales and marketing will input orders and their estimates of demand during the distribution lead time.

In the first instance, having this information will allow the centre best to allocate stocks – rather than letting the regions hold stocks for anticipated demand – around the world. Near term production schedules will then be drawn up with reference to these estimates of demand and by applying the same logic to manufacturing as was applied to stocks. If successful, it will cut stocks and improve financial performance significantly.

The system being developed is an application of 'just in time' inventory control to stocks distribution and orders worldwide. Rajagopal says that the 1980s way of manufacturing is not good enough. If it took Edwards a month to make something, now it has to take a week. Customer confidence in delivery is, he says, absolutely important. 'If the customers don't have confidence in supply then sooner or later they'll go somewhere else.' Pointon agrees.

'The old cliche is correct: getting the right product in the right place at the right time.' The new management structure, together with the changes in train for stock control and distribution, have set the direction for Edwards in the early 1990s. Behind them has been Rosenkranz, encouraging and chivying his team.

The company has occupied his mind fully since late 1982, when he assumed the role of managing director. He is clearly still engaged by the problems and opportunities the company continually throws up. And he has further plans.

'There is one I have which I believe is right for vacuum technology but the question is how to reach it by evolution and not revolution,' he says.

Mid-way through the decade he might just attempt to introduce it. He appears to command considerable respect from his senior managers. To a man they speak highly of his business acumen – his capacity for detail and the quality of his intuition. 'Before Danny none of our managing directors had credibility. He inspires loyalty and he will be a difficult act to follow.' His greater responsibilities within BOC will take him away from Edwards, although the latter remains his prime responsibility and will probably be so for some time. In his absences maybe a natural successor will come to the fore. But Rosenkranz has shown himself to be a master of the matrix and possibly the most difficult test he will have to pass is the one which measures how enduring his influence on Edwards has been once he is no longer there.

SLAUGHTERING SACRED COWS BEEFS UP BHS

By Maggie Urry

First published 11 April 1990

David Dworkin has instant recall of the date he joined BhS, the UK chain store group – November 13 last year. Only a few months after his arrival, BhS's total sales are running at 20 per cent above those of a year ago, and this at a time when retailers generally are moaning about the poor state of trade. Within the whole, sales of womens-wear are running at 35 per cent or more ahead.

It sounds too much like a miracle. But Dworkin, an American, says that 'we are not talking about brain surgery'. So far he has been making simple changes which provide 'quick wins'. He describes the first phase of action at BhS as 'tweaking' and reckons this can boost the chain's turnover significantly.

Already, he claims, this has had an enormous effect on the morale in the company. 'Many of the store managers have never seen a lift in sales. It is a new feeling for them. The pendulum has swung,' he exclaims.

Staff at BhS now wonder about the calm and softly spoken Dworkin: 'We don't understand how a man who speaks so quietly makes us run so fast.' BhS – once British Home Stores – was merged with Habitat Mothercare in early 1986 to form Storehouse. The plan at the time was to jazz up the dowdy but still significantly profitable chain with a touch of the Sir Terence Conran design flair.

Something went wrong in the process, and when Michael Julien was brought in as Storehouse chief executive in June 1988, BhS's problems had to be re-addressed.

Its profits have fallen from a peak of over £70m at the operating level to £40m in its last financial year to March 1989, with analysts forecasting at least a halving of that for the current year.

Thus Dworkin came to a business which was already in the throes of reorganisation. He admits that he was taking a risk in giving up his career in America, which includes experience with US retailers such as Nieman Marcus and Bonwit Teller, to come to BhS, but says that he was not 'totally crazy'. It still had a legacy of strengths – its well-known name, the good locations of most of the 134 stores, annual turnover at around £600m which is large enough to build on, and which demonstrates 'there must be some appeal' in BhS. And its electronic information system is used by some US retailers and is considered by Dworkin to be one of the best.

Further, on taking his first look at retailing in the UK and comparing it with his US experience, Dworkin was amazed at how many customers there were in the shops. In the US, he says, the first struggle is getting people into shops. In the UK, with fewer shops and greater population density, there is a higher level of customer traffic already.

Dworkin had done his homework before coming to BhS – 'it was no surprise to me that it was run in a very antiquated way for a retailer,' he says. Some things he found astounding – but readily reversible.

He initiated the setting up of a workshop which came up with a mission statement. This starts: 'The BhS mission is to be the first choice store for dressing the modern woman and family.' That has been followed up with an activity value analysis project (AVA) which will look at every aspect of the business to see what it contributes.

Already Dworkin has plans to get rid of the 16 warehouses which are currently holding merchandise, so speeding up the supply chain, and saving costs.

At the start of the AVA exercise two slides were presented. The first said 'there are no sacred cows'. The second, 'there is no bullshit'. The project will be complete in mid-May and is expected to bring cost savings rapidly.

The first phase is to get the business up to an acceptable profit level – though Dworkin admits he has no idea what the true base line for the business will turn out to be.

Dworkin reckons he can 'get the business into good shape quickly and cheaply'. There will be a need for some capital spending on new fixtures in the stores, but nothing more serious since much had already been spent.

The shops have been tidied up and some of the clutter caused by too many signs removed. The policy of putting other retail brands – Storehouse's own or outsiders' – into the stores has started to be reversed. Dworkin insists on 'harmony' which includes 'continuity under one roof'. The concessions, he says, 'do not have a place in the stores'. His first concern was the amount of merchandise that was sitting in stock rooms and warehouses instead of being put in front of customers. This has two elements – merchandise that did not sell and was shoved into stock rooms and new merchandise that had arrived at the back door but had not yet been put out on the shelves and racks.

Storehouse had already recognised the problem of old stock – which in the past had been trotted out again in subsequent seasons – with a savage new policy on writing down stock that was not selling. But, says Dworkin, though Storehouse 'intellectually understood that something was wrong', it did not have what Dworkin calls a 'factory floor obsessiveness' – a determination to push goods through the stores.

Before Christmas the group cut prices of stock which had not been selling well to a level where customers did buy it and Dworkin decided, against the advice of his staff, to put spring ranges – which had arrived and were waiting in the stockrooms for spring – out on the floor. The first sacred cow had gone.

The move worked. Already the shops are demanding more stock. That poses a problem in that usually British shops order most of a season's merchandise in advance. BhS has quickly had to find some new sources of stock. Here Dworkin's American experience came in handy. A trip to New York found a range of merchandise that could be delivered within four weeks, and would fit into the BhS price ranges and its margin structure.

This presented a cultural challenge for old hands at BhS. The merchandise could only be received in so short a time if the existing labels, with someone else's brand name, were kept in – changing to BhS labels would add another three weeks. Dworkin decided that that would be too long to wait, so another sacred cow has been slaughtered.

Dworkin is bemused by the British system of classifying people into social classes – A, B, C1, C2 and so on – preferring to think in terms of attitudes and lifestyles. These days, he reckons, shoppers are more ageless and classless, and too tight a targeting of a certain age group or class is merely 'painting yourself into a corner'. He plans to rework the merchandise strategy to aim at 'end user groups'.

This will involve looking at sub-sections of ranges – leisurewear, for instance, includes four or five lifestyles, Dworkin says.

In the past BhS has worked on what he calls 'dumb broad categories' – a dress buyer might have been told to go out and buy dresses, without a thought as to what kind of dresses or how they would fit into the store. By looking at what is selling, the chain can understand its customers better, Dworkin believes.

So far Dworkin has not closed any stores, preferring to see whether the worst stores will respond to the tweaking treatment. He is pleased with the 'tweaking' at the Putney store – which would have been a candidate for closure if he had simply closed the 10 worst shops. It is a small store which was trying to offer both clothing and homewares. By taking out the homewares, he says, the clothing ranges could be expanded, with, he says, great success.

There is a lot of 'fallow footage' – space wasted in stockrooms, for instance – which will be set to work. And while the goods on offer already look more attractive, picking the right merchandise, he says, is the easy part and only the beginning.

HOW TENNECO SHOOK OFF PREDATORS

By Charles Leadbeater

First published 5 September 1990

The deal earlier this summer in which Cummins, the diesel engine maker, sold 27 per cent of its equity to Ford Motor, Kubota of Japan and Tenneco, the US farm machinery, defence and automotive components conglomerate, might mark a turning point for the company.

Since the mid-1980s Cummins has been turned into a test case of the ethics of American capitalism. Henry Schact, Cummins chairman, has championed what he saw as the long-term interests of American industry against Wall Street, which he accused of having loose morals and short-term perspectives.

Yet the deal was also significant for Tenneco. Like Cummins it has been subject to a lengthy tug of war between the industrial and financial factions of the US economy.

Schact may draw some comfort from Tenneco's experience. Its involvement in the Cummins deal marks another stage in its resurgence, as its improved industrial performance has dispelled the financial uncertainty around it.

Although Tenneco's recent history does not have the tainted glamour of the more infamous leveraged bids, it was reshaped by the US takeover wave without being taken over. Its revised corporate strategy introduced in 1989 was in large part a response to rumours on Wall Street of an impending break-up bid.

Tenneco, which began life during the Second World War as an oil and gas pipeline company, moved into oil and gas exploration and production in 1946.

This was to be the foundation for the rest of the group for more than 40 years as it determinedly diversified and evolved into an industrial conglomerate. It added chemicals in 1955, shipbuilding in 1968, the JI Case agricultural machinery operations two years later, automotive components in 1977 and to cap it all, parts of the ailing International Harvester, another agricultural machinery maker, six years ago.

At that time, the company expected healthy demand for agricultural and construction machinery and rising oil and gas prices. Neither expectation was fulfilled.

By 1987 the company was in deep trouble: it reported a 54 per cent fall in operating income for the first quarter as the recession in the oil and gas business took its toll. The farm equipment business was also struggling, despite substantial investment. Tractor sales which reached a peak of 166,000 a year in 1979 fell back to 61,600 in 1986.

In 1987 operating income was halved to $505m as the company slid into a net loss of $218m. Yet the sharp decline in Tenneco's fortunes was only partly due to the cyclical decline in oil and agriculture. The plunge in 1987 marked the culmination of a steady decline from a peak net income of $777m in 1981, falling each year to $369m in 1984 and on to the loss in 1987.

Through the 1980s the company showed little return on the capital investment of almost $9bn it made between 1981 and 1985. The rate of return on common stockholders' equity trailed from a peak of 18.6 per cent in 1980 to 5.8 per cent in 1984 and a loss of 6.5 per cent in 1987.

The company became heavily geared as debt rose steeply to finance continued investment and losses. Short-term debt rose from £263m in 1984 to almost $2bn four years later. Long-term debt drifted up by more than $1bn to $6.2bn in 1987. This was set against equity of $3.7bn and preferred and preference stock of $435m.

By then the patience of shareholders and Wall Street was tested to the limit. Analysts raucously called on the company to revise its strategy, accusing it of being out of control despite layers of bureaucratic management.

The vultures began to gather. With the company's share price languishing at about $38, Tenneco's break-up value was put at $70 to $80 a share. A bid to dismember Tenneco became a real possibility.

In March 1988 the company responded to the mounting chorus of criticism by appointing Kenneth Reese, its executive vice president, to carry out a thorough review of the company's structure. He was given a mandate to leave no stone unturned – and took his bosses at their word.

Most expected the company to spin off some of the manufacturing interests, particularly agricultural machinery, in order to protect the core oil and gas business.

Reese says the figures simply did not add up. He estimated that JI Case was worth about $3.8bn, but Tenneco would have realised only half that from selling it. With the oil and gas division still making losses, Tenneco would have disposed of a prized asset to be rewarded with at best only a limited reduction in debt.

However, the oil division would still have been making a loss if oil prices had risen. The sale of the oil and gas division would raise more than

£5bn, allowing the company to reduce debt, buy back some of its stock to prevent a takeover bid and stabilise the company's finances, Reese calculated.

Reese says: 'A recommendation to sell the oil division did not go over real big with a company based in Houston, Texas.' Wall Street was taken aback by the announcement that the company was in effect staking its future on a marked improvement at JI Case, the agricultural machinery business which had lost money every year between 1983 and 1988.

Nevertheless, the sale went ahead in one of the biggest corporate auctions in Texan history. Chevron paid $2.6bn for Tenneco's oil and gas interests in the Gulf of Mexico, Petrofina paid $600m for Tenneco's south western business, while Mesa paid $715m for operations in Kansas, Oklahoma, Texas and Arkansas. Combined with purchases by Atlantic Richfield, Mobile, Amoco and Conoco, about $7.3bn was raised over three months.

With that, short-term debt was cut from $1.9bn in 1988 to $428m last year, while long-term debt was more than halved to $3.1bn.

In addition, new management was brought into JI Case, with a determination to cut costs, improve quality and produce profits as well as tractors.

Reese reflects upon the traumatic experience – which involved swingeing cuts at its corporate head office – with equanimity. 'It was like an internal leveraged buy-out without taking on all the debt and incurring all the fees. We were too leveraged. We sold a major business to reduce debt and refocus the rest of the group,' he says.

He also recognises that the lumbering industrial giant had lessons to learn from the financiers which preyed upon the company and forced it to change.

Reese says: 'We learnt a lot. We cannot continue to take on debt year on year. We cannot just continue with all our businesses regardless of the returns they make. Managers have to watch cash in and cash out. We have to pay attention to financial performance and return to shareholders as well as being interested in being good managers.' Reese still cannot understand Wall Street's love affair with leveraged bids, its apparent preference for clever financing rather than solid industrial performance. 'A lot of the LBO skeletons are just rising to the surface from the depths of the lake,' he says.

Yet he admits that the corporate raiders did play an important role in revitalising companies such as Tenneco. 'A lot of things they did were for purely selfish reasons, for their own purposes,' says Reese. 'However, in many companies managers set themselves up to be attacked by a raider because they were more interested in being professional managers than delivering returns to shareholders. Not everything that the raiders did was bad.' Tenneco's performance has improved considerably. Last year it delivered a net profit of $584m, with earnings per share of $4.46. Its stock price has advanced to more than $65, leaving only a very narrow margin between the market price and break-up price.

But now that large leveraged bids have been discredited, what discipline will be in place to make sure that industrial conglomerates like Tenneco do not fall back into their bad old ways? Reese admits that maintaining a sense of urgency is difficult, but he points to three factors. First, bureaucracy has been cut and management has been sharpened, he says. The test case will be the performance of JI Case. The company is making money, but is still yielding unimpressive returns on sales of $3bn. There is little room for further cost-cutting through factory closures in the US or savings in administration.

Having instituted sustained cost-cutting the company is working to improve its quality, after-sales service and reputation for reliability. Under the leadership of James Ashford, Case's president, the company is rationalising its base of more than 8,000 suppliers. This is where the deal with Cummins comes in: to secure a long term relationship with one of its main engine suppliers. Higher volumes from fewer suppliers should allow lower costs.

Tenneco is hoping the energy of Case's management will spread through the rest of the company, to meet ambitious targets set by central management.

Significantly, the company is now stressing the achievement of financial targets where it might once have focused on industrial logic.

James Ketelsen, Tenneco's president, set these out in its last annual report: a 20 per cent return on shareholders' equity, to improve earnings per share by 15 per cent a year and to generate cash for capital investment and dividends. Reese says: 'We have to make senior managers stockholders rather than just hired guns. We need to get the key people more deeply involved in the business.' Secondly, senior managers intend to take a more critical approach to priorities for investment.

Reese does not see any case for getting out of any of the company's remaining major divisions, including packaging, which was the only one to make a loss last year, and chemicals and minerals which accounted for only 9 per cent of turnover.

However, it will do more to move out of lower margin businesses within divisions and into higher margin activities. Ketelsen cites the sale last year of the automotive retailing businesses. The proceeds were used to acquire the shock absorber business of Armstrong, the UK engineering group.

Thirdly, Tenneco plans to internationalise its operations, especially through acquisitions such as Armstrong and the joint ventures it has formed with Bosch of West Germany and several Japanese groups including Mitsubishi.

Reese says: 'If we are going to be in a business we have to be global.' But in some areas, such as chemicals and packaging, that may be easier said than done. The rapid growth projected for the Pacific Rim and Europe will be a severe test of many US manufacturing companies. The size of their domestic market has lulled some into a complacent insularity, admits Reese.

Indeed, last year only 29 per cent of Tenneco's revenues and 25 per cent of its operating income came from outside the US. This leaves it extremely vulnerable to the state of the US economy.

Case's performance is improving, the natural gas pipeline business is delivering healthy profits and Reese says he is confident the Newport News shipbuilding business will hold up despite cuts in defence spending. He believes the company has a balanced portfolio of businesses, serving a range of customers with different spending patterns, from the US Government and farmers, to the large motor manufacturers and consumer industries such as food processing.

Whether Tenneco is well balanced enough to achieve the goals set out by Ketelsen is yet to be proved. But it is no longer under seige. For others such as Cummins, which found themselves so at odds with the financial fashions of the 1980s, that should be heartening news.

HOOVER SETS OUT TO MAKE A CLEAN SWEEP

By John Gapper

First published 23 April 1990

Mervyn Davies, a foreman at Hoover's plant in Merthyr Tydfil, south Wales, is not unhappy at the prospect of his job disappearing at the domestic appliance maker. 'It will be sad if I disappear with it, sure, but if you are talking about running an efficient factory it has to be done,' he says.

Davies spent nine years as a sergeant in the Royal Signals. He followed that with 18 years as a foreman at Hoover, nearly all in a similarly ambiguous role, stuck between officers and men; he is one of 42 foremen whose jobs are to be abolished in a work restructuring.

'I believe you are born to be a foreman,' says 44 year-old Davies. 'You have got to be a leader of men. You have got to take some flak and you have got to give it.' Born to the role or not, Hoover's foremen will soon have to get used to a different one.

For some, the new role will be redundancy. For others, it will be that of specialist tasks within the old factory on the outskirts of Merthyr, which was first built in the aftermath of the last war as a place for returning soldiers to work. The rest will join a new supervisor grade.

There is a lot of uncertainty inside the Merthyr plant these days. It is a time of old certainties being abolished without new ones to take their place. The previous order was broken by the announcement last September that 290 of the 1,890 jobs there were to go.

They have gone now, and a new factory manager has been in place since January, planning new ways of working to fit in with a £12m capital investment approved by Hoover's US parent company Maytag. Hoover is to change, but some of its workers are still unsure of how.

Ian Bonnar, general manager personnel and associate director of the Merthyr plant, wants a different factory from the traditional and aged one he has inherited. 'It is like a car that has run very well for years, then you miss a service or two, and suddenly when you put your foot down it does not take off,' he says.

The announcement of job cuts in September came from a broad review of the way Hoover works. The review was known within the US parent company as 'Backdragon' because it involved a group of senior managers standing back to look at operations from the company's Merthyr head office.

Among other things, the review concluded that Hoover was producing too much to match a downturn in demand and increased competition from the Far East. Job cuts were decided on both at Merthyr and at the company's vacuum cleaner manufacturing site in Cambuslang, Scotland.

A series of changes emerged from Backdragon, from a switch in advertising agency to a new distribution contract. It also tried to address the managers' old complaint that Hoover was led too much by its marketing side – 'We would sell machines with bells and whistles on,' says Bonnar.

But the implications of the review for the Merthyr plant – beyond the cut in jobs to 1,603 – are only now starting to emerge. They range from a change in production methods affecting 25 per cent of floor space to a set of innovations in working arrangements and supervision.

The news of another big work reorganisation prompts some disbelief from Bill Bish, the plant's union convener. Only four years ago, under Hoover's previous US owners, Chicago Pacific, it was in the throes of a project known as Phoenix under which manufacturing methods were revised.

'Quite frankly, I don't think the plant is being run as efficiently as it was in the past,' says Bish, who emphasises the unions' commitment to increasing profitability. He says production changes such as the introduction of just-in-time techniques have not been thought out thoroughly.

The main production changes for the Merthyr plant will be the use of polypropylene tubs in place of the current metal ones, and a move to buying-in pre-painted shells for the machines rather than pressing and painting steel inside the plant. This will in turn affect final assembly.

Bonnar's aim is to cut down the variety and complexity of tasks in assembly.

As part of the Phoenix project, the company moved from cycle times of 30–45 seconds in this area to times of up to two and a half minutes. The aim was to enrich the jobs of workers and cut absenteeism.

A side-effect has been to make it much more difficult to train production workers. The new cycle times require workers to carry out 5,000 operations to achieve full competence, against 50 for 30-second tasks. The company has found the commitment too heavy and wants to return to the old ways.

But Bonnar's attempt to revitalise the plant involves more than making production simpler to fit in with a re-shaped marketing effort. It also means cutting through some of the accumulated layers of tradition in a factory where the average age of workers until recently was 49.

He has identified a number of targets: More managers are being brought in from outside. There is a new technical manager at the plant and he is recruiting managers for other functions. The family traditions of Hoover have combined with the distinctive nature of the plant in the Merthyr area to keep turnover very low until now.

Craft workers are being asked to train in multi-skilling; for instance this would involve electricians doing fitters' jobs and vice-versa. The number of maintenance craft workers has been cut from 83 to 43 and Bonnar wants installation work to pass to outside contractors instead of direct employees.

The materials delivery group of 70 mainly semi-skilled workers is to be asked to work more flexibly between areas of the factory. More generally, he wants to achieve more flexibility in deploying semi-skilled workers across functions in assembly lines.

But the most dramatic change in working arrangements is the proposal to abolish the jobs of all 42 foremen at the factory in favour of an extended layer of supervisors who would be clearly identified as part of management rather than being stuck between the workforce and managers.

From long experience as an industrial relations manager in the motor industry, Bonnar talks of foremen as being 'a bit of an enigma' in many companies. Within the Merthyr plant, he says many foremen have been inadequately trained and have more or less abandoned the management of people.

Instead, they have become chasers of materials on lines. He means to remedy this by re-appointing some of them to specialist tasks of this kind while bringing in better trained supervisors with responsibility for controlling the way work is handled within sections of plant.

In the washing machine assembly area, he envisages the current 16 foremen and three superintendents – as supervisors are known in the factory – being replaced by about nine supervisors. Each supervisor in the factory would typically have responsibility for about 70 people.

'The role of the foreman over the years has moved from being a man manager to being an activity manager,' he says. 'The calibre of foreman we have here now does not meet our needs and we are left with this extra layer that slows down communication.' As one of the foremen better-regarded by the company, Davies sees some sense in this view. 'I don't think the role the foreman is playing at the moment is quite sensible,' he says. 'He is half on the workers' side and half on the management's and he needs to be all on the management's.' Bish says the company has been at fault in its treatment of foremen. One reason the foreman's role has been degraded is the company's abolition of materials progress chasers as part of a move to a just-in-time system, he argues. Foremen have simply ended up covering for the absent chasers.

The fate of Hoover's progress chasers raises a common flaw in many work re-organisations: that the remaining structure tends to absorb the absent jobs informally. Is there then a guarantee that Hoover's foremen really are to be abolished, and they will not re-emerge under another name? Bonnar believes not, if his aim of re-focusing the manufacturing process to simplify it and improve communications is achieved. For him, foremen have been one of the accumulated layers that have stifled the Hoover plant for too long, and need to be removed.

THE RATIONALE BEHIND ICI'S RESTRUCTURING IN EUROPE

By Clive Cookson

First published 7 September 1990

Imagine a European domestic appliance manufacturer designing a new range of refrigerators that do not use CFCs, the chemicals that are destroying the ozone layer in the upper atmosphere. That company is a prized customer of ICI, the UK-based chemicals giant. But until now it has been on the receiving end of a disparate barrage of approaches from salesmen and technical experts from different parts of ICI.

Then ICI announces a complete overhaul of its European organisation, which is intended to produce a far better co-ordinated approach to customers. Power and responsibility will be transferred from ICI subsidiaries in individual countries to a new regional management structure.

As a result the appliance manufacturer can expect to receive a single ICI technical and sales team to help it with the fridge project as a whole. There will be representatives from ICI Chemicals and Polymers (providing new coolants that do not contain CFCs), ICI Polyurethanes (providing CFC-free insulating foam) and ICI Paints (providing a new hard-wearing finish for the fridge).

ICI's present European structure was never designed as a whole. It has grown up since 1960 when the company first became seriously involved on the continent. The 75 separate units report in different directions to ICI's main operating businesses.

Fifteen wholly-owned 'national companies' now represent ICI in the individual European countries. But some ICI businesses work through these national companies and others operate independently through 30 different sales organisations.

According to David Beynon, the chairman of ICI Europe, the new organisation 'provides ICI with a much simpler and more cohesive structure than exists at present'. The main changes are:

- ICI Europa, set up in Belgium in 1966 to oversee the company's continental activities, will be renamed ICI Europe. It will have much more power and responsibility, since the 15 national companies are being downgraded.

    Beynon's team, based at Everberg close to Brussels airport, includes three new directors who will be responsible for personnel, finance and information systems. Beynon will chair a European Advisory Board, which will include European directors of the 10 ICI businesses.
- Six regional centres will be created to provide functional support to those businesses. The regions are: Mid-Europe (West and East Germany, Austria, Switzerland), France, Italy, Benelux (Belgium, the Netherlands, Luxembourg), Iberia (Spain, Portugal), and Nordic (Denmark, Sweden, Norway, Finland).
- All European sales staff will report directly to one of the 10 ICI business headquarters. They will no longer be managed by the national companies – mostly the case today.

Tom Hutchison, the ICI main board director responsible for Europe, supervised the planning of the new structure. He says the reorganisation is a response to both external and internal developments.

Internally, ICI realised that the expansion of its European operations – continental sales increased 100-fold from £30m in 1960 to £3.2bn in 1989 through a combination of organic growth and acquisitions – had left it with an inefficient proliferation of business units and national companies.

External factors include the prospect of a single European market and the emergence of large corporate customers – multinationals such as Ford, Philips and Electrolux – which deal with their chemical suppliers on a Europe-wide basis and do not want to bother with national companies or small business units.

'Our prime objective is to meet the changing needs of our customers,' says Hutchison. 'The single European market will affect the way in which our customers organise their own businesses. They will be looking for fewer suppliers and a more integrated relationship with companies supplying them. They will be seeking technological help to solve their product problems and develop their own markets.'

ICI sells mainly to other manufacturers; it expects the number of customers to decrease during the 1990s as a result of mergers and joint ventures. 'Overall the picture is one of fewer customers seeking fewer suppliers and expecting a total and highly responsive service package. ICI wants to meet these challenges and be a "preferred" or "first choice" supplier.'

The European chemical market is still fragmented in comparison with some of its customer industries. The top five European chemical companies (including ICI) supply only 20 per cent of the market – in contrast with, for example, the car market in which the top five producers account for 60 per cent of sales.

The study team which Hutchison set up early in 1989 to plan the reorganisation soon concluded that 'we were hugely sub-optimal in terms of functional support for European sales,' Hutchison says. 'When we went into the market-place we weren't adequately pulling together the strengths of ICI's customer services. We needed to make a change that would give us more corporate clout.' The new organisation has a relatively simple parallel structure, with ICI Europe and its six regions providing functional services (such as finance, computing, health and safety) and the 10 ICI businesses providing specialist skills. 'We decided that the day of the generalist in serving customers was coming to an end,' says Hutchison.

Although ICI executives insist that the primary reason for the reorganisation is to provide a better service for customers, the company will also benefit from cost savings, as it cuts out unnecessary duplication of facilities such as offices, computers and legal services. Internal estimates suggest that the savings could amount to £25m to £30m a year.

A significant new appointment is that of Derek Newman, who moves from ICI's computer centre in the UK where he is corporate information systems manager, to become information systems director for ICI Europe. His job will be to weld together a plethora of different computer and telecommunications systems into an effective European network.

Even though the national companies are being very much reduced in importance, they will not disappear entirely. 'It's important to retain a senior national presence in each country,' Beynon says. 'We're going to have someone called a "national manager" who will be ICI's corporate spokesman. We see this as a part-time role for a senior member of the ICI organisation in that country.'

The one business which is expected to continue to organise European sales on a national basis is ICI Pharmaceuticals, because its main customers are the national health services. (Non-tariff barriers will continue to impede pharmaceuticals trade in the EC after 1992, with each country maintaining a different regulatory process for drugs.) All other ICI businesses are likely to appoint sales managers with transnational responsibilities.

The closure of some European offices will inevitably mean disruption for staff. But the company says there should be no overall loss of jobs. The number of ICI employees on the continent has grown from 800 in 1960 to 17,000 now, and the growth is likely to continue.

'Such growth, coupled with a control of recruitment to replace leavers, will in most locations absorb the effects of a changing organisation,' Beynon says. 'But where this proves not to be possible I am determined the consequences of our changes will be handled caringly and in full consultation with staff and their representatives.' The changes will not be imposed overnight but introduced gradually, he emphasises. Some important elements, such as the location of the regional centres for Benelux, Iberia and the Nordic countries, have not yet been decided. But the aim is to have the whole organisation fully operational in continental Western Europe by 1992.

Eastern Europe (apart from East Germany) is being left out of ICI Europe for the time being, though it may be included later in the 1990s – depending on the region's political and economic progress. Only last week up ICI Poland was set up – a wholly-owned subsidiary similar to the national companies that are to be phased out in Western Europe.

The role of ICI's home territory in the new Europe is still to be decided.

'A separate study is to be undertaken to determine the most appropriate structure to meet the needs of the UK and the Republic of Ireland,' Beynon says.

'The UK needs to be integrated into Europe as a whole,' Hutchison says. 'It would be pointless to have a strategy for the European motor industry that didn't include the UK. But at the same time the UK is clearly different because ICI has its major infrastructure here.'

3 MAKING TOTAL QUALITY A WAY OF LIFE

INTRODUCTION

Quality has become one of the competitive watchwords of the 1990s. Increasingly, companies now realise that attention to detail, customer satisfaction and reliability are the factors which will separate the stayers from the also rans. Official quality standards now exist for manufacturing and service industries and to attain them is to gain the basic qualification for entering into whole new markets. It can mean all the difference for smaller and medium-sized companies as to whether they get on to the list of suppliers to a corporate giant or a government department.

However, quality – or more specifically quality standards – are not an end in themselves. Quite the opposite. Quality standards are the beginning of a process which must remain the continuous backbone of corporate life, a factor which emerges time and again in this chapter. Total quality management – a discipline which embraces the entire corporate being, from customer relations to product and manufacturing quality – should be one of the ultimate objectives of any company. However, it takes time, effort, resources and commitment.

For many companies the right route is to add layer upon layer of quality over several years before the company is finally ready to embrace TQM. Texas Instruments, Exxon Chemical and Kodak are examples discussed in this chapter, Texas moving down this road for 10 years before it felt ready to take the plunge.

One of the great ironies of quality management has now become the stuff of folklore. This is that the Japanese – from whom TQM was learned by the West, along with other management imperatives like Just-in-Time manufacturing – drew on the theory of an American for what they were to turn into pre-eminent quality performance. In the first of a series of articles on TQM, Simon Holberton, the FT's then Management Correspondent, relates how W Edwards Deming, imparted his views on quality to the Japanese in the early 1950s. In turn, the Japanese not only developed Deming's theories into formidable competitive qualities, but also named a quality award after him. Yet it was not until the 1980s that he was to achieve recognition in his own country. Then America instigated its own quality prize – the Malcolm Baldrige National Quality Award – which, while attracting a faithful following, also collected hostile reaction, the dissenters believing that it was fundamentally flawed on philosophical and other grounds. To add to the irony, Deming himself was critical of the award.

The parameters of quality have broadened significantly since the early days after the Second World War, when the Japanese first began to apply them to re-build their industrial base. Then, it was manufacturing based, relating particularly to a control process designed to iron out the variations in products that naturally occur in any mechanical production process. Today, quality is built in much more fundamentally to both manufacturing and service industries, relates to all of a company's elements – customer relations, inventory control, training, employee responsibility etc – and may well be enshrined in the corporate philosophy or 'mission statement'.

The modern concept is difficult to turn into reality, and cannot be imposed. To work properly TQM must be a continuous striving to achieve excellence. Thus, nothing can stand still, and everything is up for improvement. This can only be done if the entire workforce is carried along and is receptive to the idea of continuous monitoring of all practices (especially self-monitoring) and is willing to change. Thus it must be a bottom up as well as a top down process. If expectations among the workforce are raised, they must be satisfied.

This commitment is exemplified by Kodak, as Simon Holberton shows in an examination of the fundamental changes which the film products group found it necessary to make when it set out to improve its manufacturing facility in the UK. Theory proved to be the easy part. Putting it into practice was very much harder because it required not only a change in the way production machinery was used, but also in the relationship between managers and managed. The particular quality methodology introduced was statistical process control, one of the fundamentals of TQM. It is a management technique which leads to a reduction in the rate of product rejects. What Kodak was able to show is that such improvements are achievable even in the production of a mature product.

Amdahl Ireland, part of Amdahl Corporation of the US, makes powerful mainframe computers. A programme of change was instigated which gradually, rather than deliberately, emerged as a strategy to improve quality, with particular emphasis on building the human emphasis and on improving co-operation internally. Responsibility was widened among the workforce, leading to the establishment of self-management teams. In this case the objective was not just quality of product, but quality of management process.

This is deemed to be one of the greatest strengths of the quality movement. Rather than producing just a quality product at the end, it provides a quality means to the end.

Equally, the quality of service to customers must be given priority. Xerox, the office equipment manufacturer, introduced such a programme, finding in the process that adjustments to the organisation's structure were essential because of the need to bring its workforce closer to the customer. Dissatisfied customers can be costly, Rank Xerox, the British end of the business, reasoned. It has a large customer base, a proportion of which drops away each year. The company reckoned it could retain a significant proportion of those which it lost because they were in some way dissatisfied with Rank Xerox. It set a target to achieve total customer satisfaction under a programme it believes is achieveable by 1993.

But while the West is avidly embracing concepts first exploited by the Japanese – indeed, even leading in certain areas – the Japanese have already been moving the goalposts. Just-in-Time manufacturing, a key element of the quality armoury, is a case in point. This is the process by which a company organises its manufacture to deliver orders direct from the production line, rather than from large completed stocks, while also having its raw materials delivered by its own suppliers just in time. As Ian Rodger wrote when heading the FT office in Tokyo, Toyota, the biggest Japanese car maker, set its sights on taking this process into a new league. The company believed that quality would remain a potent competitive weapon for many years, but it also reckoned that customer demands would intensify, demanding of volume car makers much greater choice, but with almost instant delivery. Toyota believes that a custom-made order to delivery cycle of just a few days is not only achievable – but that this is where the quality movement is heading.

QUALITY IN THE 1990s

By Simon Holberton

First published between March and May 1991

Defining the crucial issues

It was Jean-Baptiste Colbert, Louis XIV's finance minister and the founder of the Sevres and Gobelins state factories, who summed up why quality matters.

Writing to the king in August 1664, Colbert noted: 'If our factories, through careful work, assure the quality of our products, it will be to the foreigners' interest to get supplies from us, and their money will flow into the kingdom.' Substitute 'company' for 'kingdom' and you have one of the main reasons for the allure of an idea that is sweeping European and American manufacturing and service companies. Total quality management (TQM) is an idea whose time has not only come but seems likely to prevail after most other management fads and fashions have been consigned to the dustbin.

Companies are turning to quality to help them cope with and survive the competitive challenges facing industry. Deregulation, the onward march of globalisation and the advance of technology have redefined industrial success.

Only those companies which are able to develop new products quickly, which can supply them at a consistently high level of quality – and on time – will command positions of leadership in the 1990s.

In order to compete at this level, European and US companies are seeking to improve their business performance by changing organisational structures and work practices. Management layers are being cut out – to save costs and to bring top decision makers closer to the factory floor – and responsibility for product quality is being defused throughout the company.

Change is the leitmotif of this trend and the desire of companies to achieve change is forcing them to confront the most fundamental managerial task: striking a new balance between control on the one hand and consent on the other. If 'control' was the dominant mode of management in the past, 'consent' – or at least a more consensual approach – is beginning to supersede it and might even become the dominant mode in the 1990s.

In the late 1940s, Philip Selznick, the organisational theorist, wrote that 'co-operative systems are constituted of individuals . . . in relation to a formal system of co-ordination'. A precondition for such a system is, however, the 'indivisibility of control and consent'. Clem Smyth, director of production for Amdahl Ireland, the computer mainframe manu-facturer, makes the same point in a slightly different way: 'This sort of change is about attitudes and you can't ordain changes in attitudes.' The origin of TQM is American and is associated largely with a handful of statisticians who, in the 1920s and 1930s, worked for the quality control section of Western Electric, the manufacturing arm of ITT.

The problem with which Western Electric was trying to grapple was variation.

Variation is the enemy of, but inherent in, any manufacturing process because mechanical processes tend to produce products which are subtly different.

The statisticians at Western Electric's Hawthorne plant sought to analyse this variation, measure it, and, where possible, modify the pro-cess to reduce variation. The techniques pioneered there today go under the name of statistical process control (SPC).

Pre-eminent among these men is W Edwards Deming and Joseph Juran, both of whom worked at Western Electric's Hawthorne plant. Philip Crosby, a former executive with ITT, Armand Feigenbaum, the man who coined the term 'total quality control' and was head of quality at General Electric of the US, and the late Kaoru Ishikawa, a member of the Japanese Union of Scientists and Engineers, complete the list of the first division of the so-called 'quality gurus'.

Until the 1980s it was the Japanese who had most consistently applied the principles of quality management. At the end of the Second World War, it was Deming, Juran and Feigenbaum who had educated Japanese industrialists in the tools and techniques of quality management, as part of the Occupation's attempt to breathe life into Japanese industry.

Much later, it was the Japanese excellence in manufacturing – partly derived from their adoption of these tools and techniques – which spurred Western manufacturers to seek out Deming, Juran, Feigenbaum and Crosby and re-learn what they had forgotten.

Today, TQM is a term which embraces much of current best practice in manufacturing. Its scope has broadened from its early concentration on statistical monitoring of manufacturing processes.

Now it can include just-in-time inventory control, the emphasis on customer service (both internal and external customers), and a change in the way people work which emphasises teamwork, training and greater employee responsibility and involvement in the work process.

These are all related devices aimed at re-orienting the production process so that it delivers products or services of consistent quality, in a timely fashion, which at least meet customer requirements. Indeed, focus on the customer – as a direct result of competition – is one of the main areas into which TQM has developed over the past few years.

'Customer expectations keep you on your toes,' says Vernon Zelmer, managing director of Rank Xerox in the UK. 'If you have found a way to do something in two steps you can be sure that someone in the Far East has found a way to do it in one. Satisfying the customer is a race without a finish.' In Europe and the US during the 1980s achieving high quality was thought to be an additional cost of manufacture; by the late 1980s it came to be realised that quality saved money. Industry is now at the point where quality is seen as affording a competitive edge.

'By the end of this decade you will go out of business if your quality levels are not up there with the best,' Peter Wickens, director of personnel and planning for Nissan UK, told a recent conference. 'High quality will be the price of entry (into a market).' Wickens' comments strike a resonant cord in many sections of industry. Car companies – especially Ford – have been at the forefront in Britain of forcing industry to improve the quality of what it makes. Demands by Ford in 1986 that its suppliers improve quality and productivity – by reducing manufactured defects through the application of techniques to measure performance – have paid handsome dividends.

Mike Bowes, director of supply for Ford UK, says that quality has been the single most important aspect of his business and life over the past five or six years. 'Quality is the one thing we have stuck to consistently over the years. It helped get the levels of supplier productivity we want and it has increased the ease of doing business.' Ford's push for quality has potentially drastic consequences for poor performing suppliers. By the end of this year any supplier which does not come up to Ford's quality standards will not receive any orders above those it currently has; if by August next year suppliers are not up to standard then Ford will begin terminating their contracts.

Under pressures such as these, industry has been forced, often more against management than shop floor intransigence, to implement programmes to improve quality.

The allure of total quality is beguiling but it disguises the difficulties companies face in trying to introduce it. The message is up-beat and can-do but it does not take account of the problems companies face in managing an organisation-wide change. Its advocates produce a vision of the company that is at once ideal but extremely difficult to achieve at shop-floor and office level.

They proselytise a holistic approach to management – hence the 'total' in TQM. This emphasises shallow hierarchies, teamwork, worker self-regulation, together with systems and techniques for measuring success and continuous improvement of tasks.

TQM is too often presented by salesmen as a black box solution to all problems, but companies find it to be more of a Pandora's box; expectations are raised only to be dashed. Where the introduction of quality has failed, companies are left with layers of their management and workforce more cynical and demotivated than before the exercise was started. The 'blitz approach', as John Oakland, professor of quality at Bradford Univer-sity's School of Management describes it. You raise employees' expectations but they are invariably not provided with any means to do things differently, he says.

'They walk around wondering "What can I do today that was different from yesterday?" The problem is one of raised expectations. People talk the language of quality but the capability of the organisation doesn't live up to the language – it is still using lousy systems and materials.'

Failure often occurs when companies seek large-scale organisational change without first understanding the thing it is they want to change: their own organisation. Successful introductions of total quality programmes, such as those in the UK by Heinz, Kodak, Exxon Chemical, Rank Xerox, and Amdahl, have worked – although none of those companies' managers would claim total success – because they spent time analysing their companies' competitive situation and defining their long-term business goals.

The experience of these companies also underlines another, little spoken of, aspect of TQM-driven change: it takes a long time. The quality programme at Texas Instruments in the UK has been under way for 10 years; at Kodak the process began in 1983, but it was not until 1985 that TQM was first introduced.

At Exxon Chemical, the process began in 1979 as a hard-nosed look at the company's future and it was not until 1984 that TQM was introduced. Xerox first introduced its quality programme worldwide nearly 10 years ago, but, according to Zelmer, the big benefits have only really begun to flow in the past three years.

The length of time needed to implement a serious quality programme also highlights another characteristic of success: the length of a manager's attention span. As Michael Cross, a businessman and research fellow at

Manchester Business School, says: 'A manager may grasp the idea very quickly, but in reality it is five years of factory time. The question is whether many have the stamina to see it through.' Some do. In Ireland, the European manufacturing arm of Amdahl, the US mainframe computer manufacturer, has taken the pursuit of quality to an altogether different plane. Its total quality programme – which began in earnest in 1985 – has got to a situation where the senior executives at its Dublin factory are attempting to design an organisation capable of spontaneous change and improvement – one that, in a sense, leads itself. But the process by which Amdahl arrived at this point was evolutionary and incremental.

'We never set out to do this in 1985,' says Smyth. 'But when you encourage people to take responsibility for their work and its improvement then sooner or later they know what to do for themselves.

'This is a knowledge-based culture – not a rules-based one. Our method was one of evolution and incremental change. If we made a mistake we could take one step back and correct it.'

Kodak's quest for consistency

There is no getting around it: if you want to become a quality manufacturer or service provider then you have to make a commitment to long-term change.

This change has to happen on many fronts and one of the most important is changing the way you think about the way you make things.

Concretely, this means re-learning the 'how' of what the company makes.

Techniques for doing this are today known as 'statistical process control' (SPC) – a method of using data about a manufacturing process to control and improve the process.

'Data', 'control', and 'improve' are the important words here. Data gets around the problem of opinions and, if everyone participates with good faith, it places discussions about work and work processes on a professional footing. As Clem Smyth, director of manufacturing and test operations at Amdahl Corporation's manufacturing plant outside Dublin, in the Republic of Ireland, says: 'Opinions are like left feet: everyone has one'. 'Control' refers to the control of variability in the manufacturing process.

All manufacturing processes are inherently variable, mostly because of the performance of equipment, but also because of the way it is used.

To mitigate the first form of variation, management can invest in more advanced machine tools or methods of manufacture which operate at higher levels of tolerance and specification. But what SPC seeks to define and then control is the latter source of variation: that which comes from humans interacting with machines – how they operate, maintain and feed them.

Once understood and controlled, a manufacturing process can be 'improved'.

With the same degree of co-operation – and the best manufacturing experience shows that this co-operation can be achieved only through cross-functional work teams – finer specifications can be applied and product quality enhanced.

That is the theory, but the difficult part is doing it. Once companies embark upon the analysis and correction of variation they soon find out that management style has to change. They find that they are forced to re-evaluate the relationship between managers and managed and this involves a different, more participative, form of interaction.

As Jack Frost, director of manufacturing for Kodak in Britain, notes: 'We all used to treat direct labour as idiots for years. Now we are giving people a share of the action. They have a lot of good ideas.' Frost is talking about Kodak in general, but his views are drawn from the experience he gained when he was the plant manager at the company's chemicals plant in Kirkby near Liverpool in the 1980s. His view on the past is uncompromising: 'Management has been at fault.' The company decided it had to change in 1982. It dabbled with SPC for some years but did not get really serious about it until 1985. According to Steve Neve, a product controller at the Kirkby plant, the plant produced chemicals which needed a lot of rework. 'We didn't understand the root causes of variability so poor process understanding and control led to variable yields. In the mid-1980s 10–15 per cent of work needed reprocessing. We couldn't forecast our production and we couldn't be confident of what we produced.' Eighteen months ago Kodak gave the Kirkby plant the prime mandate for the worldwide production of a chemical known as 'HO' around the plant – it is a complex organic chemical which goes toward sensitising Ektacolor photographic paper. The plant currently produces hundreds of tonnes of HO a year – more than half is exported to the US, Brazil and Australia – and is the major chemical now manufactured there.

HO is a mature product, some 20 years old. At that point in a product's life most management text books would tell you that large improvements in the productivity of manufacture would be hard won, if achievable at all. But Kodak's experience at Kirkby shows that, consistently applied, SPC in tandem with a team approach to work and just-in-time inventory control can produce some remarkable results.

Says Charlie Kelly, manager, synthetic chemicals: 'We have achieved a lot, given the chemistry. We have made improvements in efficiency, in cycle time, and we've got extra volume.' These achievements stem from Kodak's 1985 decision to send selected individuals on a six-week course of study in SPC. Stephen Duffy, factory manager at Kirkby, says that good interactive skills and shop-floor credibility were the key qualities that Kodak looked for in the people it sent.

The message that the new 'quality improvement facilitators' came back with underlined to top management that SPC, whatever its considerable merits, was not going to be a quick fix.

'They came back and said to management that they needed a plan and the commitment of management,' recalls Duffy. 'They pointed out that SPC was not a quick fix option. Getting a process under control would take time. First, they had to figure out why it was out of control and what level of capability was needed to get it under control before they set about correcting it.' On their return they trained 60 colleagues in elementary SPC at a one-day course. However, Kodak was still left wondering how to translate that knowledge into action. At the beginning of 1986 a series of workshops was set up involving not only managers but technicians, engineers and operators.

'Everyone had a say,' says Brian Charters, one of those attending the main SPC course. 'The object of the exercise was directed at improving the process, but equally to confer ownership of it on the people operating it.' Charters says the main problems were cycle time (speed of manufacture), and the need for a technical review of process and manufacturing procedure. The workshop in question made sure everyone was doing it the same way, and looked at how to reduce variability. Participants then listed their concerns, ranked them, decided on actions and set deadlines. Then they looked at the process again, seeking the critical areas, and what needed to be done to control the process.

Refocusing the attention of managers, technicians and operators in this way has produced some impressive improvements in the productivity of manufacture of HO at Kirkby and made it one of the most efficient plants in Kodak's worldwide portfolio.

Over the period 1986 to 1990 the cost of manufacture has fallen 40 per cent, the yield from raw materials has risen from 86 per cent to 91 per cent, for three successive years the plant has hit its delivery schedules 100 per cent of the time, and, most important, the measurable quality has improved.

According to Neve, the specifications the makers of HO work to now were recently applied to the chemicals produced in 1987. 'If we use 1990 specifications then 70 per cent of what we produced then would have failed,' he says.

'We had a mature product, but the specifications were getting tighter. The customer wanted improved products. A major effort was put into understanding variability. We got together in workshops to look at variability everybody was involved. If you get process and quality right then yield improvement follows.'

Teamwork at Amdahl

Total quality management has two prerequisites. One is to introduce a recognised system for standardising production and imparting the skills needed to monitor work processes; the other is to train management and the workforce to operate in a less hierarchical and a more co-operative environment.

Quality consultants and experts alike refer to the first as the 'hard' skills and second as the 'soft' skills associated with TQM.

Many companies believe that they can be 'quality' manufacturers or service providers simply by getting accreditation to BS 5750 – an industrial standard developed by the British Standards Institution in the early 1980s.

But this does not guarantee quality; it is quite possible to be a BS 5750 company and produce poor-quality goods systematically.

Teaching skills to workers, such as statistical process control – 'Pareto charts', 'fishbone diagrams', 'root cause analysis' and the like – is, therefore, a necessary but not sufficient condition for quality manufacture.

Although improvement can be gained by implementing only the 'hard' skills associated with TQM, for superior performance – performance which comes only through a shared sense of purpose and a single-minded orientation towards the customer – companies have got to embrace the 'soft' processes as well.

As Armand Fiegenbaum, who 40 years ago coined the term 'total quality control', said in London recently: 'Quality is a way of managing, it is not a technical activity.' David Hutchins, managing director of a UK consultancy specialising in TQM which bears his name, agrees: 'People often think that getting the systems and processes right is enough – they often ignore the human side. No one could accuse Amdahl Ireland of that.' The subsidiary of Amdahl Corporation of the US and manufacturer of high-performance mainframe computers has directed much of its efforts to getting the 'human side' of work and management right.

In so doing, Amdahl has redefined what managerial success means: promotional opportunities depend on managers' abilities at participating in cross-functional teams, not their ability to build empires within functions.

Furthermore, the progress management has made in training Amdahl's workforce is such that the company has set the objective of turning the 300 or so workers engaged in manufacturing and testing its computers into 'self-managing' teams. By December it hopes to have the 120 workers involved in testing Amdahl's computers operating in self-managed units.

Self-management is the antithesis of the so-called 'scientific management' associated with Frederick Taylor and still so widespread in industry today.

Instead of breaking down a computer into parts which are assembled serially on a production line, self-management, Amdahl-style, puts the people who work in production and test operations into teams which build large-scale assemblies. In a sense, it is an attempt to reintroduce a notion of 'craftsmanship' in a late 20th century factory.

But for all that, self-management is also something of a misnomer. The men and women who manufacture, assemble and test Amdahl's computers do not decide what to build and when to build it. They do not control completely the work schedule. But there are spaces in between where they have significant control, such as in factory layout, managing their time (the factory works on a 'flexitime' basis), their level of skill (they can be trained to do as many operations as they wish), together with a total responsibility for the quality (that is, perfection) of the work they do.

'We didn't set out in 1985 (when Amdahl embraced TQM) to do self-management,' says Clem Smyth, director of production and test operations. 'We didn't even know that it existed as a concept.' But what Smyth does know is that self-management is the logical outcome of the change that has occurred at Amdahl over the past five years. This change, which has been driven by training and teamwork, has resulted in Amdahl's production and test workers moving from a position of being able to monitor their own output and correct errors to one of prevention of errors and the improvement of processes.

'As production and test people got more proficient they identified problems and solved them before a manager knew they existed,' says Smyth. 'They experienced a growth in autonomy – the problems they solved weren't selected or approved by management – but we had not set out to create that growth in autonomy.

'As they got into improvements and enhancements of work processes they took total responsibility for quality and for the scheduling of work. They didn't need to get approval for overtime let alone needing a supervisor to organise it . . . So why do they need a supervisor around when he is often dysfunctional to the working of a group?'

The growing autonomy that production and text workers achieved has led Amdahl to reconsider the role of supervisory and middle management. The roles of these managers have changed from inspection and giving orders to guidance and enabling. It is planned that the two or so 'managers' who will oversee Amdahl's test area will be there primarily to help solve conflicts between teams, if and when they arise.

The supervisor's role has changed from being the centre of control and decision-making to being a leader, a provider of resources and a facilitator. The supervisor is becoming part-manager; it is hard here to find a plant supervisor who doesn't have a company-wide perspective.

Supervisors are spending 50 per cent of their time in cross-functional teams on issues that do not relate to their area. With this knowledge it makes them more promotable. Teamwork pervades Amdahl. Managers spend up to 60 per cent of their time in cross-functional teams, and in some cases much more. Smyth claims that 'any change that is being seen through is done in teamwork, not through the functional structure.' This, in turn, has had an effect on the way Amdahl defines managerial success.

Smyth says the more thoughtful managers learn that the way to get on is to be on a well-functioning team rather than through empire building. The criteria for moving up are different. 'Where individual stardom is rewarded it leads to people not sharing information. Teamwork makes that sort of behaviour redundant. If they are rewarded on the basis of motivating and leading teams then that's what they engage in. Departmentalism and territorialism are seen as dysfunctional . . . delinquent. Achievement through collaboration is what's rewarded here.'

So how successful has this all been? By 1987, the goal of 'zero' defects was close to being achieved. In that year, Amdahl's workers achieved 0.05 defects per assembly (that is, one defect in every 20 assemblies). Since then, such measurements have moved on to the parts per 1,000 and parts per million as corrective action techniques were replaced with prevention techniques.

The introduction of teamwork and 'just in time' inventory control has had equally startling results. In 1985 it took Amdahl 135 days to build a mainframe computer; in 1990 it took 59 days. In 1985 the weekly volume of work orders – internal invoices for parts or assemblies – averaged 800; last year it averaged 14.

Before the inception of TQM, Amdahl management used to budget for overtime equal to 6–7 per cent of work time. Now overtime is 0.4 per cent of time worked, and this at the same time as output has risen.

'People here take responsibility. To be behind schedule is not something they are proud of. It is an embarrassment not to function properly and it is not seen as an opportunity to earn more by doing overtime.' But Smyth is emphatic that TQM it is not about making gains in productivity. For him it is about global competition and effectiveness, where effectiveness is defined as customer satisfaction.

'The definition of quality is when your market share increases, when people come back to you and recommend your products to others. It's a wrong mind-set to say you will introduce TQM to get schedule adherence, or cut out middle management or make cost savings. And you don't get people to do things you create an environment where they enjoy what they are doing.'

Customer service at Rank Xerox

Few phrases have seized the corporate imagination more in recent years than 'customer service'.

Honoured, perhaps, more in the breach than the observance, serving customers better has been elevated to the top of many lists of top corporate priorities for the 1990s.

Customer service – which is a way of life in Japan and, to a lesser extent, the US – is often confused in Britain with servility. It should not be.

Customer service is the hard-headed pursuit of market share by winning the loyalty of customers.

Serving customers better, Total Quality Management theorists and practitioners maintain, is the proven path to increased profitability. They cite studies which show that well served customers are more likely to make repeat purchases of goods and services than those who are not.

Throughout the 1980s, customer service as a concept has broadened TQM; proponents applied it to the internal operations of an organisation as well.

Like many management ideas, this is a self-evident proposition but a powerful one, nevertheless. Loyal, or repeat, customers can have a significant effect on a company's profitability. Studies show that they not only tend to spend more over time, but that they are also more cost-effective. This is because the costs of customer acquisition – marketing and advertising – can be spread over time.

There are other benefits. A satisfied customer may tell up to eight others of the good service he has received; a dissatisfied customer may tell up to 15 others. As a study published last year by Bain & Co, a management consultancy, noted, 'just avoiding this negative publicity has value – although quantifying it precisely is not possible'.

For the past six years Xerox, the office equipment manufacturer, has been trying to live up to its goal of making customer satisfaction its top business priority. It has found that the pursuit of this goal has led it to reconsider its organisational structure and the way it remunerates its employees. The former is designed to place the whole capabilities of the company – especially the service side of its business – closer to the customer, while the latter aims to reinforce its rhetoric with real financial advantages to employees.

In Britain, Rank Xerox's way of getting closer to the customer has been to divide the country into five regions and bring together sales, service and administration.

In the words of one recent management presentation to staff: '(The regions) must exercise local, pro-active, situational decision-making in order to be truly responsive to our customers.' It added that, in a business where the office equipment market is fast becoming a commodity market, 'customer service, support and application capabilities are now the key factors that influence customer buying decisions.'

Those buying decisions, says Rob Walker, director of quality and management systems for Rank Xerox UK, can be worth a lot of money. Last year, customers discontinued using 5,500 Xerox machines out of about 140,000 installed. If Rank Xerox had retained them all, the impact on its bottom line profit would have been an extra $8.5m in 1990, and, over three years, an extra $30m.

'If you then add in the opportunity cost, the effect on the bottom line is large,' says Walker. 'Not all of this is, however, controllable and recoverable. But we reckon that 30 per cent of it is. So the financial impact of dissatisfied customers is large.' Rank Xerox spends a lot of time trying to understand its customers, especially the dissatisfied ones. At present the company estimates that 7 per cent of its customer base is dissatisfied, and it is aiming to reduce that level of dissatisfaction to zero by 1993.

It attempts to measure the level of customer satisfaction/dissatisfaction through the responses it receives to two surveys conducted for it by an independent market researcher. The first is an annual survey, sent out to more than 130,000 customers. Last year, this survey had a 39 per cent return rate. 'We take the dissatisfied responses and try to determine the root causes for the dissatisfaction,' says Walker.

The second is a questionnaire sent out 90 days after a Xerox machine has been purchased. (Before that the purchaser should have been called by a customer care officer, and the salesperson responsible for the account should also have made a call to see that everything is functioning correctly.) A 'vulnerable' report is completed which highlights dissatisfied customers. These are acted upon by people in the regions, who meet, decide an action plan, and agree with the customer what needs to be done to remedy the problem.

The nature of the complaints is also analysed to see if there are any generic problems with equipment or service delivery. Walker says the company has set up three cross-functional teams – comprising people from sales, service and administration, management and non-management from all levels throughout the organisation – to look at reliability, the order-to-install life-cycle, and response time. Their job is to improve the process.

Surveys, teams and analysis may be a rational way of understanding customer satisfaction/dissatisfaction and alerting management to problem areas, but senior management at Xerox soon discovered, in the words of Vernon Zelmer, managing director of Rank Xerox, that 'it is hard to distinguish customer satisfaction from employee satisfaction. You can't have one without the other. Without happy and satisfied employees, who believe in what they do and who can see the managers "walk as they talk", then the message will fall on stony ground.' For the past two years, therefore, Rank Xerox has been working on employee satisfaction. This has involved work on role clarification (understanding what the job is), employee involvement (being involved in the job specification), training, reward and recognition, and measurement.

One of the more intriguing aspects of this has been the decision to tie a percentage of all Rank Xerox's 4,000 UK employees' pay to the achievement of customer satisfaction targets. The percentage of pay affected by this increases as employees become more senior in the company. Directors have 30 per cent of the value of their package riding on attainment of pre-set goals.

'We look for incremental improvements in customer satisfaction each year,' says Walker. 'Last year we set ourselves a target of growth of 4 percentage points for 1991. Xerox Europe has just told us they want it up by 6 points.' He claims that the company works hard at not allowing managers to make trade-offs between attaining customer satisfaction targets and ones relating to purely functional and financial goals. 'If we deliver customer satisfaction all the other things will follow,' he says. This is probably the most difficult time since 1980/81 but we are still making investment in customer satisfaction.' Zelmer is convinced that tying part of his employees' pay to the attainment of service goals is the right way to go and is working. He says there has been a positive correlation with the introduction of the new pay scheme and the company's market share in the UK.

Although he believes that customer satisfaction ought to have been Xerox's prime aim from the moment it embarked on its quality drive – some 10 years ago – he is certain that to have tied remuneration to customer satisfaction goals would have been wrong. 'You can't do that until people have some control over what they do,' he says.

Management evaluation has also changed. Zelmer subscribes to the view that 'experience shows that 90 per cent of the time it is management that's the problem, not the people.' Xerox, among other companies, has introduced a form of assessment where the managed evaluate the managers. Known as the 'management practice survey', employees are asked to rate their manager. The results are anonymous and the manager sits down with his staff and goes through them.

Yet this survey, and others, have shown up the gulf that still exists between the aspirations of people who work at Rank Xerox and the reality of working there. As Walker notes, the four things that employees most value – fairness and respect, reward and recognition, career opportunities, and pay – are the things managers are least successful at delivering.

'We are trying to understand what the employees are saying to us and the role of management in motivating them,' he says. 'We want the role of manager to change from director to teacher and counsellor. But we still have a long way to go; you don't change behaviour overnight. Employees have to see senior managers behave in the appropriate way. It's difficult – it's the next big leap for us.' Though Walker maintains that people are always capable of stepping outside the boundaries of their jobs/ responsibilities they will do so only if they are given support. 'They won't if you step on them the first time they do it.' And that is a real challenge for management. While senior managers accept, intellectually, the new style and behaviour the company wants them to exhibit, '60 per cent of them got to where they are under the old style,' he says.

TOYOTA'S FRESH LOOK AT JIT

By Ian Rodger

First published 10 September 1990

Few management innovations in the post Second World War period have been as widely admired and imitated as Toyota Motor's just-in-time (JIT) production system.

Developed originally in the 1960s by the now legendary Taiichi Ohno as a way of reducing inventories, JIT quickly evolved into an overall system for eliminating waste and maintaining high levels of reliability and quality in the total production process.

Yet market conditions and technology march on, and even as basic a development as JIT is subject to important changes in the environment for world class manufacturing.

For example, the system was designed at a time when all of Toyota's manufacturing was done within a 50 kilometre radius of its headquarters in Aichi prefecture. The company was able to set up a network of suppliers close to its plants, making it easy for them to deliver just the right number of parts at just the right time on a daily basis.

In the past few years, and in response to market and political conditions, the company has opened plants in the US and is building others in the UK and in remote areas of Japan. This is making the logistics of timely delivery of components more difficult and is thus putting into question the whole JIT system.

Also, for all its effectiveness, the system operates with surprisingly primitive tools. The famous kanban are nothing more sophisticated than cardboard inventory bin tickets that delivery men carry back and forth between suppliers and the assembly line. Computer and telecommunications technologies have scarcely been explored.

Toyota began to take a fresh look at its production system when it set up the New United Motor Manufacturing Incorporated (NUMMI) joint venture with General Motors in the US in 1984. The tentative conclusion from that experience was that, even though the supply of parts was nowhere near as efficient as it was in Aichi, it was still worth attempting some form of JIT. 'We do not reduce inventory to a minimum for its own sake, but to maintain good production discipline,' says Tadaaki Jagawa, director of Toyota's production planning department.

In other words, the US experience put into relief the real value of the system. If sub-contractors know that there will be no surplus parts on the assembly line, they tend to make sure of the quality of their output.

If assembly workers know there is no surplus personnel to fix their machinery, they keep their eyes open for problems and do something about them when they emerge. (A characteristic of the Toyota system is that every worker has the right, indeed, obligation, to stop the line if he detects a problem.) 'Stocks made people feel safe. We want them to make every effort to prevent mistakes, to get to the root causes of problems,' Jagawa says.

Two years later when the company started up its own plant in Kentucky, it decided to install the whole JIT production system, despite the risks and higher costs involved. That has meant that on occasion, when an ordering error is made, parts have to be flown from Japan at great cost.

Also, the company found that US parts suppliers were unwilling to deliver every day, so it set up depots in Detroit and Chicago where the suppliers could make more irregular deliveries. Toyota itself would make daily collections from the depots for delivery to the plant. What Jagawa calls a milk-run was introduced to bring parts on a JIT basis from suppliers located near the plant.

Although all this caused significantly higher costs, especially at the outset when scheduling errors were frequent, Jagawa says the benefits are already apparent. 'We have achieved unexpectedly high output in Kentucky. When we started, we thought we would get about 200,000 cars a year from the plant. With the same equipment, we would get about 250,000 units in Japan. Now, we are already at 240,000 in Kentucky.'

'American workers have turned out to have a sort of Yankee spirit. If they have a target, they are just like the Japanese – they put their energies together to achieve it,' he adds.

Then there is what he calls the kanban plus alpha effect. The introduction of just-in-time in Kentucky forced the company to start using modern technology. At the simplest level, kanban from the US destined for Japanese suppliers have to be sent by facsimile to save time.

High volume data communication links have been installed connecting Kentucky to Toyota City, enabling the head office to monitor overall production and even the real time performance of some sophisticated machines, such as body-assembly robot lines. 'Because we are far away, we cannot see what is going on, but we want information. This has given a new dimension to the kanban,' Jagawa says.

Based on the Kentucky experience, the same sorts of system will be installed at the Derby plant in the UK and at the two domestic plants announced last month. Jagawa believes a milk-run system will be adequate for the UK-based parts suppliers, but depots will be needed for European suppliers. As for the Hokkaido and Kyushu plants, ships can be used for some parts, the national rail and trucking networks for others.

With the increased complexity of the production network, the need for more sophisticated data-handling systems is becoming more apparent. 'We are starting to automate the information transfer process, installing automatic readers and sorters with our large suppliers. This is not so much to increase efficiency as to reduce the possibility of accidents,' Jagawa says.

He acknowledges that the company has been slow to automate but says with a wry laugh that Ohno, who died in May at the age of 78, was very conservative. 'He hated computers.' Jagawa is now leading a major programme, expected to take several years to complete, to turn just-in-time into real time at Toyota. The goal is to have a production system that can produce cars in response to real orders in the shortest possible time. 'Our stocks for tomorrow should be based on what we are going to sell tomorrow, not on what we sold yesterday,' he says.

He believes that competition in the world car industry will continue to be based mainly on the quality of a maker's products for the next decade or so.

However, both European and US producers are already beginning to achieve the high standards the Japanese have set, and so the quality issue is bound to fade in importance. Thereafter, the key to competitive success will be timeliness of delivery, he predicts. 'Customers will want their cars the day after ordering them.' The challenge for a volume car-maker is to build a production system capable of responding to that sort of demand as well as being able to operate effectively 100 per cent of the time. 'If we wanted to create a system with 80 per cent uptime, that would not be so difficult,' Jagawa says.

Toyota believes that, just as in JIT, the minimising of inventories holds the key to the success of this project, and so it feels it has an advantage over others. Indeed, even without a real time system, it already has a remarkably responsive and flexible production process. It can adjust its production schedule for any given day only three days in advance. Other Japanese, European and US companies still require a week to 10 days.

CONTRASTING VIEWS OF THE BALDRIGE AWARD

By Martin Dickson

First published 3 February 1992

Apostles such as Robert Galvin, chairman of electronics group Motorola, call it 'the most important catalyst for transforming American business' methods.

Dissenters say it is nothing of the sort and may even represent a religious fervour of dangerous, destructive proportions.

In its four-year life, the 'Baldrige' prize (more formally known as the Malcolm Baldrige National Quality Award) has become the subject of controversy among US management experts – a debate which has intensified in the pages of the Harvard Business Review.

The controversy is hardly surprising, since the award – ceremonially handed over by the US president to up to six companies a year – centres on a kind of corporate religion.

The creed in question is Total Quality Management – TQM to the faithful – which has been one of the hottest topics in US business theory for the past decade. At its simplest, this means focusing all a company's energies on improving the quality of its work.

The Baldrige gives awards to companies which have excelled at TQM, and winners undertake to share their knowledge with other US businesses.

'More than any other initiative, public or private, it has reshaped managers' thinking,' says David Garvin of the Harvard Business School. It has set off 'America's rediscovery of co-operation as a national strength', adds Donald Petersen, Ford Motor's former chairman.

Critics, however, fault it on a number of counts, complaining variously about its methodology, focus and philosophy.

The most cynical point out that it has been won by subsidiaries of several large US companies which at present are hardly examples of financially successful American businesses – IBM, General Motors and Westinghouse Electric.

All three are struggling and their shares have performed dismally in recent years. Indeed, some on Wall Street view a Baldrige award as the kiss of the death for a company's shares.

The debate may find some echo over the coming months in Europe, which has copied the idea of the Baldrige: next autumn, the Dutch-based European Foundation for Quality Management will hand out its first award for TQM.

The origins of the Baldrige lie in a simple American emotion: fear of the efficiency of the Japanese industrial machine and a desire to emulate it.

There is great irony in this, since modern theories of quality control originated in the US between the first and second world wars. But US companies largely ignored the ideas and it was left to the Japanese to apply them rigorously, a lesson they learnt from US advisers sent to rebuild the shattered economy in the late 1940s.

In the early 1950s, the Japanese instituted their own quality prize and named it after W Edwards Deming, the foremost of those American advisers.

The US finally followed suit in 1987 with the Baldrige award, which was named after a US Commerce Secretary who died in a rodeo accident.

It is run by an offshoot of the Commerce Department, the National Institute of Standards and Technology, and gives up to two awards a year in each of three categories – manufacturing, service and small business.

Companies nominate themselves and have to submit a lengthy application form describing their quality practices and performance. Those which score well are visited by a team of examiners for a detailed look at their operations.

What are the Baldrige judges looking for? Firstly, adherence to the underlying tenets of the quality movement. These include a belief that the customer is the most important judge of a company's quality.

It is also deemed important for the company's top management to create clear quality values, that the workforce be fully involved, and the whole enterprise aim for continuous, long-term improvement.

Companies should also be trying to build bridges with outsiders, such as suppliers and the local community, and be responsible corporate citizens.

The judges examine a business under seven categories, awarding points in each area. In order of priority, these are: customer satisfaction, quality results, human resource development and management, management of process quality, leadership, information and analysis, and strategic quality planning.

The current controversy was set off by the Harvard Business School's Garvin, a former member of the Baldrige's board of overseers. In a lengthy article in the Harvard Business Review, he claimed criticisms of the award represented 'deep misunderstandings', and concluded the Baldrige was positioned just right. That sent many management gurus rushing to their word processors. The issues in the ensuing debate include.

• Financial performance. Garvin and his supporters say it is meaningless to fault the Baldrige for not rewarding financial success since it is not meant to measure this, but total quality management processes. Financial success can depend on other factors, such as luck. Nevertheless, Garvin reckons the award is a 'strong predictor of long-term survival'.

• Critics say the award does not honour superior product or service quality, pointing to the example of General Motors' Cadillac division, which won the award at a time when surveys showed American consumers did not rate its cars very highly.

• Again, Garvin dismisses this as beside the point, saying the Baldrige is not meant to reward product excellence alone, but more a company's management systems and processes. The Baldrige bashers say this approach sends the wrong message to corporate America. Says Phil Pifer, of management consultants McKinsey: 'The Baldrige needs to reinforce that "just do it" is not enough if you don't do it right.'

• The critics say that no coherent philosophy underlies the Baldrige, unlike its Japanese equivalent, which is based firmly on the ideas of W Edwards Deming – himself a strong critic of the American prize. Since the world of TQM is so full of clashing academic egos, each with its own approach, the organisers of the award merely lay down a list of broad quality criteria, without prescribing how a company should achieve them. Garvin defends what he calls this 'non-denominational approach, with a strong ecumenical flavour', but says it does not mean that the award lacks a general philosophical direction.

• The impact on US companies. Defenders of the Baldrige say that it has had a significant effect in waking up American managers to the need for TQM – a prime reason for starting the award in the first place. According to Robert Galvin at Motorola, another past winner: 'Those companies that embrace the Baldrige are beginning to make giant strides. The difference between the alert business leader's attention to quality today versus 10 years ago is like night and day.' However, the critics say there is a grave danger that the Baldrige, with most of its points going to management processes rather than market place results, will simply encourage a knee-jerk, 'check the box' approach to quality issues.

McKinsey's Pifer warns that his consultancy is 'seeing a disturbingly large number of companies whose total quality management programmes are failing to show signs of meaningful business impact. More and more senior executives privately express reservations or concerns to us about the eventual impact of their quality activities.' An important contributory factor, he says, is a blind pursuit of TQM, when quality or the other benefits of such a programme may not be the most important priority for a company. 'The Baldrige award contributes to this problem, by perpetuating the religious fervour and universal appeal of TQM.' Garvin, however, gives short shrift to such apostasy. And to those who argue that the Baldrige is stuck in the middle ground, neither a reward for all-round corporate excellence, nor narrow, traditional quality control, he says that that is precisely where it should be: any narrower and it would not attract the attention of top management any broader and it would become impossible to judge.

He does acknowledge one flaw – the award is a competition with a limited number of winners, rather than a qualification prize which any number can achieve.

The latter approach, he says, would enhance the co-operation among businesses which the Baldrige is meant to promote.

Yet Garvin's satisfied tone itself seems at odds with the spirit of the award, with its strong emphasis on the need for companies to strive for continual improvements in their working practices.

As Shoji Shiba, a visiting professor at MIT's management school points out: 'When you consider something "ideal", you lose the opportunity to improve it.'

Part Three

PEOPLE PLANNING FOR THE NEW AGE

4 MAKING SENSE OF HUMAN RESOURCES

INTRODUCTION

One of the basic principles of people management for most of the 20th century was to narrow an individual's task down to a small, heavily monitored, transparently cost-effective unit of work. This was particularly the case in many areas of manufacturing, where it was felt to be a necessary route to greater competitiveness. It left the individual with little chance to show any initiative. Today, that tenet is being turned largely on its head. Much more is expected from employees; their value to a company's well-being is increasingly acknowledged, even if not necessarily properly recognised.

This transition has been accompanied by the emergence of 'human resource management', a term not universally acknowledged as representing much more than 'personnel management', but one which does signify a broader remit than in the past.

Just how much broader is discussed in this chapter, along with the widely differing attitudes of trade unions to human resource management, and the issues that management must confront. Also examined are the issues that have been preoccupying human resource managers themselves. An example is the rapid emergence of new technology, which puts pressures on workers that cannot always be easily resolved.

It is in the nature of good management practice that nothing, in isolation, provides the answer to every prayer. As John Gapper relates, British Airways, which lays claim to being the world's favourite airline, has embraced human resource management to what is generally considered to be good effect. It sees its employees as front-line troops in the competitive battle with other airlines. Its overall success is acknowledged, witness its ability to produce profits while rivals notch up huge losses.

Gapper traces the pressure to re-think heavily monitored, narrowly-defined work patterns as having come from Japan, where the team approach, with decisions made by consensus, is acknowledged to be a potent competitive weapon. Much of the shift is due to the fact that traditionally structured principles are incompatible with rapid technological change. This is especially so in service industries, where labour accounts for a large majority of total costs, and where employees can be at the forefront of enhancing standards of service.

The mixed attitudes of unions to HRM emerge against a background of distrust. Inevitably, if responsibility is pushed further down the organisation, with established lines of authority being eroded, the unions' traditional role is called into question.

This suspicion is exemplified by a national officer of the Transport and General Workers' Union, who also accuses employers of often having as their real motivation the desire to weaken collective strength. An academic's view is that HRM sits uncomfortably with industrial relations since, among other things, managers will endeavour to by-pass unions to achieve their ends.

But not all unions are opposed to HRM, one particularly perceptive view being that it is inevitably an acknowledgement by management that workers should be more involved in decision-making. A rider to this is that it brings managers under greater pressure to deliver and opens them to accusations of merely paying lip-service to the concept if they prove unhappy about being challenged.

A further view is that HRM in the United Kingdom is a pale shadow of the regimes that exist in Continental Europe, since the 'power' offered to workers is rather illusory and allows little scope for feedback from workers to upper echelons of managment.

This argument could well be supported by attitudes which are reported in Christopher Lorenz's article about whether or not a value can be put on human resources and if, indeed, management really wishes to do so.

Lorenz points to the growing number of chief executives who are at least paying attention to concepts which enhance the status of employees. But he questions whether this has any more substance than is revealed by the perfunctory acknowledgement in so many company annual reports of how valuable employees are to the organisation.

One of the inevitable outcomes of 'empowerment' of employees is that they will make mistakes and that they should be left (or helped) to learn by them. Yet this prospect helps make some managements draw back from delegating real power of decision further down the line and thus from taking HRM to its proper conclusion.

In a world of rapid technological advance, human resources play a crucial role – but not just in ensuring that the latest piece of technology performs. They are also a barometer of what is achievable and what is not, as Michael Dixon illustrates. What is particularly clear is that employees' reactions to new technology must be read carefully if they are not to be misinterpreted. For, however impressive any technology might be, some of its technical possibilities may have to be sacrificed in order to match what employees are happy – or can be persuaded – to work with.

Even in companies where HRM becomes very much the chief executive's remit, much of the responsibility for ensuring that employees' views are understood by management still falls to the human resource manager. Many managers still feel vulnerable in the organisational hierarchy, however. Simon Holberton suggests that while they know what their role should be, many human resource managers find themselves insufficiently informed by their companies to design programmes to meet managers' demands.

Significantly, training is at the top of the list of their priorities. And while, since Holberton's article was first published, the economic climate has changed considerably for the worse with budgets slashed or put on hold, training is still widely perceived to be one of the most pressing requirements if a wide swathe of companies is not to be left unprepared to take advantage of an economic upturn.

AN IDEA WHOSE TIME HAS COME – HUMAN RESOURCE MANAGEMENT

By John Gapper

First published 28 January 1991

Mr Robert Ayling, British Airways' human resources director, would prefer his job not to exist. 'The ideal company would not need a human resource activity, just as an ideal world would not require doctors,' he says. Like a world in which nobody became sick, a company which had no need to alter its workers' behaviour would be happier. But even Mr Ayling is resigned to BA falling short of perfection.

Indeed, BA faces distinct problems in managing its workers. 'Many of our employees are thousands of miles away, and there is no manager there to tell them what to do,' Mr Ayling says. The company obviously cannot prescribe how a flight attendant should behave with a particular customer, and yet its sales pitch is based largely on the individual service each passenger receives.

One response would be to leave them to it, an approach BA came close to adopting in the past. 'I remember 10 years ago, standing at the gate, handing out boxes of food to people as they got on the aircraft. That's how we dealt with service,' says one manager. BA now trains employees intensively in customer service, re-arranges work to give them more responsibility, and teaches managers that handling customers and employees is their main role.

This approach to cultivating workers' abilities has come to be known as human resource management (HRM), an American creed of which BA is the best-known British exponent. The company is discussed reverently at Harvard Business School on the HRM course taken by all those studying for a Master of Business Administration degree. BA has assumed its place alongside Rank Xerox, People Express and Lincoln Electric as an example of a company forging a competitive advantage through its workforce.

The human resources concept swept through US companies in the 1980s, promising an alternative to the bureaucratic world of personnel management.

Human resource managers would not merely hire and fire or negotiate slow advances with union shop stewards. They would be at the forefront of business planning, persuading employees to change their ways of working. Now the evangelists are winning converts in Britain.

The gospel has provoked both enthusiasm and scepticism among personnel managers. Many are attracted by the idea of a new prestige for their job, and sick of being regarded as the 'maintenance crew for the human machinery'. Yet others see HRM as hot air rather than substance. They say personnel managers have always wanted to involve employees in work, and include training in business plans. At most, HRM is personnel management done better.

Human resource management is clearly not an original notion. Rather, it is a set of ideas which have become attached to a phrase. That vagueness is risky: for each case of a company like British Airways investing enormous sums and effort in changing the way it manages employees, there will be many others who do no more than re-title their personnel directors.

The common thread in many British and American companies which have adopted HRM is a recognition that 'scientific' line management – devised on early US steel and car production lines – has serious shortcomings. It saw the most productive way of managing workers as removing as much control of their own work from them as possible. Managers split work into fragmented tasks with the help of time and motion studies. These tasks were carried out by employees according to detailed instructions.

Japan's formidable success in industrial productivity and the organisation of work has done more than anything to challenge this orthodoxy. Japanese companies have shown that quality comes from a combination of outstandingly designed products and a shrewdly motivated workforce. The emphasis on team-working and employee involvement in quality improvement has been a salutary example to those American industries that have maintained strict distinctions between managers and workers. In Japan, quality is typically the responsibility of all workers in the 'scientific' approach, quality goals are the responsibility of the system itself and of those supervising it. There has been much copying of the Japanese approach in the US – General Motors' team-working at its Saturn plant is a case in point.

In addition, changes in technology are making it increasingly difficult for manufacturers to organise work according to 'scientific' management principles. Flexible manufacturing systems controlled by computers require fewer line operatives carrying out isolated tasks. Instead, modern production lines work best with teams of multi-skilled workers that can band together to manufacture, repair, and solve problems. This demands involvement and understanding, and it undermines the logic of making work simple and repetitive.

In services – which now employ three times as many people in Britain as does manufacturing – the logic of managing people differently is even more compelling. Labour forms above 60 per cent of total production costs in services, and companies compete by offering quality, tailored service. Many jobs are not amenable to being closely controlled, even if companies want that. In activities such as consultancy and design, employees use their initiative to create products.

Beneath the HRM banner, then, there is a great diversity of experiment and experience. Broadly, however, the approaches can be divided into the schools of 'hard' and 'soft' human resource management.

Hard HRM preaches that companies gain advantage primarily by using workers effectively. The management of people is too important to be left to personnel managers. Instead, a company's strategy should involve – even centre on – the best deployment of its workers. At lower levels, line managers should assume responsibility for how employees work and develop.

Hard HRM emphasises that managers and workers should communicate directly, rather than through personnel managers and union shop stewards.

'Every BA manager is a human resources manager,' says Mr Ayling. 'His job is to manage people, and he does not negotiate with them through the medium of a personnel manager.'

Mr Alan Popham, human resources director of the retail group Kingfisher, talks of British managers being 'almost castrated' by working agreements. 'Because there was a collective relationship between company and unions, the line manager got cut out of the process,' he says.

Many companies associate HRM strategies with a move away from dependence on unions. HRM has been linked to 'union-busting' in the US, although the techniques have also been used in unionised companies to raise levels of trust between managers and workers. Some have instituted team briefings and carried out attitude surveys to try to reduce dependence on worker representatives.

In Britain, HRM can be a covert attempt to bypass shop stewards. Industrial relations and HRM techniques often sit uneasily together. Mr Keith Sisson, professor of industrial relations at Warwick University, talks of a tension between styles. 'You have managers doing industrial relations firefighting in one room while the young MBAs are trying to win hearts and minds down the corridor.'

Soft HRM says workers are most productive when they are committed to the company, informed about strategy and trading conditions, involved in deciding how tasks are done, and grouped in teams that work without strict supervision. But it stops short of advocating worker participation in company decision-making. For this reason, HRM is a distinctively Anglo-American package of ideas, which sits uneasily with traditions of worker participation in Europe.

These soft HRM ideas are now common. Companies in the coatings group Courtaulds are trying to match multi-disciplinary teams of workers to projects, according to Ms Gill Lewis, the company's human resources director. 'You can see the more rigid structures disappearing,' she says. Mr Jim Prophet, human resources director of the oil company Burmah-Castrol, says it is trying to compete 'by making our people better, improving their knowledge and their commitment'.

This core of human resources chiefs is increasing its grip on British industry. Already entrenched in foreign multi-nationals and non-union companies, it is spreading in the unionised private, and even the public, sector. The car maker Jaguar has a human resources executive and an employee relations manager under its personnel director. The London Borough of Hillingdon has appointed a head of human resources. Yet the growth of the terminology begs the question of how far people-management techniques are actually changing.

The problem of HRM being 'talked up' because it sounds good is widely acknowledged. HRM techniques have been estimated to cover no more than 23 per cent of the US workforce. Its enthusiasts often cite the same small set of case study companies in emphasising its importance. Surveys of the spread of quality circles and team briefing in Britain have found them being used in an ad hoc manner in large companies, with only patchy commitment from line managers.

Mr Sisson talks of 'a massive cynicism' about HRM techniques among middle managers. 'If my bonus depends on financial results, you can tell me I should be a facilitator and developer until the cows come home,' he says.

The everyday pressures of management can easily sap a theoretical commitment to employee involvement: Mr Ayling admits to a tendency for managers to slide from their training in how to treat workers when 'back in the whirlpool'.

Because it is easier to change the title of the personnel department than the way people are managed, it is likely that much of what passes as HRM is simply old wine in new bottles. Yet companies such as BA have clearly expended effort in altering management techniques, because workers' attitudes were seen to be integral to their competitive position. A genuine change may be harder to bring about at companies in which labour costs account for less of the total, or tasks are less sophisticated.

Indeed, HRM may by definition be of only limited application. It may imply paying more than competitors and recruiting the best available workers.

Conversely, few HRM advocates appear to have considered the process in reverse, with committed workers willing to accept pay sacrifices. 'If we are to change the culture, we have to identify ourselves with high-value people,' says Mr Prophet. 'We aim to be in the upper quartile of pay and benefits.' Since not every company can be in the upper quartile, the HRM club is bound, in this respect, to be somewhat exclusive.

There is, then, especially in Britain, some considerable gap between the grandeur of the human resource management vision as taught in business schools and real company practice. But there is no doubt that the faith is spreading among companies attracted by the search for a new way forward in the old struggle between workers and management, but one which stops short of the social partners approach of mainstream European social democracy. But in seeking to break the bonds of the collective relationship between personnel managers and unions, many companies are destined to struggle for some time with one of the most intractable issues in British industrial management. For companies that generate more than hot air and fancy titles, however, the rewards could be enormous.

UNION REACTION TO PARTICIPATIVE SCHEMES

By John Gapper

First published 11 February 1991

Ron Webb is recounting his reaction to the suggestion of Unigate, the dairy company, that it introduce employee briefings at a plant in Chadwell Heath, Essex. 'Our immediate response to that, quite frankly, was "not on your nelly",' says Webb, a district officer of the Transport and General Workers' Union.

Webb's opposition to one of the employee involvement techniques increasingly bundled under the heading of human resource management (HRM) is in one respect typical. It shows the suspicion with which unions often greet attempts by companies to change the ways employees are managed.

But in another respect, it is unusual. For his comments are on a video film made by the TGWU for its shop-stewards. The video is one of the innovative ways in which the union is trying to limit any damage being done to collective organisation by the spread of HRM techniques through British industry.

Although many of the ideas under the HRM banner are also found in companies with traditional personnel departments, unions often associate the term HRM with an explicit challenge to their strength. They see it as an attempt by managers to bypass stewards and deal directly with workers.

As HRM techniques spread, unions are also trying to plan responses to make the best of the challenge. Some argue that unions can learn from techniques such as employee attitude surveys. Others believe the adoption of HRM and its rhetoric of employee involvement make companies more vulnerable.

HRM is not overtly anti-union, and managers often emphasise that they are happy for shop-stewards to remain in place. Yet they seek a workplace in which managers are not dependent on unions to communicate with employees, and in which collective relationships are replaced by individual ones.

The implication is that unions may simply wither away in a company run entirely according to HRM principles. They will certainly not be afforded the level of employer support in companies which have traditionally reinforced shop-steward power by disseminating information through them.

'It sounds plausible, that is what is so difficult for us,' says Fred Higgs, a TGWU national officer. 'It can be a genuine attempt to involve workers, and of course you cannot do anything other than welcome that. But the real motivation of companies is often to weaken collective strength.' The TGWU's video warns its stewards to be wary of attempts to introduce communication and involvement ideas such as team-briefing and quality circles, or consultation mechanisms like works councils, which do not involve unions. It also warns against easy acceptance of team-working and multi-skilling.

But the video acknowledges that the union has faced real challenges in HRM, and suffered setbacks. It cites examples of employees accepting new working agreements which shop-stewards have opposed, including broad changes at Norsk Fertilisers in Immingham which were linked to a single union deal.

David Guest, professor of occupational psychology at Birkbeck College, London, says HRM sits uncomfortably with industrial relations management because it assumes workers' and managers' interests are not inevitably at odds. He says it presents three specific forms of threat to unions.

First, managers will try to pursue goals through channels which bypass unions. They may encourage individual performance rather than collective pay awards they will have team briefings rather than communicate through stewards they pay attention to employee development through training.

Second, the general improvement in the quality of people management will reduce tensions and conflicts which drive workers towards belonging to unions. The pay mark-up which is the most obvious benefit of belonging to a union may be established without worker pressure.

Third, at non-union sites and in new plants, HRM may obviate the need for unions. Rather than having alternative communications and consultation structures, managers will be able to establish their own. They may not even need the cover of a non-independent staff association.

Furthermore, there is a danger that unions which have been used to exploiting traditional forms of work organisation by building up pay based on demarcations and skill differentials may be wrong-footed by team-working and multi-skilling. They can find themselves opposing things that workers like.

A warning was sounded in the bargaining 'new agenda' drawn up last year by John Edmonds and Alan Tuffin, leaders of the GMB general union and UCW postal union, respectively. They said unions had to 'escape from a self-defeating fixation with tightly specified job description and embrace adaptability'.

Despite all this, some union leaders remain sanguine about the development of HRM. They say employers make themselves more vulnerable to unions by embracing HRM because they admit the legitimacy of workers becoming involved in work decisions, but then fail to deliver the promised new world.

Edmonds talks of the 'false prospectus of HRM' in companies promising consultation and involvement, but in practice only wanting to establish new forms of control away from unions. This problem 'is exposed to most workers the first time they actually disagree with managers,' he says.

'The HRM package does not actually handle the views of employees at all well,' says Edmonds. 'It is quite good on communicating managers' views, but not too good on feedback, and no good at all on allowing the real questioning of managers' decisions.' He argues that this unwillingness to allow real worker participation in management decisions is characteristic of the American roots of HRM ideas.

In contrast, European-owned companies such as Nestle offer GMB members a better chance of taking part in proper discussions about work.

This view that HRM may exert little long-term damage to unions because of managers' failure to accept its more painful implications is shared by John Monks, deputy general secretary of the Trades Union

Congress, who says HRM presents 'extremely fertile territory' for unions.

Monks believes there is limited scope for companies to marginalise unions by providing good enough employment conditions to make them unwanted. He says only market leaders which have policies not squeezed by 'the vicissitudes of the trade cycle' may have the luxury of doing so.

Instead, he says human resource items such as the emphasis on single status employment conditions can be exploited by unions. 'Unions have attacked the divide between white-collar and blue-collar workers, but the distribution of perks to executives is another fertile area,' he says.

This view of human resource management as a creed – which in practice does not threaten union organisation – has been adopted by some unions in the US, notably in the car industry. Local branches of the UAW union have co-operated with quality improvement programmes in the big car-makers.

Such developments have also spread in the car industry in Britain, where Ford's employee development and assistance programme and its quality improvement drives have both been backed by unions. Car companies have spent some effort reassuring unions of their intentions.

Some unions go further than this, and argue that they can learn some new HRM tricks themselves. Clive Brooke, leader of the Inland Revenue Staff Federation, says HRM techniques, which include employee attitude surveys, show 'a degree of sophistication that unions ignore at their peril'.

Brooke argues that by adopting their own versions of quality circles and worker involvement, unions can strengthen themselves and ensure members take part in decision-making. He says unions can use this strength of consultation to challenge companies to improve their quality of management.

'The natural response to HRM is to dig in and oppose it, but that is a short-term view,' says Brooke. 'Unions have got to address the issues HRM raises. It is the sort of thing we have been calling for in management, so we should go with it and make the most of it.'

SHOULD HUMAN ASSETS BE ON THE BALANCE SHEET?

By Christopher Lorenz

First published 24 June 1991

Take a look at the chairman's statement in most companies' annual reports.

Tucked away after all the verbiage about financial performance, takeovers and so on, there has always tended to be a bald statement along the lines of 'our people are our greatest asset'.

Most such declarations have been as empty and ritualistic as they are brief.

Significantly, few of the chairman's other communications with the outside world during the business year have made any mention of people issues, except those relating to his top team – unless, of course, he has muddied his hands with redundancy announcements, something most chairmen leave to their underlings.

Now, however, the chairman is under pressure – competitive, shareholder and otherwise – to make his (or, occasionally, her) organisation flatter, faster and more flexible. So his annual statement is starting to make more elaborate references to the 'people-centred' nature of the business.

And, in speeches and statements throughout the year, he and his boardroom colleagues are starting to make mention of such fashionable 'human resources' concepts as empowerment, trust, and team-building.

Empty rhetoric again, dressed up in flashier clothes? Or something more substantial that will actually affect the future competitiveness of the organisation? For the sake of every organisation, one very much hopes the latter. After all, the only way an organisation can survive is to learn, and change, more rapidly than the rate of change in its environment. And the only learning tool that an organisation possesses is its brain – which consists of its people, not just at the top, but at every level.

Lest this all seems over-philosophical, consider the following picture, painted by Professor Charles Handy, best-selling author and adviser to countless boardrooms, of the sort of organisation that will thrive in future.

Addressing an Association for Management Education and Development conference earlier this month on Creating 21st Century Organisations, Handy forecast that the core staff of future organisations, whether in manufacturing, services or both, would consist of highly qualified and trained professionals. They would operate, as do many professionals today, either on their own, or in project or task teams.

Since today's 'professional' organisation is the model for the future, Handy advised companies to take a close look at how consultancies and other partnerships, universities and even media organisations manage themselves.

Given what motivates most people in such professional organisations, and the flatness of the structures in which many (though not all) work, they have to be trusted to take the right decisions, rather than be controlled at every stage by managers above them. They have to be 'led, rather than managed'.

Control is often exercised after the event, not before – in other words, through performance. Many kinds of mistake must not be punished, but written off to experience, learning and renewal.

In some professional organisations, people do not play single roles but combine several in a shifting portfolio. Nor do they work mainly in the organisation's status hierarchy, which in any case consists of only a few levels.

Instead they operate in a hierarchy which is related to the changing requirements of each task or project, in which junior people sometimes lead their seniors. Examples are a consultancy, where a senior partner works part-time on a task group run by a junior associate, or a theatre, where a famous actor is directed by a young newcomer.

In such organisations a fundamental priority is for people to requalify themselves continually and always to keep at the front of their fields.

Supporting Handy's prescription at the conference was the association's chairman, Bob Garratt, himself a consultant. Like brains, which learn, rather than machines, which ossify, organisations needed to become more open at all levels, both within themselves and towards the outside world, he said.

Few of today's younger company chairmen would argue with that. More controversial altogether, though, was Handy and Garratt's advocacy that organisations should demonstrate their 'people-centredness' by putting the value of their corporate learning, and of their people, on their balance sheets.

The fear (or incentive) of takeover is certainly, as Garratt argued, driving some companies to value, or revalue, their accumulated learning – either their brands or other forms of intellectual property. But valuing people for balance sheet purposes is extremely difficult, as Tottenham

Hotspur has found. Paul Gascoigne has shown how hazardous transfer valuations can be.

More appropriate for most companies could be Handy's suggestion of emulating the example set by WPP, the advertising group, which has valued its 'fixed intangible assets'. This represents, in effect, the value of the brands of its main constituent companies, part of which includes a valuation of their people.

An ad agency's human assets are far from fixed, of course – which is one reason why most accountants dislike the idea of putting them on the balance sheet. But, as Handy told the conference, the idea of human asset values is hardly more far-fetched than was environmental accounting a decade ago.

Any chairman who has the courage and accounting dexterity to find a way of putting 'his' people on the balance sheet will certainly be committed to taking them – and their continued development and learning – as seriously as any of the company's other investments.

Along with real delegation and empowerment, it would certainly help his slogan of 'people as assets' to take on real meaning.

ATTITUDES OF HUMAN RESOURCE PROFESSIONALS

By Simon Holberton

First published 27 June 1990

The name may have changed but the problem remains the same. Human resource managers, once known as personnel managers, still appear to feel vulnerable and on the margin.

They believe they have a significant role to play in the company – 'pivotal' is the word and 'value added' the claim – but they are witnessing a devolution of their traditional role, especially in recruitment and training, to line management.

The argument they make sounds reasonable: if a company does not have a coherent approach to its human resources it may not be able to fulfil its business needs. However, it is one which the finance director or the production director could easily make for his area of special interest.

In the struggle to be heard, the human resource manager will have to rise above the obvious.

These are some of the impressions gained by reading a systematic attempt to discover what human resource practitioners believe to be the main issues facing them.

The study, of 6,000 companies and public sector bodies in the UK, France, West Germany, Sweden and Spain, was devised by the consulting arm of Price Waterhouse and Cranfield School of Management, the UK business school. It drew on the resources of leading business research centres in the countries surveyed.

It asked human resource professionals for their responses to questions covering their companies' human resource strategy, its methods and attitude toward recruitment, pay and benefits, training and development, employee relations and flexibility and working patterns. Some of its key findings are: Human resource professionals are on the boards of companies (between 60 and almost 90 per cent representation in all survey countries except West Germany), but few are involved directly in influencing or determining their companies' corporate strategy from the outset.

With the exception of Sweden (and Sweden is the exception for most things relating to personnel management), most companies do not have a written corporate strategy. Personnel responsibility is increasingly being devolved to line managers, particularly in the training and development of workers and managers. Line managers' responsibilities have also grown in recruit and benefits. Their responsibilities have shown a much slower growth in industrial relations, health and safety and workforce expansion and reduction issues.

The report argues that human resource professionals have a role to play in ensuring personnel strategies are applied consistently. But the growth in line management responsibility for key areas of staff development suggests that human resource professionals are being side-stepped in an area which a priori would have appeared central to their role.

The Swedes, who score among the highest in questions relating to the relevance of human resource professionals to companies, accept that line management implements training schemes. They see their role as one of listening to managers' demands and designing appropriate programmes. In this way they retain a level of control over in-house training.

The report quotes one Swedish personnel professional: 'Customer service skills are really important in modern personnel work and the line managers are your clients.' Employers across Europe have increased significantly their investment in training, especially for managers and professional staff, though there is little systematic evaluation of training. Training of manual staff received the smallest increase in funding.

But the survey showed up a large lack of knowledge among human resource professionals as to how much their organisations are spending on staff training and development. The French were the best informed and that appears to be because French law requires companies to spend 1.2 per cent of the wages and salaries bill on training.

The survey provides evidence of companies systematically analysing their training needs – between 60 and 90 per cent of respondents said they did this. The demand for training appears to be driven more by the needs of line managers than by human resource professionals initiating training programmes.

The evaluation of training tends to be informal. The most common form of evaluation comes from the responses of trainees and their managers to the particular training experience. Tests and more formal systems are less used.

During the next three years, the skills employers think they will need most in the coming three years are: people management, computing and technology, business administration and strategy and the management of change.

Managers are currently being trained across a broad range of skills which appear to be for people management. Team building, delegation, staff communications and performance appraisal score highly. Possibly reflecting the business opportunities that may come with the liberalisation of markets for goods and services after 1992 the learning of languages scores highly in most countries, with the notable exception of Britain.

Looking ahead, people management is expected to dominate in most of the countries surveyed. In France, Sweden and the UK training managers in the 'management of change' is seen as a high priority.

Variable pay is on the increase in all countries surveyed, with merit pay and individual bonuses the most frequently used incentives.

The report notes that employers are moving away from rigid pay structures.

Variable pay packages are on the increase in all countries, especially Sweden and Spain. Fringe benefits are becoming an important part of remuneration in all countries except France.

Profit-sharing is widely available, but predominately to managerial and professional staff. Bonuses, whether individual or group, and performance-related pay are popular in all countries.

The Price Waterhouse Cranfield Report is a thought-provoking document. It argues for a greater role for human resource professionals in shaping and responding to the training and developmental needs of companies.

CAN PEOPLE ADAPT AS FAST AS TECHNOLOGY?

By Michael Dixon

First published 30 April 1990

Managers are fast learning to treat excited laughter in the workplace, not as an outbreak of high-spirits to be kept in check, but as a sign to dread.

Nowadays, the cause is less likely to be some happy event than that the computer system has gone phut.

What most executives seem slow to learn is that the problems arising from technical breakdown are small beside those implied by the snickering that greets it. Psychologists have found that laughter on such occasions is apt to mean the staff resent the system their bosses have imported, and are resisting the change it requires.

Even when the resistance is obvious, managements typically discount it as mere reflex dislike of new ways. With trade-unionism subdued, technological progress tends to be viewed as ultimately irresistible. Sooner or later employees will adapt to it, and any who cannot will be readily replaceable with others who can.

The strength of high-rank faith in humanity's adaptive powers was illustrated by the senior managers from two dozen of Europe's best known businesses at a recent conference held by the Index Group. The theme was 'the Market/Customer Driven Company', and all attending were clearly committed to converting their companies to that type.

Repeated references were made to reports that, in Japan, a customer can go to a Toyota showroom on a Monday, order any model in any colour with any combination of options, and collect same by the end of the week. It was largely accepted that companies failing to emulate Toyota's legendary service are doomed to an early grave.

It was also largely accepted that survival hinges on technology. For example, one speaker pictured sales representatives as a fatally archaic means of doing business with customers. Every sales transaction – from specifying a suitable product and promoting its advantages, through taking the order and answering inquiries about its progress, to registering delivery, invoicing, chasing up payment and scheduling after-sales service – could be far better done electronically by staff at terminals linked to a constantly revised database.

While reps would still be essential, the speaker said, their role would no longer be nuts-and-bolts selling and otherwise handling details. Their job would be purely 'relational', promoting goodwill between company and customers on a general plane.

Many of the audience nodded agreement. But half a dozen questioned later were unable to cite a single rep on their payrolls who was fitted for the radically changed role. All they could think of was several thousands who were not.

If their companies press on with the electronic development the speaker outlined, it is to be hoped evolution will supply reps with the right abilities in time. Otherwise it could well be lower-tech competitors who have the last laugh – and not just because the effects of reduced birthrates and so on are likely to make able recruits of any sort hard to find.

Another and deeper reason is that executives overhasty to ring in the new are ignoring a warning bell that has been sounding for a long time.

In Britain it first clanged in the late 1940s when the recently nationalised coal industry began introducing 'longwall' mining. The engineers and managers were determined to exploit every advantage offered by what was then the latest technology, and rejigged the miners' working methods to suit.

It soon became obvious that something was wrong. Besides unexpectedly high costs of installation and low gains in output, there were increasing absentee rates and other signs of worsening morale. It seemed that the members of each shift were working against, instead of with one another.

The Tavistock Institute of Human Relations was called in to investigate. And what it learned not only eased the problem in the mines, but has since been applied by a good many, even though still a small minority of organisations across the world. The main lessons are twofold.

First, unless there is no need for humans at all, every technical system requires a social system to run it. Second, there is a point where the two systems become incompatible, with the result that attempts to maximise the technology stir up counter-productive antagonisms in its operators.

'So some of the technical possibilities must be foregone to meet the people's individual and social needs, and some of the people's preferences must give way to the strengths of the technology,' explains Dr Frank Heller, director of Tavistock's Centre for Decision-Making Studies. 'In practice, the technical and social systems aren't separate. Rather than maximise either, you have to view them as one socio-technical system and optimise their workings in conjunction.' One result of the 1940s discovery of the socio-technical principle was that Volvo and Saab began having vehicles built by groups of workers, with fair leeway to decide who did what and how, instead of subjugating them to machine-paced assembly lines.

Heller says that long after being exported to Sweden, what were then called 'semi-autonomous groups' have been re-imported. 'The Japanese took and improved them, mainly by adding a strong training element still unusual in the West, and they're now known as quality circles.

'But managers mostly stay addicted to the technological fix and maximising mechanistic returns. That's probably because of the third element in the mix – the economic system which at present rules that results are measured by the short-term bottom line. And while socio-technical approaches can pay off by that yardstick, it isn't a necessary consequence.' On the other hand, he adds, the longer-run costs of the technological fix have repeatedly been shown by research. Classic effects are that staff gain less satisfaction from their jobs in general, feel dulled by the lack of variety and challenge in their work, and resent being barred from using numerous of their abilities.

A 1960s study of Detroit car workers found that all three effects were significantly linked with reduced mental health. The most baneful was apparently the under-use of abilities.

More recently, joint US-Swedish studies have shown that increased risk of cardio-vascular heart disease is linked with 'low decision latitude'. The term describes jobs in which workers have little control over their task or their conduct while doing it. Moreover, no matter how hectic the work, the link with heart trouble emerged solely when the job also had low decision latitude.

Ian Angell, Professor of Information Systems at London School of Economics, sees the technological fix as especially hazardous when applied to computerisation. 'In this new technology, more than ever before, the use of machinery cannot be separated from human intellect, aspirations, culture, philosophy and social organisation. There must be increased emphasis on a policy for the effective management and utilisation of personnel at all levels in the organisation,' he says.

'Not only must this policy ensure that misplaced optimism in the benefits of technology does not run roughshod over human aspirations, but also it must release the potential fount of ideas and innovation in the workforce as a whole. To do this, we really need to understand how technological systems affect both business and individual performance.' Martin Bauer, a social psychologist at LSE, suspects that many managers debar themselves from gaining the necessary understanding by their attitude to resistance to their designs. They tend to view it as an enemy and attack it by one of two means.

The first is to overpower it, with the potential drawback that the people resisting will build up countervailing force. The second tactic is to open a second front by raising a different issue that distracts the opposition, which can often be done at less cost.

Bauer thinks that, in the longer run, it is more productive to change the analogy and view such resistance as pain – a signal that something is wrong.

In which case it is unlikely to be eradicated by warfare, but needs to be sensitively diagnosed and set to rights.

The diagnosis may well be difficult, he adds. In a small company he studied in Switzerland, staff initially showed their opposition to a system imposed on them only in general ways such as by laughing when breakdowns occurred.

It took patient handling by the management to get them to make their real complaints specific.

As a result, the system was scrapped and replaced after a mere three years.

'The replacement was chosen by more sophisticated criteria, and one in every three of the factors used was human as distinct from technical, compared with only one in eight the first time around.' Professor Angell doubts that one in three is enough. 'A better balance would be eight in nine,' he says. 'It is the human factor, not technology, that makes the difference between commercial success and failure, and between acceptance and rejection of a system.'

5 TRAINING ON TRIAL

INTRODUCTION

As with many initiatives, there were high hopes and expectations when the government-inspired programme to raise the quality and availability of vocational training was launched in the UK at the end of 1990. Its parameters had been set after studies had been made of the American Private Industry Council (Pic) initiative, and the programmes run by the German Chambers of Commerce movement.

The FT set out to track, with regular up-dates, the progress of the British initiative in which responsibility for training has been handed back from government to employer-led councils. It called on correspondents also to provide the backdrop of experience in the US and Germany, highlighting their weaknesses – and indeed, mistakes – but also their strengths.

Employers were eager to participate in the UK government's scheme, lining up to offer their chief executives to serve on what are known as Training and Enterprise Councils (in Scotland, Local Enterprise Companies). The Tecs were given the responsibility of spending the Department of Employment's training budget, and were setting out, as one of those involved put it, to 'change the tide of history'.

Numbers given vocational training in the UK compare unfavourably with those in Germany and France, and the Tec movement accepted that a fundamental under-skilling in Britain's workforce was the challenge it was having to tackle.

In this objective, the Tecs started out with not only the support of employers, but also wide political and industrial support. As Lisa Wood and John Gapper, principal authors of the FT's series, explained at the outset, the Confederation of British Industry backed the movement, as did most unions, which said they would be prepared to join Tec Boards. The Labour Party was also enthusiastic; it committed itself, had it won the 1992 election, to placing vocational training at the top of its agenda.

The Lecs in Scotland were given a much wider remit. This is because they were born out of the demise of two development bodies and thus have a more direct role in the country's economic development.

The American experience, on which the UK Tec plan was partly based, has many structural similarities, particularly in terms of drawing upon local business people – who, as with Tecs, must be in the majority on the board of what are termed Private Industry Councils (Pics). Also mirrored in the UK – as the FT's Martin Dickson reported from New York – is the American requirement that most of the training work be contracted out to outside organisations, which must bid for the contracts.

But one of the fundamental weaknesses of the US system, or so its critics would have one believe, is that the system of rewarding the outside contractors on the basis of how many people they place in full-time employment meant that contractors chose only those who would probably get jobs anyway.

Even the German training system, often held up in the UK to be of a quality that Britain would do well to emulate, has its British detractors, as David Goodhart found. Too much formalisation and too broad an objective were two criticisms he uncovered. Overall, however, Goodhart found the British view to be that the legally-backed, compulsory membership, well-funded chamber of commerce system of training in Germany produced higher training standards and results.

Certainly, the stability of the German system contrasts with the roller-coaster progress of the Tecs. The scrapping of a central Tec body has left many companies complaining about having to deal with Tecs on a time-wasting individual basis. Tecs have also faced uncertainty because of reduced government funding for programmes, and have claimed that quality of training will suffer and that they will not be able to guarantee, as they are supposed to, training for all young people.

Tensions built up between government and G10, the group of ten chairmen which represents the movement, because of funding uncertainties, and also because the G10 felt it wanted more say in the formulation of government policy.

However, it took only three months for the mood of the chairmen and chief executives to switch from a point at which they saw the initiative being in danger of collapse to a feeling that the future was reasonably assured. Inevitably, though, there continue to be deep political under-tones to many of the issues surrounding the development of the Tecs, from how they should be coordinated to the tenure of executives on their boards. In late 1992 the subject remained a subject of debate in the pages of the FT.

CLOSING THE INTERNATIONAL GAP

By James Buxton, Martin Dickson, John Gapper and Lisa Wood

First published between November 1990 and January 1991

Turning the tide of history

Tim Evans, one of the business leaders embarking on Britain's biggest training shake-up for 25 years, does not underestimate the task. 'The problem of failure to invest in training has cropped up since the 1850s. What we have to do is change the tide of history,' he says.

That tide has been running strongly of late. Britain is entering the 1990s burdened by a lack of skills. As the economy sinks into a cyclical downturn, it is still suffering from the wounds inflicted by the last recession on what was an ailing system of vocational training.

Manufacturing skills were one victim of the 1979–82 recession. As companies under threat of closure attacked over-manning and inflexible working practices, they laid off skilled workers and ended youth apprenticeships. By the end of the 1980s, output was suffering as a result.

Over the same decade, the government used publicly-funded training more to reduce unemployment than to raise skills. Despite refinements, Youth Training achieved less than the apprenticeships it replaced. Training for the adult unemployed offered most of them little more than work experience.

It is hardly surprising that the government has now decided on a new course, but the timing is difficult. British businesses are being asked to turn back the tide of history amid trading conditions which are prompting many simply to batten down the hatches and hope they will survive the storm.

None the less, a new course has been set. Drawing on the experience of Germany and the United States, responsibility is being handed to a network of employer-led councils. Each will cover a population of at least

100,000, organising public training and encouraging more in the private sector.

The first responsibility of these Training and Enterprise Councils (Tecs) will be to run local versions of government schemes such as Youth Training.

These schemes have been organised until now by the Training Agency, a branch of the Department of Employment.

Evans, deputy chairman of the engineering group Foster Wheeler, is one of 1,200 business leaders who have agreed to sit on the boards of the 82 Tecs planned to cover England and Wales. Thirty six Tecs have started work, and the others should be running by next April. In Scotland, responsibility will fall to 22 Local Enterprise Companies (Lecs).

The Tec initiative is the latest in a long line of attempts to improve training, although it is the most significant shake-up since Industrial Training Boards were set up in 1964. These constant efforts have been prompted by a series of studies showing the inadequacies of Britain's education and training record compared with other countries.

Unease about Britain losing ground to overseas competitors led to the establishment of a Royal Commission on Technical Instruction in 1884. That concluded that the neglect of education and training by the state in Britain was one of the key reasons for a lack of economic competitiveness.

The comparative advantage of other European countries has only widened in the past decade. France has made a strong effort to raise standards of youth vocational training to those of Germany. Some 82,000 French students a year now achieve the A-level standard Technical Baccalaureat, while only 25,000 British young people pass the BTec equivalent.

About 120,000 workers in what was West Germany gain engineering and Technology craft qualifications each year, against 35,000 in Britain.

Everyone under 18 in Germany is entitled to a day's vocational training a week, but the number of British manufacturing apprentices has fallen from 236,000 in 1968 to under 100,000 today.

Why has Britain failed to produce a well-trained workforce in the past, and why is that failure deepening? The factors include: Education: Vocational training has long had a second-class status in Britain compared with academic education. The education system was geared to produce an intellectual elite for entry to professions such as the civil service, rather than helping the bulk of the population acquire skills for industry.

Youth training: Many young people have left education for jobs that offer little or no training. The apprenticeships that were intended to fill this gap have been in serious decline. Those left have also been criticised on a number of grounds. They are thought to lead to narrow craft skills and be based too heavily on time-serving.

Industrial structure: British companies have become concentrated in product markets with relatively low skill requirements. There has been a long-term shift away from manufacturing towards services, where many jobs are part-time. This has cut both manufacturing craft training, and the demand for specialist skills, Financial markets: British companies often complain that they are driven by the City of London to maximise profits and dividends, and so are pushed into a short-term approach. This has made it harder to invest, and has placed particular pressures on training budgets, which appear as costs on balance sheets.

All this means that Tecs and Lecs face a substantial task. Their raison d'etre is the government's view that the private sector is better placed than politicians, civil servants, or bodies such as the former Training Commission (a forerunner of the Training Agency) to motivate managers and workers and cajole employers.

So far, it has been relatively easy. The managing directors and chief executives invited to sit on boards – personnel directors were thought too junior – have come forward eagerly. All the Tecs should be running by next April, two years ahead of the schedule set last year.

Relations between the government and Tec leaders have even survived tough negotiations over the latitude the Tecs will get in handling public money.

The original guidelines laid down by civil servants were thought too restrictive by many Tec leaders. Tecs have now won freedom to spend public money on improving and subsidising private sector training.

But the real test is about to start, as Tecs grapple for the first time with the widely-acknowledged and deeply-rooted problem of under-skilling in the British workforce. This is far from the first time that there has been a consensus about the problem, but a solution has always proved elusive. Their models are the Private Industry Councils (Pics) in the US, and Chambers of Commerce in Germany. Pics are business-led groups which run schemes mainly aimed at the unemployed and poor, while the Chambers of Commerce have broad supervision over training for young people in their areas.

Tecs will be expected to assess the needs of their local labour markets, and be their main delivery mechanism for government schemes including Youth Training and Employment Training. They will take responsibility for spending the Department of Employment's training budget – £2.5bn for 1990–91.

Government funding is to be pruned progressively over the next few years. The Employment Training scheme for the adult unemployed is being cut in size, and the government wants Tecs to persuade local employers to spend more. Employers are estimated to spend about £18bn on training currently.

Tecs will try to improve training of the adult employed, particularly among small businesses which have been notorious for 'poaching' trained staff from larger companies. However, they will not have legal powers to force companies in their areas to take part in training or co-operate with others.

The councils will attempt to form links with education authorities in an attempt to match local education better to the needs of business. They will also be responsible for a variety of local enterprise initiatives, including counselling and financial help for small businesses starting up in the area.

The staff administering Tec activities will largely be civil servants. Two thirds of each Tec board will have to consist of chief executives from private industry – a requirement seen as a snub by local authorities, unions and voluntary groups. But many have taken the opportunity to join when asked.

Indeed, the idea of Tecs and Lecs has gained wide political and industrial support. The Confederation of British Industry, which has been increasingly worried at the effect of poor training arrangements, has backed it. Most unions have declared themselves willing to join Tec boards.

The Labour Party has also said it will retain the Tec network if it wins the next general election. The party has placed improvements to vocational training along with education at the top of its agenda. It wants the government to go further, giving workers' legal rights to training.

This broad backing means Tecs have a weight of expectation on them to improve Britain's training record. But a number of areas of debate are emerging as they start work: Funding: The Department of Employment has been under pressure from the Treasury to cut training budgets in line with unemployment. The department's budget is being cut by £300m in real terms next year, with the brunt falling on adult training budgets. Tec boards have demanded more flexibility in the way the money is spent in return; Links: The responsibility for training and local enterprise means Tecs will have a complex relationship with various government departments, local authorities, and other employer groups such as Chambers of Commerce. One sensitive area will be education links, with Tecs open to accusations of altering teaching to suit business needs.

Targets: Many Tec chairmen want the government to commit itself again to national targets for skills set by Sir Norman Fowler, the former employment secretary. These were abandoned by Michael Howard, his successor, on the grounds that it did not have any control over the national level of qualifications.

The government's critics claim the true reason was that the targets would cost more than the government would pay. 'You cannot have world-class targets for training with a Third World budget,' says one Tec chairman. Some fear the government is now free to lower standards rather than raise them.

So the Tec initiative is being launched at a delicate and critical time, amid widespread agreement that the problem of underskilling must be addressed, and that employer-led councils may be well suited to do so.

But there is broad consensus about the magnitude of the task facing them.

INITIATIVES DOWN THE YEARS

1884. Royal Commission on Technical Instruction concluded that neglect of training was a key reason for Britain's lack of competitiveness.

1964. Industrial Training Boards set up with the authority to operate a levy/grant system on employers.

1973. Manpower Services Commission set up to run public employment and training programmes.

1975. Job Creation Programme established to provide worthwhile work for those otherwise unemployed.

1976. Work Experience Programmes instigated for 16–18 year-olds.

1978. Youth Opportunities Programme and Special Temporary Employment Programme (STEP) set up to replace Job Creation and Work Experience Programmes.

1979. Most ITBs abolished 7 remain.

1981. Community Enterprise Programme replaces STEP.

1982. Community Enterprise Programme becomes The Community Programme.

1983. Youth Training Scheme created to replace YOP and offer one year training for young people.

1988. Employment Training set up for adult unemployed. MSC abolished.

1990. Youth Training replaces YTS. National Vocational Qualifications instigated and Training and Enterprise Councils set up. 6 ITBs abolished, leaving only Construction Industry Training Board.

Who runs the Tecs?

Why are they doing it? It is the most intriguing of the questions hanging in the air as chief executives and managing directors of many of the best-known British companies take on responsibility for the country's industrial training. They are not being paid, and have little time to spare. Yet there is no shortage of volunteers.

Sceptics prefer to remain anonymous in the initial rush of enthusiasm for Training and Enterprise Councils. 'Most of my colleagues from the private sector are superb,' says one local-authority chief executive. 'They have a lot to give, and they give of their time generously. But I wonder what a few of them are doing it for. Perhaps it's the kudos they're after.' It is more than a matter of idle curiosity. The 1,200 chief executives who have so far volunteered to sit on the boards of 82 Tecs in England and Wales will decide their success or failure. If they lose interest, or become disillusioned, the fate of Tecs might mirror that of the Private Industry Councils (Pics) in the United States which inspired them.

A deterioration in the calibre of the business leaders involved is one reason for the patchy quality of Pics. For Britain to break with past failures in vocational training, and improve the management of publicly funded training schemes, one overriding uncertainty must be overcome: the long-term commitment of Tec directors.

The reason why the government wants the directors is clear. It hopes to end decisively the chequered history of joint control of training which was established in 1964 with Industrial Training Boards. Trade unions and local authorities have been excluded from equal participation. Instead, the government has insisted that chief executives will comprise two thirds of Tec boards.

A full-time chief executive – about half of them civil servants on three-year secondments – will control day-to-day running of Tecs. The boards, led by private-sector managers, most meeting once a month, are there to apply management skills and establish a strategy. They must combine public and private funds to raise the level of skills in their regions and towns.

The government hopes these business leaders will impregnate a crusading spirit into their communities and persuade other managers of the importance of training. It wants them to encourage workers to demand better training, and improve the way in which local providers such as colleges of further education and training agents operate.

It trusts that business leaders such as Mr Alastair Morton, chief executive of Eurotunnel and a man known as a tough negotiator rather than an idealist, will improve the priority given to training. Tec boards have already proved capable of fiercely lobbying the government on funding and the rules governing publicly funded training.

Mr Roger Dawe, chief executive of the Training Agency (the arm of the Department of Employment which is handing over responsibility to Tecs) says the government believes the best way to influence attitudes to training is to give managers control. He says Tec boards should become missionaries for enterprise rather than simply supervising existing training programmes.

The motives of senior managers for joining Tec boards will govern whether they operate effectively, and whether they lose interest. A simple wish for recognition is one acknowledged motive. One Tec chief executive says he actively fosters competition to get on the board. The prestige of being seen as a local business leader has stimulated many.

So far, only 20 Tec board members are said to have resigned those solely seeking recognition may follow as soon as their names appear on an honours list. Tecs that do not succeed quickly risk losing board members who only want to be associated with a prestigious venture. Virtuous circles of success – and vicious ones of failure – may develop.

However, most Tec board members say they are motivated by something more.

Many speak of the venture in terms of national idealism. That card – the chance for business leaders to take part in remedying a persistent cause of Britain's industrial failure – was played successfully by Sir Norman Fowler, the former employment secretary, in the early days of Tecs.

'I was at a dinner and I heard Norman Fowler speak about world class objectives in training. I was impressed,' says Mr Charles Darby, a director of Bass, the brewing and hotels group, and chairman of Birmingham Tec. The government has tried to reinforce the feeling that board members are participating in a historic venture through advertisements and briefings.

Mr Eric Dancer, chairman of Devon and Cornwall Tec and managing director of Dartington Crystal, was already convinced of the need to participate. 'My company trades all over the world, He says. I see the strengths of the international competition. As a nation we really do have to improve our performance, and I want to play my part.' That visionary atmosphere may lead to difficulties in sustaining long-term commitment to Tecs. Among the main ones is the limit on what many Tecs will be able to achieve in practice. Mr Michael Howard, employment secretary, has abandoned the targets set by Sir Norman, and public expenditure that would help Tecs to achieve them has been cut.

Some doubt whether Tec directors who are imbued with the spirit of idealism will manage effectively. Mr Richard Guy, chief executive of South and East Cheshire Tec, says directors who see their work as charity may avoid hard decisions. 'If you join a board because of a vague view that you want to do good, you will not rock the boat,' he says.

As the initial fervour fades, the work of Tec boards may also become harder, and less inspiring. 'It was very exciting discussing principles, structures, allocation of funds and writing the plan,' says Mr Darby. 'Making it work is going to be a long, hard haul, and we are going to have to deliver. That could mean we may have to be more hands-on.' That might be testing for non-executive Tec directors from companies in which training policy is the responsibility of personnel directors. So far, Tec chief executives say there has been little lack of competence among directors. 'It has not been an issue for us,' says Mr Gregory Hyland, of Thames Valley Tec.

'Directors would be hard-pressed perhaps to conduct negotiations with training providers – but that is not what they are about,' he says. Mr Guy talks of a partnership between chief executives and directors. 'My board needs advice about the workings of programmes, but they bring to me high-level strategic thinking,' he says.

Many Tecs are feeling their way gingerly in the relations between directors and staff. A cultural gap has been opened by the government's insistence on Tecs' taking staff seconded from the Training Agency. Although Tec directors admit that civil servants bring practical know-ledge of public schemes such as Youth Training, they fear divided loyalties.

Civil servants have been trained in a culture of offering service to the public. The aim of many Tec directors is to alter training to get the best value from limited funds – possibly selecting the people they regard as most suitable for training. One chief executive says wryly that some of his staff complained about that as 'not fair'.

There is, equally, a prospect of tension within boards in relations between the two thirds of directors who are private-sector managers and others. Many of the latter directors – including local education authority officers, union officials and people from voluntary organisations – believe they represent interests as well as lending expertise.

Ms Anne Weinstock, chief executive of the Rathbone Society, a mental handicap charity, is a director of Manchester Tec. 'I thought it would take too much of my time to get the message of equal opportunities across to boards of business people,' she says. 'But colleagues said if people like me did not get involved who would represent their voice?' In the early stages, such potential tensions have largely been contained.

Many Tecs have also built up links with councils and local education authorities. The government did not include those – or other big public-sector employers such as the National Health Service – among obligatory Tec members.

But many local authorities, like trade unions, have made the pragmatic decision to get involved with Tecs. Mr Stephen Clark is chief executive of Labour-controlled South Tyneside Metropolitan Borough Council, and was nominated by councillors as a member of Tyneside Tec. His presence has been accepted by the private-sector managers on the board.

A growing mesh of informal working relationships is being forged between his authority and the Tec. However, all Tecs face the prospect of local authorities believing their authority in areas such as education is being usurped. 'There are no irreconcilables between us,' says Mr Clark. 'But it would be unrealistic to claim that there are no tensions.' The unusual powers now being accorded to private-sector managers through Tecs face little prospect of being seriously disturbed. The Labour party not only supports the idea of Tecs but thinks it would be wrong to change the structure of boards into equal representation for local authorities, unions and businesses.

'We do not plan to go back to the old tripartite approach but we do want some flexibility,' says Mr Henry McLeish, Labour's training spokesman. 'We support the concept and recognise that employers make important contributions. The arrangements could be ruptured if we took any hasty actions for party political reasons.' That means the experiment is likely to continue for some time. It will only seriously be threatened if Tec directors start to lose interest and resign en masse. The government will have to ensure that the difficulty and variety of tasks facing directors does not lead to disillusionment when the initial enthusiasm wears off.

High ambitions in Scotland

Lex Gold, one of the men at the centre of the web of Local Enterprise Companies (Lecs) springing up in Scotland, makes a crucial point: 'Lecs may sound like the English Tecs (training and enterprise councils) but they are actually very different they have a far wider remit and will be much more powerful.' While the Tecs, progressively being established across England, will concentrate on training, the Lecs will not only handle training but also take on many of the powers for economic development of the Scottish Development Agency (SDA) these include advice and funding for businesses, property development, land reclamation and provision of factories.

The Lecs are part of a sweeping reform whereby both the SDA and the Highlands and Islands Development Board are disappearing, merging with the Scottish functions of the Training Agency to form two new bodies: Scottish Enterprise in the south, and Highlands and Islands Enterprise in the north.

The structure will come into existence at a stroke next April 1. Scottish Enterprise, based in Glasgow in the old headquarters of the SDA, will be the core body for 13 Lecs, and Highlands and Islands Enterprise for a further nine.

The Lecs now exist in embryo, their boards headed by senior local businessmen and with private sector representatives holding at least two-thirds of the places. Scottish Enterprise's Lecs recently submitted three-year plans all costed for what they intend to do. These amount to competitive bids for the Lecs' share of the £320m out of the £406m Scottish Enterprise budget (the rest goes to the central body). The total budget represents no increase in real terms on the previous year's spend.

Of the £320m rather more than half is destined for training, with tight statutory strings attached, while the ex-SDA portion is more discretionary, though Lecs must obtain authorisation from Scottish Enterprise for items of more than £250,000.

'Scottish Enterprise is being created in the belief that it is going to be more effective than what was being done before,' says John Condliffe, the ex-SDA director who is joint managing director of the core body, along with Gold, who formerly ran the TA in Scotland. Next week their chief executive, Crawford Beveridge, a Scot headhunted back from California, moves in.

Professor Neil Hood, who has left a senior post at the SDA, recently described Scottish Enterprise as a 'morass of complexity' full of 'tensions and uncertainties'.

These are some of the main questions being asked about the initiative: Will the core body exercise strong central control over the Lecs, or will the Lecs have reasonable autonomy? Will the training and economic development functions genuinely be merged? How different will what the Lecs do be from what the SDA and the TA do now? How much flexibility will the Lecs have, especially in spending their training budgets? Will they have enough money for all they want to do? Will Lecs attract private sector finance, as the government wants? Although the Scottish Enterprise core body will retain functions such as responsibility for attracting inward investment to Scotland and venture capital finance, as well as close supervision of the Lecs' activities, Condliffe underlines the Lecs' autonomy.

'There will be a strong core to deliver the national programmes, but where a programme can be delivered locally it will be,' he says. 'We would rather see lots of performance even at the price of things being a little unco-ordinated.' In Dundee, William Low, a former textile industrialist, is chairman of Scottish Enterprise Tayside, which covers the Tayside region. He is not proposing big changes in the already well-established operations of the SDA and the TA in the area, although the two bodies will move into a single new office.

'We are determined that there will be no stop-go, so the SDA will carry on here with its projects as if it were going on forever,' he says. Scottish Enterprise Tayside has informed all the organisations which currently carry out training operations for it that their contracts will be renewed for 12 months from next April.

Low sees the advantage of the new structure in the fact that 'we understand local requirements. In the past staff were always on the train to Glasgow to get permission from the SDA to do things, or asking the boffins at TA headquarters in Sheffield.'

The picture is rather different at Enterprise Ayrshire, south-west of Glasgow. Here an organisation is being created almost from scratch in an area where the SDA was never strong. A driving force is John Lord, the former TA director for the area, who is chief executive-designate. His chairman, John Hornibrook, who runs a Roche pharmaceutical plant, says: 'We've gone for a single team in which hopefully people won't remember whether they are ex-SDA or ex-TA.' The merger is reflected in the management structure of the new body. Under the chief executive there are two directors of 'business and human resources development', with heads of training and of business development reporting to them. The two directors each cover different geographical areas or industrial sectors which have yet to be decided.

Enterprise Ayrshire is terminating all contracts with organisations or companies which provide training and reassessing which of them should be re-hired. 'There are some training activities giving people skills for which there is no demand in this area,' says Hornibrook. 'Training has got to be refocused.' He sees Enterprise Ayrshire helping small companies in

Ayrshire 'which have started up successfully but do not grow'. In Aberdeen, Ian Wood, who runs the Wood Group, a large private company in oilfield services, is chairman of Grampian Enterprise. Unlike many areas of Scotland which have serious unemployment, parts of Grampian suffer from labour shortages. Though he feels that more should be done to help indigenous businesses exploit the oil services market, Wood sees the encouragement of diversification away from dependence on oil as a priority.

Grampian Enterprise has appointed a chief executive from outside both the SDA and the TA. Wood, who is also on the board of the SDA, plans to rationalise training, cutting the number of training providers from about 30 to about ten.

He sees Grampian Enterprise as a means of co-ordinating the proliferation of economic development bodies, some run by local authorities, in the area.

Almost uniquely in the Scottish Enterprise organisation Grampian Enterprise has its own members, about 200 in all. They include companies, local authorities, colleges, trades unions and individuals.

'I don't expect much private sector money to be contributed to Grampian Enterprise, apart from membership subscriptions,' says Wood. But the private sector will invest in projects alongside Grampian Enterprise. 'The greatest thing that can happen is if they will invest more money in human resources in their own companies.' Now the Lecs are waiting to see whether the core body approves their first year business plans and spending proposals. Wood is not alone in being worried that cuts in the training budget in line with demographic changes and falling unemployment will prevent Grampian Enterprise from doing much beyond its statutory duty to provide Youth Training and Employment Training.

At Scottish Enterprise headquarters Condliffe acknowledges that the amount of money which the Lecs are seeking is far in excess of the total available, but it does not bother him. 'We can say to the Lecs: your proposals fit our overall strategy it's up to you to prioritise them according to your budget. There will be practical reasons why not all projects will go ahead in year one or even later. Year one will be difficult for Scottish Enterprise. The time to judge it is the middle of year two. If we still have problems then it will be serious.'

Flaws in international role models

The initial appearance is highly deceptive: you proceed down a thickly carpeted corridor, lined with blandly tasteful art, into a bright, freshly painted room where smartly dressed women are busily tapping away at an array of new word-processors. Welcome to a typical corporate office in Anytown, USA.

In reality, this is a training centre for some of America's least privileged citizens in the gritty Connecticut town of Bridgeport. The women at the word-processors are single black mothers on government welfare, learning the skills of the office workers they hope to become.

The centre's resemblance to a real office is a quite deliberate device to build their self-confidence. It is also a tangible demonstration of a successful partnership between business and the Southern Connecticut Private Industry Council (Pic), the local arm of a federal job training programme aimed primarily at the poor.

The word-processors are part of a $165,000 gift of equipment and software from International Business Machines, while the furniture, artwork and other equipment have all been given by local donors. Even some of the women's clothes have come from business people the centre insists that trainees dress in a manner suitable for an office and maintains a wardrobe for those who cannot afford their own.

The educational process is as much psychological as practical. 'On day one we tell them, "you're in charge of your destiny",' says Joyce Thomas, who runs the centre and has a good record of getting Pic graduates into work and keeping them there.

A similar self-help ideal – that local private enterprise is best suited to determining local training needs – underlies the entire Pic movement in the US, which has served as the inspiration for Britain's new Training and Enterprise Councils.

However, the Bridgeport Pic is regarded as one of the best in the US and many of the 620 others scattered across the nation have a very chequered record. Their problems suggest that while the American system offers some good ideas to the UK, it is a far from ideal role model.

Pics emerged in the early 1980s out of the Job Training Partnership Act (JTPA), a Reagan administration reform designed to produce greater private sector involvement in manpower training.

The board of each Pic has to have a majority of local business people. They, working together with a minority of representatives from government and community groups, and a full-time executive team, decide how to allocate federal training funds.

Equally important is the role of the private sector in the training itself. For the Pics do relatively little teaching themselves, instead delegating most work to outside organisations – ranging from private businesses to union groups – which bid for contracts.

The contractors have to show that there is a local demand for the training they are offering – for example, through letters of support from potential employers – and they are paid in part by the number of trainees they actually place in jobs. According to the theory it is the marketplace that rules, rather than bureaucrats.

At its best the system does much very valuable work, as the example of Bridgeport shows. But the system is highly dependent on the quality of the individuals involved, and fails to reach those most in need of help.

The Bridgeport Pic is particularly blessed. First, the geographical area it covers, together with a New England sense of community service, means there is no shortage of business talent willing to serve on its board. In fact there is a waiting list.

However, in some other parts of the country, critics say initial enthusiasm for the scheme seems to have faded, that the seniority of businessmen serving on Pic boards has consequently dropped, and that momentum has been lost.

But attracting the right businessmen depends crucially on the quality of the individual executives running a programme and on their diplomatic skills.

Here, too, in contrast to some other areas, the Bridgeport scheme has been fortunate. Its director, Henry Durell, is an enterprising man with a hard-headed commercial background in retailing and, having been with the Pic from the beginning, he gives it a sense of continuity. Other staff members radiate enthusiasm for their work.

Durell believes that having businessmen in the majority on the board works extremely well. For one thing, he says, it has removed budget allocation decisions from the political arena, with its lengthy squabbles over who gets what. And his board members – who range from senior figures in local banking to small entrepreneurs – provide not only strategic direction and a feel for the business climate to the Pic, but can also give day-to-day practical advice and support services 'which money can't buy'. But, in spite of all this support, the Pic's budget has been shrinking since 1984 because federal contributions relate to local unemployment levels. Those fell sharply in New England in the late 1980s.

However, in another display of enterprise, Bridgeport has tapped the state of Connecticut for funds, and some 35 per cent of its $5m budget now comes from this source and is aimed at more welfare-oriented programmes, such as improving the employment chances of the Hispanic population.

But the budget squeeze has also forced the Pic to cut back on some of its more high-risk programmes, aimed at those who are hardest to train. And this highlights a major attack that has been made on the Pic system by critics who argue that it has basic flaws.

In particular, they say that rewarding private contractors for the number of trainees who get placed in jobs has created a 'top skimming' bias contractors choose for training those who would be most likely to get jobs anyway. John Donahue, an assistant professor at Harvard Kennedy School of Government, says it is as if doctors 'were presented with a large population of patients suffering from complaints ranging from tendonitis to brain tumours, were invited to choose two to three per cent of them for treatment, and paid on the basis of how many were still breathing when they left the hospital'.

A report by the Department of Labor's Office of Inspector General in 1988 concluded that although the JTPA programme had led to 70 per cent achieving employment it was 'not focusing on hard-to-serve individuals – the population segment where potentially the greatest returns on investment can be realised'.

In Bridgeport, Durell acknowledges that 'of the eligible population referred to them, they (the contractors) are probably going to take those they think are most likely to succeed'. But he points out that the Pic tries to screen out those who would probably get jobs anyway all those accepted fit the deprivation criteria – and their places could be filled three times over if the budget permitted.

The Pic programme in general is also attacked for emphasising short courses that will put people in jobs quickly, rather than longer term training that will produce more enduring results. The average training period is just three to four months.

Durell says this problem is built in by the JTPA law, which does not allow Pics to pay trainees living allowances, and that in turn limits the time they are able to remain in a programme. 'We once tried a one year auto mechanics training course, but they all dropped out,' he says.

In some parts of the US Pics have also been strongly attacked for wasting resources, for example, by subsidising companies for training people they would have hired anyway. According to the Labor Department study this applied to about 60 per cent of on-the-job trainees.

None of these criticisms brands the Pic programme as a failure. It is certainly more successful than its predecessors in finding jobs for the poor, but it does have major flaws if it is regarded – as it should be – primarily as a welfare programme.

What it is most certainly not – and was never intended to be – is a national training programme which addresses the serious deficiencies of America's school-to-work transition in an age that demands a more highly skilled working population than before.

This was underlined in a high-powered report published last year by the influential National Center on Education and the Economy, which said that the JTPA programme was well intentioned, 'but because the programmes are designed exclusively to aid the disadvantaged and dislocated populations, benefits are marginal in the labour market'.

Instead, the study called for the establishment of state and federal Employment and Training Boards to take a comprehensive look at the nation's critical manpower problems. Perhaps in a few years' time this new enthusiasm will cross the Atlantic too.

THE NEW CONSENSUS ON TRAINING

By Lisa Wood

First published 13 July 1992

In stark contrast to just three months ago, chairmen and chief executives of Training and Enterprise Councils have been talking as if Tecs had a future.

In April a confidential memorandum from Tec leaders to Mrs Gillian Shephard, the new employment secretary, claimed that the initiative was in danger of collapse.

Last week more than 500 representatives of the employer-led movement, which was set up two years ago with the ambition of revolutionising training, were talking at their annual national conference about a five-year agenda.

What, if anything, has changed? Behind closed doors, Mrs Shephard was left in no doubt about the damage that would be inflicted by additional spending cuts – as suggested in her speech to conference.

For a start, Mrs Shephard, a woman with considerable inter-personal skills, raised Tecs' expectations that she would bring a new momentum to training, and she received an enthusiastic welcome at the conference. Prior to the general election, Tecs had been demoralised by a brutal round of spending negotiations, preceded by 18 months of government inertia on training issues.

The conference revealed the new thinking on both sides since the election.

Mr Nigel Chilcott, head of the small secretariat which services the Tecs, said after the conference: 'We are drawing up an agenda of what Tecs believe they want from government and it, in turn, is making explicit what it wants from Tecs.' The government offered a mixed bag of policies, a few of which could make Tecs' financial situation sounder.

Mrs Shephard hinted at possible financial sweeteners – she would try to persuade Mr Michael Portillo, chief secretary to the Treasury, to accept that Tecs needed three-year funding commitments on the lines of National Health Service hospital trusts. This would help them and their providers of training to plan more effectively. She also said she wanted more result-based payment to Tecs. These are both strong ambitions of Tecs, but are likely to be resisted by the Treasury which prefers finite funding over a single year. Although Mrs Shephard is a junior cabinet member, she has experience of the Treasury and is a personal friend of the prime minister.

The secretary of state invited Tecs to join two working parties on help for unemployed adults and education and training for young people.

While this gesture of partnership was warmly received by Tecs, they will have to make contributions quickly. The Department of Employment has been reviewing both areas and the Treasury has intervened considerably in the debate.

Mr Michael Heseltine, trade and industry secretary, announced that he wanted Tecs to contract with his department and to be the lead strategic body in the creation of 'first-stop shops'. These will group the different agencies providing advice to business, including chambers of commerce. He hinted that the DTI might place some of its small business initiatives with the shops if they were successful.

Although Tecs are pleased with the new relationship with the DTI, they understand that they will have to work quickly to bring sparring parties to one table. Mr Heseltine admires Continental-style chambers of commerce, and could ask chambers to be the lead bodies if Tecs are slow.

While the government lobbed a couple of balls into the Tecs' court, they showed they were becoming more effective at returning them. The government was asked, for example, to give a lead on Investors in People (IIP), the scheme to improve training of people in work, by introducing it into all government departments.

Tecs have been starved of resources to promote the scheme, and at the conference they decided to sponsor research into how different time-limited incentives – such as levies, tax and national insurance options – could stimulate the take-up of IIP. Such a study could be a powerful tool in their fight to get the scheme more widely accepted.

Representatives also showed growing sophistication in discussing what they wanted in training programmes and the relative cost-effectiveness of different programmes. In the lively debate over Employment Training, the training scheme for long-term unemployed, Tec directors said the argument with the government should not be over who was trained, but over training quality.

But if there was a new mood of consensus, there was also a strong demonstration of the division which might hinder the development of the Tec movement, whose 82 members are fiercely independent.

The argument was over whether they should press for a new intermediary body between them and the government – which advocates believe would give Tecs more political clout and greater freedom from government interference. The debate ended in disarray, although members agreed to consult on the issue.

The conference may have illustrated that Tecs were putting more forcefully their own agenda to the government. But they need a more effective national umbrella body.

As one observer noted: 'This is the first time Tecs have publicly confronted the fact that there are major divisions. The next stage in the maturing process will be for Tecs to realise on this issue it might have to come to a vote.'

Part Four

CRITICAL DILEMMAS UNDER SCRUTINY

6 CORPORATE GOVERNANCE – STRIKING THE RIGHT BALANCE

INTRODUCTION

How can one ensure that companies operate within a framework of accountability while not stifling innovation and entrepreneurial drive? This question is at the heart of the debate on corporate governance which has developed increasing heat in recent years.

In the United Kingdom the inspiration for the intensity of the debate has been a series of corporate disasters, most notable being Polly Peck and the Maxwell companies. Both were headed by charismatic chairmen – Asil Nadir at Polly Peck and the eponymous Robert Maxwell. When they crashed, the roles of company executive and, more particularly, non-executive directors came in for increasingly detailed scrutiny. Also under the microscope were the auditors and bankers and all those involved in controlling and reporting on corporate activities.

In the UK a committee headed by Sir Adrian Cadbury and including representatives of interested bodies, spent a year considering how corporate governance might be improved. Its recommendations were essentially uncontentious, advocating self-regulation rather than legislation, and focusing largely on aspects of financial monitoring and reporting. As is clearly evident in this chapter, key players in the corporate community, including fund managers and auditors, were dissatisfied that more radical solutions had not been found for what they deemed to be radical problems. But the Cadbury committee had taken the view that several key questions which had been subject to much debate prior to publication of its report – directors' pay, whether non-executive directors should have powers to police executives – had not been part of its remit.

Nevertheless, they are issues which have refused to lie down, particularly pay. The heads of the formerly nationalised utilities – gas, electricity and water – have faced particularly strong criticism as, following privatisation, their salaries have risen very sharply. The ethics of their action and the example they do, or perhaps do not, set have been the subject of fierce debate.

The wider issues of corporate governance also remain open to scrutiny and continue to polarise attitudes. Under intense discussion in 1992 were not only questions of balance in the boardroom (executives *vs.* non-executives) and how much directors should be paid. There was also heated debate on whether there should always be audit committees to monitor their performance, and whether shareholders (particularly institutions) should exercise more actively their 'ownership' of companies. If this was so, it was asked, what sort of extra powers might they need?

Concentration of power in the boardroom can be a two-edged sword. A powerful and charismatic chairman who is also the chief executive is, in the best of all worlds, able to drive a company forward, essentially drawing all others in the boardroom and below along with him. In the worst of worlds (*viz* Robert Maxwell), such power can be destructive. So the debate rages as to whether the roles of chairman and chief executive should be divided.

This can be further complicated in the larger multinationals when more prosaic structures are introduced – for example, when the roles of chairman and chief executive are vested in one person, but with another taking on the role of either managing director or, as more commonly termed in the US, chief operating officer.

Ironically, one advocate of both this structure, and of a board with a strong non-executive contingent, was to find himself the victim of it. Robert Horton had very grand ambitions for BP, the large UK oil and chemicals group, when he took over as chairman and chief executive in 1990, with David Simon becoming deputy chairman and chief operating officer. How Horton envisaged BP should be governed was clearly spelled out in an article in this chapter written by Steven Butler in 1990.

Just over two years later, however, Horton was to be ousted by the non-executive majority on the board, not because his grand plan was deemed to be entirely wrong, but – as the FT's Resources Editor, David Lascelles, relates – largely because of the aggressive and arrogant style in which he executed it. It was, for example, felt by many critics that while he was an advocate of the theory of empowering more people to take charge of their own destiny, he was incapable of leaving enough of them alone to assume their responsibilities.

A clear lesson that emerged was that the theory of corporate governance is only just the beginning of the story. Putting all the elements into practice is where really hard work begins. If, in the implementation, the style of the individual or group of individuals at the top is at odds with the plan as perceived by those around them, then its success is put in very real danger.

What the BP incident illustrated was the sheer unpredictability of the management process. However well laid the plans for the governance of a company, events can change rapidly and the board must be ready and able to adapt to and exploit those changed circumstances.

But corporate governance does not always take place in an abrasive atmosphere. After SmithKline of the US merged with Beecham of the UK in 1989 to create a large multinational drugs company, changes in the board structure were deemed necessary. Simon Holberton describes how the combined board was reduced in size. The chairman, Henry Wendt, opted for a majority of non-executives, which meant some executive directors losing their places, while new non-executives were brought on board. Wendt had sound reasons for such a structure and had a clear vision of how it should be achieved. But while non-executives theoretically wield the majority power, their performance is monitored and judged in precisely the same way as it is for the executive members.

The sheer scale of the corporate governance challenge that now faces large companies in particular is outlined by Richard Giordano in an article by Christopher Lorenz. Giordano, an American at the head of the UK-based BOC industrial gases group, believes that to master organisational scale and complexity is going to be one of the biggest tasks facing management in the 1990s. The trick is going to be to exploit all the advantages of scale with an ability to remain responsive to the needs of individual markets.

SMITHKLINE BEECHAM – THE SHIFTING BALANCE OF POWER

By Simon Holberton

First published 21 December 1990

There continue to be all too many reasons why corporate governance should be one of the major business issues. The boardroom high-fliers of the 1980s have been shown to demonstrate the failings of Icarus, and financial scandals have proliferated. Investors are therefore increasingly rating companies by the degree of transparency of decision-making at the highest level.

Transparency in this context means, at the very least, ensuring a proper balance between the interests of the managers and the owners. This can be achieved most visibly by having more independent directors than executive directors in the boardroom.

The board changes announced last week by SmithKline Beecham, the Anglo-American health care multinational, underline the hard thinking that Henry Wendt, SB's chairman, and Bob Bauman, its chief executive officer, have done about the governance of SB.

The merger of SmithKline of the US with Beecham of the UK in July 1989 created a multinational drugs company with sales from continuing operations of nearly £4.3bn. These are derived from activities in pharmaceuticals, animal health, consumer brands and clinical laboratories.

At the time of the merger, SB's board consisted of 20 members. The composition of the board had all the appearance of a Solomon-like judgment 10 directors from each of the merging companies, 10 executive and non-executive directors, 10 Englishmen and 10 Americans.

'There was nothing wrong with 10/10,' says Wendt. 'It was a good way to start. But we thought that 20 was too large and that a smaller board of 15–17 was about right.' Wendt also had other items on his agenda. SB is a trans-national company and Wendt thinks the board should reflect that cultural diversity. More controversially, he also believes that non-executive directors should be in the majority.

The changes to SB's board mean that from January 1 next year, there will be 16 members of the board, nine of whom are non-executives and six of whom are executives. This has meant that three executive directors of SB have had to relinquish their board posts. Two non-executive directors have departed and have been replaced by one.

As a move towards altering the Anglo-American nature of the board, Alain Gomez, chairman and chief executive of Thomson SA, the French electronics and defence equipment manufacturer, has been appointed. The only other non-native English speaker is Jan Leschly, chairman of SB's pharmaceuticals division, who is a Dane.

Wendt plans to push further the bias in favour of non-executives – he would like to see non-executive directors comprising two-thirds of total board numbers – and to increase the multicultural nature of the board in line with where it does business. The geographical spread of SB's sales is 40 per cent US, 40 per cent Europe and 20 per cent the rest of the world, mostly Japan.

A penetrating interrogation. But playing with numbers and nationalities could be seen as just cosmetic.

The non-executive directors need to have responsibility and a clearly defined role in monitoring management. To this end, the structure Wendt and Bauman are setting up does appear to be designed to put management on its mettle.

Wendt says he wants the non-executive directors to conduct 'a penetrating interrogation of management'. Bauman emphasises the role of the board in monitoring management's performance. Both are aware that by placing the executives in the minority the non-executives have been given a lot of potential power to change management.

'The litmus test for them is accountability,' says Wendt. 'The non-executive directors should look at performance and how we accomplish it,' adds Bauman.

Says Wendt: 'Their most important role is to ensure that the proper management is in place. If they were in a minority that would be difficult to do.'

SB's directors meet six times a year. On five of those occasions they meet in conclave for a whole day, having supped the night before. On the sixth they meet for three days. All directors receive monthly management accounts.

With the new board structure Wendt also wants non-executive directors to specialise in parts of the business. They will focus their attention on one of SB's four core business activities for three years – they will be encouraged to make two or three visits a year to relevant SB operations – after which they will redirect their attention to another core activity.

'We don't expect them to be management, just conversant with the issues,' says Wendt. 'We also want them to get to know the senior management, because one of their key roles will be succession management.' The non-executives also have other responsibilities. SB's remuneration and audit committees are chaired by the company's two vice-chairmen, both non-executives, and membership of both is restricted to non-executive directors. Wendt says he liaised closely with the non-executive directors over the appointment of Gomez.

Wendt says he had never met Gomez before he was invited to join the board. SB had employed an executive search agency to find an appropriate executive. It worked to a specification drawn up by Wendt and agreed by the non-executive directors, especially the vice-chairmen. 'We saw a lot of names and biographies before we settled on him.' SB is asking a lot of its non-executive directors. Less than full attendance at board meetings will not be good enough and, most intriguing of all, the performance of non-executive directors will be subject to approval as well.

Wendt says this has not been discussed fully by the board. But, he says, 'just as management is appraised on an annual basis so too should be the performance of non-executive directors.'

BOC'S GIORDANO ON THE ORGANISATION AS A GLOBAL 'NETWORK'

By Christopher Lorenz

First published 9 February 1990

When the chairman of a large company holds forth on how it spent the 1980s renewing and reviving its existing businesses, regaining technical excellence, and penetrating new geographic markets, one may be forgiven the reaction 'so what?' Such Herculean feats are certainly impressive. But in today's global economy they are merely qualifications for playing the competitive game – not for winning it.

Richard Giordano, boss of the BOC gases group, as good as admitted as much last night in an illuminating analysis of the difference between the challenges which BOC confronted over the past decade and those it faces now.

Delivering the first of this year's Stockton Lectures at the London Business School, Giordano argued strongly that the organisational mastery of scale and complexity was probably the most difficult task facing companies – British and otherwise – during the 1990s.

Companies must master forms of organisation which reach beyond traditional concepts of delegation and profit centres, Giordano said. Such organisations would have to be internally flexible ('interactive and interdependent'), and would be required to do business across great distances, across national boundaries and cultures.

'We need to find ways of organising and managing bureaucracies effectively,' said Giordano. 'That is what our international competitors have achieved. This is what has driven their successful product strategies all over the globe.'

BOC itself has expanded its core gases businesses from an Anglo-US base deep into Asia and the Pacific, and has continental Europe next on the list. So it faces this organisational problem writ large. It needs to maximise the flow of technology, and other forms of skill-sharing, across its global empire, while remaining responsive to market differences from country to country.

In Giordano's own words, 'the scale of our businesses simply could not afford local self-sufficiency nor a traditional managerial pyramid over the whole group driven from the centre nor some form of an expensive matrix.' BOC's solution to the problem bears the overworked label of 'networking'. As Giordano explained it: 'We expect managers and technologists in our companies throughout the world to take on their shoulders the responsibility for accessing group technology wherever it resides, and to keep appraised of and implement best practices in every aspect of their business.

'Our job at the centre is to facilitate communication and (to) occasionally audit,' he continued. Among other activities, the BOC head office creates ad hoc short-lived committees 'to draw managers' attention to what is available and what is changing'. For each specific area of technology or operational problem, it appoints a 'lead house' – the most knowledgeable unit on that topic, be it in Sydney, Osaka or elsewhere. That unit then has responsibility for disseminating the knowledge to other parts of the group around the world: 'We don't expect its work to be duplicated by other group companies,' Giordano stressed.

A small staff is retained at the centre in Britain 'which acts on occasion as a traffic policeman, sometimes as an orchestra conductor, infrequently as an auditor, and very often as a cheer-leader'. Such networking was fast, efficient, but not easy to sustain, said Giordano.

It required managers to live with 'more than average ambiguity and sometimes conflicting objectives'. It required give-and-take: 'individuals are often called upon for contributions that have no immediate benefit to their profit and loss'. Networking necessitated a high degree of co-operation and trust, rather than authority, the BOC chief emphasised.

Lastly, said Giordano, it was important to recognise that the links in the network were often sustained by technical personnel, and by other non-managers. 'Their quality and experience are increasingly important to the success of our business. We have had to fashion rewards for them that reinforce their importance.'

SHARING EXECUTIVE AUTHORITY AT BP – THE HORTON PLAN

By Steven Butler

First published 7 February 1990

When Robert Horton becomes chairman of British Petroleum next month, BP will have not only a new leader, but a new style of leadership and a new structure of authority.

Horton has decided to split the job of his predecessor, Sir Peter Walters, in two. He will be chairman and 'chief executive', while David Simon will become deputy chairman and chief operating officer. Horton will concentrate mainly on strategy and external relations while Simon will focus on making sure the operating parts of the business perform up to expectation.

The titles have a decidedly American flavour to them. They are commonly used in the US, and Horton confirms that the idea of reshaping the pinnacle of BP's executive power derived from his experience as chairman of Standard Oil, BP's US subsidiary, that has since become BP America.

Titles aside – and there is plenty of confusion at large about the various and contradictory uses of chief executive, managing director, and chief operating officer – the arrangements at BP raise important issues about the management of large, complex and geographically diverse corporations.

Michael Knight, of the Corporate Consulting Group, believes that changes in the corporate landscape, and external pressures likely to develop in the 1990s, may encourage more companies to adopt a similar structure.

Knight, and his colleague at Corporate Consulting, John Scott-Oldfield, call the prototype of Horton's approach a 'one-over-one' arrangement. This means that the chief executive (the boss) has only one top man directly reporting to him – the chief operating officer.

Horton had a COO beneath him in Cleveland, where Standard Oil has its headquarters, and he liked the arrangement.

His explanation for the set-up is simple, albeit laced with Americanisms: 'I am tremendously in need of time expansion,' he says. BP has become too big and complex for one man effectively to perform all the roles of the traditional chairman/chief executive.

Horton expects to be travelling about 40 per cent of the time as chairman.

He believes that in the 1990s BP will face a number of external challenges that will absorb most of his attention: dealing with pressures on the environment, increased government regulation, and the need for strategic corporate alliances in the face of continued change in the oil industry.

Although David Simon will oversee the operations of the company, Horton clearly intends to be in charge of it, to project himself as the single leader.

'One person has to be the boss if there is not going to be confusion,' agrees Michael Knight.

As chairman, Horton will naturally be responsible to the board for the performance of BP. He has an expansive personality, and in addition to focusing on strategic direction and external relations, wants to have the time to project his personal presence throughout the group (120,000 employees in 90 countries), in part to lead a transformation of BP's corporate culture and management style.

The details of this programme – the first phase of which was dubbed Project 1990 – are under consideration by a small group directly under Horton. He clearly has it in mind to be the charismatic leader who transforms the group.

This method of splitting the task of the chief executive is unusual in Britain. While management consultants applaud the broad sense of the arrangement and especially the deliberation with which it will be instituted, they have trouble naming a precise parallel among British companies.

A more typical arrangement has been to have a chairman and chief executive – in the manner of Horton's predecessor at BP – who manages strategy and external relations, as well as the internal parts of the job. Sir Peter has had a number of managing directors beneath him responsible for various divisions of the company.

Another common arrangement is to have a part-time chairman, who may take a leading role in presenting the company to the media or the city, but with a full-time managing director who is chief executive (the boss) and runs the company.

The most extreme example of this approach is Lord Weinstock, managing director of GEC, who has all aspects of the company well under his control.

Hugh Parker, a long-standing expert on board structures as a former UK head of McKinsey, the management consltancy, and now chairman of Corporate Renewal Associates, traces four transitional stages in UK corporate development, beginning with a simple combination of chairman and managing director (or CEO), followed by a stage of part-time chairman with full-time managing director.

The third stage is characterised by full-time chairmen and managing directors, and a fourth stage by the concept of multiple chief executives, such as in Royal/Dutch Shell, Unilever, and BP, beneath an executive chairman.

Horton's changes at BP add another twist to the final stage – splitting the job of chairman, with multiple chief executives beneath the chairman and COO in the operating divisions, such as BP Exploration or BP Chemicals.

The arrangement bears similarity to a structure of leadership just adopted at Pearson, the diversified financial and publishing group that owns the Financial Times. Frank Barlow, formerly chief executive of the FT, has been appointed managing director and COO of the group under Lord Blakenham, the chairman – to whom the group's oilfield equipment business reports directly, however.

There also appear to be similarities at British Aerospace, even though Professor Roland Smith is not a full-time chairman. He plays a much fuller role than many non-executive chairmen in influencing the group's strategy and external relations, while BAe's chief executive, Richard Evans, has a brief that is similar to David Simon's at BP.

In the days when Sir Raymond Lygo was still chief executive at BAe, and Roland Smith had just become chairman, the balance between the two roles was rather different.

A slightly different balance – not always harmonious – applies to the relationship at British Airways between the energetic Lord King, whose chairmanship is officially non-executive, and Sir Colin Marshall, his chief executive, whose role is not confined to strictly operational matters.

There are innumerable variations on these themes, and there is certainly no single 'right' structure for any situation. 'To some extent it is a function of personality and to some extent it is a function of size,' says John Scott-Oldfield.

At BP, Bob Horton and David Simon stress the importance of their personal relationship and mutual understanding in making the split of authority work.

They see a fit between personalities and circumstances.

While the two have prepared a list of duties and responsibilities for the jobs, both stress that it is not a rigid demarcation.

'We are very clear about what our duties are,' says Horton, but adds: 'There is a space between David and me which is very difficult to define.'

'You don't introduce a system just for the sake of a system. To say that you have here a certain type of structure is dogmatic,' says Simon. 'The terms of reference (for the two jobs) are really more important for people outside. Basically we are working as one unit.'

THE FALL OF HORTON

By David Lascelles

First published 27 June 1992

'They were anxious to be gentlemanly about it,' says a British Petroleum official.

The boardroom coup which ousted Robert Horton from the joint position of chairman and chief executive of BP on Thursday was indeed swift and relatively painless. The messy part came in a confrontation earlier this week. But once the news was broadcast to an astonished world, it was all over and the parties to it maintained a dignified silence. This was broken only by Lord Ashburton, the new chairman, who spoke of the board's 'great sadness' at Mr Horton's departure.

Mr Horton spent yesterday at his Thames-side home in Oxfordshire. 'Life goes on,' he told the local newsagent when he slipped across the road to buy the newspapers with his name all over the front pages.

The coup was also a classic display of the way the business establishment dispatches those who have outstayed their welcome. By showing that a board can bring down even a man who holds all the reins of power, it marks something of a triumph for corporate democracy. The intention, of course, was to do BP some good. But while that seemed to be the general expectation in the City yesterday, large questions about the future of the UK's leading, but financially stressed, company have still to be answered – hence the £1.8bn by which the market value of BP plummeted between breakfast and lunchtime yesterday.

Mr Horton's downfall came as a total surprise, as much to senior people within the company as to outsiders. He had only been in the job since March 1990, and even though he made more enemies than friends with his high-handed manner and aggressive cost-cutting strategy, there were few signs of the pressures that were building up in the boardroom.

It transpires that Lord Ashburton, better known as the City merchant banker Sir John Baring, and his non-executive board colleagues, had been nursing misgivings for some time. Not only was BP faring noticeably worse in the recession than its main competitors – profits were down 85 per cent last year – but Mr Horton's personal style was hitting morale and adding to the problems.

The misgivings were strongest among the other business representatives on the board, people like Sir Patrick Sheehy, the chairman of BAT Industries, Dr Carl Hahn, chairman of Volkswagen, and Charles Knight, chairman of the US company Emerson Electric. After sharing their concerns last week, they confronted Mr Horton at the beginning of this week. According to one account of the meeting, Mr Horton quickly understood that he was being given little choice, and offered to resign.

His resignation was accepted at a full board meeting on Thursday afternoon.

This was attended by the other seven executive directors – the heads of BP's various divisions – who all supported the changes and the new appointments.

Although it was the non-executives who took the initiative on Horton's ouster, they seem to have had little trouble in getting the executives on side, a further indication of Horton's isolation.

Lord Ashburton himself appears to have played the key role. Scion of the Baring family and former head of Barings merchant bank, he is a leading City figure and former director of the Bank of England. He is also the longest-serving BP non-executive director with 10 years on the board, which gives him considerable influence. His style is languid. But a banking colleague says: 'He has strong feelings about companies being run properly and effectively. He would be the sort of man to act in a situation like this. He has high standards.' The boardroom drama, rare in a UK blue chip company, would rank as a significant corporate event at the best of times. But it also comes at a moment when corporate governance is a fashionable topic, after the recent Cadbury Report on board accountability.

The BP coup showed two things. It reinforces the view that non-executive directors can play a key role in keeping the executive directors in check.

BP is particularly strong on non-executives. They are in the majority on the board by nine to eight, and only they sit on the board's auditing and compensation committees which oversee the accounts and directors' pay.

It also bears out the Cadbury recommendation in favour of splitting the role of chairman and chief executive. Even though the British corporate tradition tends to separate them, the two positions have always been combined at BP.

But Mr Horton's dominating style highlighted the dangers of concentration of power. In future BP is to have a non-executive chairman, Lord Ashburton, and a full-time chief executive, Mr David Simon, until now the chief operating officer.

'This creates a good balance,' said Mr Simon. 'My executives are fully in agreement that the change is appropriate.' But as well as providing for a more balanced distribution of power within the group, the changes are also intended to bring about a shift in style.

Although people inside BP say that talk of Mr Horton's arrogant manner is overdone – he has often shown acts of great personal kindness – his evident enjoyment of power, his lack of tact and irritating name-dropping habit alienated many of his colleagues. Whether this was due to a supreme self-confidence or the exact opposite was a matter of debate within BP, but it led to much anti-Horton sniping, culminating in a famous spoof of an FT article, put together with evident relish on some internal BP desk-top printer, depicting Horton as a power-crazed eccentric.

David Simon could hardly be more different. A quiet-spoken organisation man who lost out to Horton in the 1990 leadership stakes and operated in his shadow thereafter, he has never had a chance to show the full range of his leadership qualities. But insiders say that while he will be more user-friendly than Horton, he can be just as tough. The adjectives used to describe him are wily, subtle, diplomatic, and knowledgeable about the undercurrents of the British establishment, something for which Horton had little time.

'Simon knows all about dynamic positioning,' said an official, referring to the ultra-precise techniques used by floating oil rigs to adjust to ocean currents and winds, and stay stable in a storm. 'He has an ability to stay right over the hole. Horton had to be tethered down.' On a broader level, Simon's appointment may be welcomed. The removal of friction on the board should make it function more smoothly. He is widely approved of by the staff. And the City likes a financial man. But goodwill alone will not be enough to resolve BP's problems. These centre mainly on the group's high level of debt – the result of expensive acquisitions and a share buy-back in the 1980s – and a high cost structure. Ironically, the earlier success of its oil exploration activities has also tilted it towards oil production, which makes it more vulnerable to changes in the oil price than companies which have a better balance between their production and retailing sides.

The crucial question is whether the change of faces at the top will lead to changes in strategy – and the message from BP is no. The unpopular cost squeeze instituted by Mr Horton will go on, and so too presumably will the job cuts.

The biggest uncertainty is in the stock market, where BP's share price fell by 14 per cent yesterday on fears of a dividend cut and a possible £1bn-plus rights issue to ease the debt problem.

Industry observers tended to dismiss the rights issue danger. Mr Paul Spedding at Kleinwort Benson Securities points out that for tax reasons, it is cheaper for BP to borrow money in the US than to raise more equity capital. 'It doesn't make sense,' he says.

But they are more divided over the dividend. Under Horton, BP steadfastly refused to cut its pay-out even though it had to pay part of it out of reserves after the latest fall in profits. By halving the dividend BP could save itself several hundred million pounds a year, reduce its debt, and give itself a fresh start. A cut announced at the interim results in a month could also be blamed on this week's upheaval.

BP's new chiefs are insisting that no changes in dividend policy have been decided. Simon himself is committed to not cutting the dividend. He told an analysts' meeting last September: 'We will not, save *force majeure*, cut our dividend. We have done it only once in our history and that was in the first world war.' What is more certain than dividend policy is another legacy of the Horton era. Simon sent out an internal statement yesterday to senior managers reaffirming the process of cultural change known as Project 1990, and laying stress on greater teamwork and openness. Project 1990 aimed to replace BP's bureaucratic 'command-control' style of management with one based on a 'delayered' structure and a atmosphere of what Horton called 'openness', care, teamwork, empowerment and trust. It is also understood that Simon stands by the proposed cuts in BP's corporate and business head offices, which are seen as an integral part of the group's existing strategy.

Simon's fortunes will ultimately depend on the oil price. Horton told investors at the beginning of this year that all BP's businesses had been 'tested against $18 a barrel oil and found to be robust'. Since then a new spirit of co-operation within Opec has helped push the oil price up over $21 a barrel, which helps. The institutional view in BP is that the price should continue to rise in the long term, though not to dizzying heights. This suggests that this week's drama was only a prelude to better times at BP.

'We aim to be extremely competitive,' said Simon, 'but we're fighting a difficult market.'

THE TOOTHLESS WATCHDOGS IN AMERICA'S BOARDROOMS

By Martin Dickson

First published 7 February 1990

American Brands, the tobacco and consumer goods conglomerate, last week announced a reshuffle which will bring it into line with most large US companies in giving outside directors a majority of board seats.

The move gave a quick fillip to the group's share price, but that may well have been due more to takeover speculation than any expectation on Wall Street that the new structure would promote a dramatic improvement in performance.

For, as a new book on US corporate power suggests, the mere creation of a board with a majority of independent directors does not in itself produce more dynamic, efficient leadership.

Far from it, argue Jay Lorsch, a Harvard Business School professor, and research associate Elizabeth MacIver, in *Pawns or Potentates: The Reality of America's Corporate Boards*, which is based on detailed interviews with over 80 independent directors and postal surveys with 900 more.

Many boards, they say, are ineffective and under the thumb of powerful chief executives they lack the power and sense of common purpose needed to oversee their companies as they should. Important issues are not discussed openly, or sufficiently quickly, and small management problems fester and tend to grow into crises.

While the study is confined to the US, it has lessons for Europe, where circumstantial evidence suggests that similar attitudes are all too prevalent.

Admittedly, the position in the US is not as bad as it was 20 years ago, when one survey described directors as simply 'ornaments on a corporate Christmas tree', a cosy club filled with the company's own employees, advisors and the chief executive's chums.

Today 69 per cent of US directors are complete outsiders (in Britain non-executives are usually in a minority), there has been an increase in board committees which scrutinise particularly sensitive issues, such as auditing, pay and appointments, and board members view their responsibilities much more seriously.

But, say Lorsch and MacIver, there is still far too much rubber stamping, rather than pursuing the director's most important tasks,which are to oversee the chief executive, determine strategic direction, and ensure the company is acting legally and ethically.

The most obvious restraint on outside directors is the entrenched power of the very person they are meant to be governing: the chief executive, who, in 80 per cent of US companies is also the chairman and thus controls the agenda of board meetings, decides what information is received in advance, and leads discussions in the boardroom.

Furthermore, he often plays a key role in the selection of new outside directors – despite the growth of nominating committees. And since 63 per cent of the outsiders are themselves chief executives of other companies, they may have an in-built bias to the management, doing unto other chief executives as they would have done unto them. The chief executive has a knowledge of the group which the part-time outsiders (dedicating around 14 days a year to the company) cannot hope to match. Many in the authors' survey said their contributions were constrained by lack of expertise or information, inadequate preparation time and, most important of all, lack of discussion time at the board meeting itself.

And this is compounded by a taboo against open criticism of the chief executive – 'about how he or she is shaping the agenda, conducting the meetings or, at a broader level, adequately developing a successor or being forceful enough in correcting performance problems in a faltering division'. Outside directors, add the authors, are confused and divided over their accountability – particularly following the takeover wave of the 1980s and the rise of the risk arbitrageur, wheeling and dealing short-term in bid stocks.

Traditionalist directors say simply that, following legal convention, they are responsible first and foremost to shareholders – even though the law on this is changing from state to state. Others consider themselves accountable to wider 'stakeholders', such as consumers and employees.

'More and more people,' says one director, 'are coming to the realisation that the shareholders are really a bunch of 26-year-olds sitting behind their trading desks, and that the people who have the best interests of the

company and its employees at heart are really those in management.'
Lorsch and MacIver produce plenty of proposals to remedy matters. One
set would simply tinker with the present US system: reduce the chief
executive's power to nominate directors and widen the pool of candidates; make sure that lawyers spell out precise accountabilities in the
various states; introduce strategic planning committees; have an annual
review of the chief executive's performance and more open board discussions.

Sensibly the academics also suggest separating the roles of chairman
and chief executive, a division common (but by no means universal) in
British companies.

But they brush aside the idea of board seats for institutional investors,
which has rather more to recommend it than they allow.

Equally questionable is their support for the fashion among some US
states to enshrine in law directors' accountability to groups other than
shareholders. For once you start widening the circle, where do you draw
the line? It is a trend which could take responsibility for corporate
America out of the market place and into the hands of the judiciary – and
in the process allow the very boardroom complacency which Lorsch and
MacIver are so keen to combat.

THE NEW BITE AT BOARD LEVEL IN AMERICA

By Martin Dickson

First published 13 April 1992

A remarkable display of muscle-flexing by non-executive directors of
General Motors is sending shock waves across corporate America and
may lead to a big shift in the balance of power in US board rooms.

The potential winners: shareholders and non-executive directors. The
losers: entrenched management.

The GM board's non-executive members, tired of the company's heavy
losses and impatient at its pace of change, took matters into their own
hands.

Led by John Smale, a former chairman of Procter & Gamble, the consumer products group, the directors demoted two of the company's top

managers, including the right hand man of Robert Stempel, the chairman.

They also changed the functions of the board's executive committee – which theoretically wielded power between board meetings but in practice never met – to make it a more active body to offer advice to Stempel. And at its head they installed Smale.

The upshot is that while Stempel is still running the company on a daily basis, he has a powerful group of directors breathing down his neck – and one which is plugged in to a more comprehensive flow of information about the business.

This, coupled with the demotion of his lieutenant, Lloyd Reuss, GM's 55-year-old president, sends a simple but powerful message: perform, or else. Reuss was replaced by Jack Smith, head of GM's international operations, who has also been appointed chief operating officer.

America's non-executive directors have a well deserved reputation as 'rubber stamps', passively accepting the decisions of day-to-day management. Yet over the past few years an increasing number have been trying to shed this image.

Directors of the motor manufacturer, Chrysler, recently resisted efforts by Lee Iacocca to stay on as chairman after his retirement date. And last autumn the board of Compaq Computer dismissed Rod Canion, chief executive and co-founder of the business, in a clash over poor results and management style.

But such behaviour at a company like General Motors, the largest industrial business in the US, is nothing short of revolutionary. For decades, the company has been a by-word for insularity and bureaucratic complacency.

So the GM directors have created a powerful example which other companies may now follow. 'This is a landmark development for the US,' says Howard Sherman of Institutional Shareholder Services, a Washington-based group which advises large US investors on corporate affairs. 'An act like this will really galvanise a lot of boards.' In the US, as in the UK, non-executive directors are meant to act on behalf of shareholders as a supportive check on the managers hired to run the business. But too often, say critics, they are merely 'the parsley on the fish'.

It is impossible to quantify just how influential non-executives have become because much of the action takes place behind closed doors. Dressing-downs as public as that delivered at GM remain rare.

Still, ISS's Sherman says his extensive discussions with outside directors make clear that 'they see their jobs very differently from just two years ago'.

An important factor is the increasing importance in the US of institutional investors demanding better 'corporate governance' – insisting that managers should be more responsive to shareholders.

The corporate governance movement was given a fillip by the 1980s takeover wave. On the one hand, this encouraged managers to introduce anti-takeover 'poison pills' which protected their positions, but did not necessarily best serve shareholders. On the other, it made investors realise that it could be cheaper, and more effective, to simply change the management of a poorly performing company than go through the loops of a bid battle.

In its early stages the corporate governance movement concentrated on correcting specific abuses by management, such as 'poison pills'. But over the last two years it has begun to say that a much more comprehensive change in the way boards are constituted and run is needed. Fix the board, runs the argument, and most other problems will fix themselves.

But that is a great deal easier said than done. The first problem is the nature of the individuals chosen to serve as non-executives. A company's outside directors will typically consist of senior managers from other businesses, often friends of the chief executive, together with a sprinkling of retired politicians, celebrities and worthies.

Graef Crystal, one of America's best-known critics of management pay-scales, has described boards as '10 friends of management, a woman and a black'.

'Directors are picked because the chief executive knows them and knows they are likely to be on his side,' says Robert Monks, a leader of the corporate governance movement, who highlighted the issue last year when he independently fought an unsuccessful campaign to get a board seat at Sears, Roebuck, the ailing stores group.

In theory, investors have the ultimate say over the choice of directors, since a shareholder vote is necessary for them to be elected to the board.

Until recently, investors tended simply to nod through management's nominees but there are now signs of growing dissatisfaction with this process.

For example, some corporate governance activists have been trying to set up a data base of potential outside directors. Investors also played a big role in selecting nominees for the board of Lockheed, the aerospace group, when it found itself under threat from a corporate raider a year ago.

But even if some independent spirits do make it on to a board, they are likely to find it hard to take effective action.

Most large American companies have a majority of non-executive directors on their board but most also combine the positions of chairman and chief executive. This gives a company's top manager immense powers to set the agenda of the board which is meant to be monitoring his performance.

Here too there are signs of incipient shareholder revolt. At Sears, Roebuck, shareholders have put down resolutions for next month's annual meeting calling for the roles of chairman and CEO to be split.

Institutions are also trying to limit the power of chief executives by ensuring that board sub-committees, where much of directors' most important work is done, are controlled by outside directors.

For example, the California Public Employees' Retirement System (Calpers), the largest US public pension fund, and United Shareholders Association, another corporate governance group, recently pressured Ryder System, a large truck leasing business, into changing its corporate by-laws to ensure than a majority of directors, and all members of its pay and nominating committees, are non-executives.

Yet even if such reforms are carried out, non-executives can remain ineffective if they lack information. A powerful chief executive can keep a great deal from his board, whose non-executive members are busy people with limited time to spend digging around the business.

The GM board's action in this area is particularly intriguing. First, Smale appears to have spent many hours inside the company conducting a survey on senior executives' performance before launching last week's bombshell.

Second, his assumption of the executive committee chairmanship means that non-executives should be better placed to receive quick intelligence of what is going on.

Ross Perot, the combative Texan billionaire who was ousted from the GM board in 1986 after criticising management, used to describe his fellow directors there as 'pet rocks'. Last week the rocks stirred, and the result could be a small earthquake in many boardrooms.

THE NEED FOR MORE 'HYBRID' MANAGERS

By Alan Cane

First published 26 January 1990

Ian Glenday, communication and computer services director for Esso UK, is one of the first of a new breed of manager in the UK whose unusual blend of skills could prove decisive in the battle to sharpen Britain's commercial competitiveness.

Glenday, an unassuming 45-year old with a self-deprecating sense of humour, is what is becoming known in some management circles as a 'hybrid': an executive who combines broad experience of general management and leadership with competence in information technology.

Glenday's company is running one of the first UK programmes designed to produce 'hybrid' managers. Its experience suggests that others could benefit from its example.

At present there is only a handful of these 'hybrids' in the UK. In the view of the British Computer Society (BCS), the professional body for the information technology industry, this dearth must be overcome if UK businesses are to get the best out of their investment in information technology – which is now running at 5 to 7 per cent of sales in some major companies.

A working group set up by the BCS which included Glenday and other 'hybrids' – Colin Palmer, formerly deputy managing director of Thomson tour operations and now an independent consultant, John Hanby, director of information technology at the Post Office and Geoffrey Dart, a divisional director of Marks and Spencer – concluded recently that the UK needs to produce at least 10,000 'hybrids' by 1995 and that by the turn of the century, some 30 per cent of all managers will have to be 'hybrids'.

This may seem to be special pleading. But Robb Wilmot, former managing director of International Computers and now chairman of Oasis, a consultancy specialising in helping companies to manage their information resources more effectively, points to four business trends which explain why a failure to generate sufficient 'hybrid' managers will prove disastrous for the UK.

There has been a fundamental change in the way companies add value to their products. Direct labour costs are shrinking as a percentage of total cost just as materials and capital have increasingly become commodities. As a result, he argues that for the company of tomorrow information management will become the major source of value-added for professionals and skilled staff, as well as the primary source of competitive differentiation.

Corporate hierarchies are becoming dramatically compressed. Large corporations with six or fewer levels in their hierarchy achieve this by using information systems which remove much of the administrative role of management, thereby allowing managers to focus on competitors, customers, staff and innovation. Companies where the information systems are not up to this will find themselves at a competitive disadvantage.

Globalisation – including the ability to integrate production and sales strategies across many countries and time-zones – demands sophisticated information systems. The corporation that never sleeps and uses every minute of the day to achieve its global ambitions is already with us, Wilmot warns.

Moves to standardised computer systems are cutting the cost of computer hardware and software so dramatically that companies will no longer be limited by their information technology budgets but by their ability to conceive effective business applications and implement them quickly. Speed will become critical, Wilmot says, as strategic options become fewer.

Each of these trends would be challenging enough in itself from an information systems design and management point of view. Exploiting them all in combination requires the new type of manager that Wilmot has in mind, and which Glenday and co represent.

One of the main reasons why it is so hard to create this new breed is the dauntingly broad gulf of ignorance and distrust which separates UK general managers from information systems specialists.

The gulf has its origin in the early days of computer systems when the data centre emerged as a self-contained, self-perpetuating company within a company, run as the data processing manager's private fiefdom with little reference to the rest of the organisation. Line managers felt themselves cut off from data processing (through their own ignorance) and had little interest in coming to terms with a discipline which seemed divorced from the company's core business.

In the US, where technical functions tend to have a higher status and specialist professionals frequently enjoy parallel career paths to those of managers in other disciplines, the problem is less acute.

The UK attitude is one Ian Glenday understands well from personal experience. An Esso man all his working life, he trained as a chemical engineer and joined the company as a petroleum engineer, becoming manager of operations at Esso's Fawley Refinery near Southampton by 1976.

It was a job which gave him a sound understanding of project management but no contact with information systems: 'In 12 years at Fawley, I do not believe I ever spoke to a single person from our information systems department although we had about 200 programmers and systems analysts,' he admits.

In 1978 he became corporate planning manager with the responsibility for Esso's long-term strategic plans in the UK. In 1980, he spent a couple of years in mainland Europe working on exploration and product planning.

This was followed in 1982 by a new job as departmental head of corporate planning, government relations and public affairs. It was a critical period government interest in the energy resources of the North Sea was at a peak and Glenday found himself working on better ways to harmonise relations between the company and the Government and, indeed, the public.

These varied responsibilities over the years gave him a broad understanding of the petroleum industry and Esso's role within it. In 1984, however, he was given charge of Esso's new information systems (IS) department, a role for which he had no training or experience.

As in many companies, the responsibility for data processing had lain with the finance department and had been principally concerned with the back-office of the business – accounts, payroll and so on. There was no central information systems function.

The decision to establish an IS department seems to have come from Esso's chairman and chief executive, Sir Archibald Forster and the Esso main board, which realised the importance of computer systems designed to support 'front office' activities like sales, distribution and marketing as well as accountancy and personnel. Glenday now reports directly to the finance director Jim Alcock.

It would have been an impossible task without his background knowledge and experience. Esso sent Glenday to the US for a year to work with Exxon, Esso's parent company, during which time he had virtually a carte blanche to study the best available data processing practices in the US.

His experiences went on to form the basis of Esso's own 'hybrid' manager programme, which aims to move each year some 10 per cent – 15 to 20 people – of his IS complement of 200 out into the business and bring in some eight or 10 general line managers.

A critical development, however, and one which seems to have set the tone for the diffusion of information systems within Esso was the decision in 1985 to instal an IBM electronic office system throughout the UK organisation.

The project was, by all accounts, a great success. Glenday says now it was the new IS department's 'passport' to being able to pursue innovation throughout the company. Now tanker drivers have computers in their cabs.

After only three years, Glenday says, he already has 50 ex-IS staff working in various line management jobs, while half his current top 15 systems people have come from line jobs, or have had line assignments.

How does he measure the success of the 'hybrid' programme so far? IS projects are notorious for providing 'soft' benefits which are difficult to evaluate, rather than hard evidence from the bottom line. But Glenday says that 75 per cent of IS projects are now completed on time and within budget, compared with 60 per cent before the programme started. Most UK companies would be delighted if half their projects came in on time and on cost.

In other respects, too, he also says he has been able to measure an increase in 'customer satisfaction' from IS users within the company. And there has been a low rate of attrition among his data processing staff.

However wedded he may be to the 'hybrid' concept, Glenday is careful to give due weight to the importance of data processing specialists in the company's IS initiatives: 'It is the blend of information systems professionals and 'hybrids working together that has made us successful,' he affirms.

THE UNHAPPY LOT OF NON-EXECUTIVE DIRECTORS

By Richard Waters

First published 19 April 1991

Wanted: a large army of experienced, independent-minded, part-time businesspeople to infiltrate boardrooms across the UK. Ability to restrain unbridled chief executives an advantage.

This, or something close to it, was the message delivered by the UK's institutional investors, which between them own two thirds of all UK listed shares. Acting through their recently-reconstituted umbrella body, the Institutional Shareholders' Committee, the institutions were adding their voices – the most important yet – to the debate on corporate governance.

This has developed as a curious side issue to the debate on relations between companies and their shareholders. Its origins can be traced to two causes: the seemingly endless arguments about short-termism (whether or not the providers of capital are unwilling to take a sufficiently long-term view of their investments) and a lingering feeling that some of the excesses of recent years should not be repeated.

What makes the debate on corporate governance odd is that the institutions appear to want it both ways. They want to regularise the way some companies are run, particularly by reining in some of the more powerful chairmen/chief executives. But in the process they do not want to lose any of the shareholder gains that can be generated by strong, entrepreneurial leadership.

There is a noticeable sound of barn-door slamming in all of this. Periods of corporate or financial excess are generally followed by reregulation. Come the next boom period, these lessons are quickly forgotten. If the institutions can't have it both ways, then it is a fair bet that, come the next bull market, they will forget many of the lessons they are now preaching in the scramble not to be left out.

In the meantime, it is to non-executive directors that the institutions have turned. These hapless people are expected to labour under the institutions' own unresolved paradox: they must at once bear equal responsibility with other directors for a company's performance, but they must also act as an internal check on the power of executive directors.

The ISC's paper, *The role and duties of directors: a statement of best practice*, contains ample evidence of this paradox. Non-executives, it says, should be independent. This is defined as 'free from bias, involvement or partiality'.

Yet the paper also comes down firmly on the side of unitary boards, rather than the two-tier structures seen in countries like Germany. It says: 'All directors have an equal responsibility in helping to provide their company with effective guidance and leadership and it is recognised that they must, and in almost all cases do, act at all times entirely in the best interests of the company.'

Is it really possible for a non-executive to bear all the responsibility that this suggests and yet remain 'free from bias, involvement or partiality'? Leading members of the ISC admitted yesterday that this was expecting a lot.

'An increasing amount is being expected of non-executive directors,' said Michael Sandland, chairman of the ISC and chief investment manager of Norwich Union.

He said that the pool of available talent was probably not big enough to provide suitable high quality directors for all UK companies, and suggested two ways of easing this shortage: companies should make more of their senior executives available to act as non-executives elsewhere, and companies should pay non-executives more for their efforts. 'The traditional £5,000, £10,000 or £15,000 is not enough, given what is expected these days, 'Sandland said.

Who, though, will decide how much to pay the non-executives? This is yet another paradox at the heart of the ISC position. Non-executives, who are expected by the ISC to set the pay levels of executive directors, will themselves be paid by the executives. Any guesses on the effect that has on the level of executive pay?

THE CADBURY REPORT

By Norma Cohen

First published 28 May 1992

At its heart, the Cadbury Committee report on the Financial Aspects of Corporate Governance relies on the threat of public censure to force companies to improve the way they are governed and to tell shareholders more about their affairs.

Sir Ron Dearing, chairman of the Financial Reporting Council and a member of the committee, concedes that the final document, presented as a draft for public comment, is a consensus view and will fall short of the sort of reforms that some have been seeking.

The report, for instance, stops short of urging companies to give shareholders greater say over executive pay. It also does not challenge the House of Lords' ruling in the Caparo case that auditors have a duty of care only to a company's management, not to individual shareholders.

Sir Ron said more radical reforms would not be complied with voluntarily and would therefore require legislation, which would stifle innovation and enterprise. He said: 'We felt in the end that the best way to go was the co-operative route encouraged by the Stock Exchange.' The main body of the report consists of a code of practice that seeks to force companies to disclose the extent to which they comply with the code and to explain themselves where they do not. 'Had such a code been in existence in the past, we believe that a number of the recent examples of unexpected company failures and cases of fraud would have received attention earlier and might have been avoided,' the committee says.

The Stock Exchange, which was represented on the committee by Sir Andrew Hugh Smith, exchange chairman, intends to add a new rule to its 'yellow book' which will make such disclosure a listing requirement. The rule will take effect almost immediately and will cover accounts filed for the year ending 31 December 1992 and beyond.

The 19-point code of practice covers four main areas: responsibilities of boards of directors; the role of executive directors; the role of non-executives; and accounting controls and reporting mechanisms.

Among its main points are: Corporate boards should have a clearly accepted division of responsibilities. When the roles of chairman and chief executive are combined, there should be 'a strong independent element' on the board, with an appointed leader.

Non-executives should be of a high enough calibre and appointed in sufficient numbers to give their views weight on a board. The majority of them should be free of any business or financial connection with the company and it is advisable that they should not be eligible to participate either in stock option or employee pension schemes. Their nomination should be approved by the board as a whole and should be the result of a formal selection process.

Non-executives should be able to seek financial or legal advice from professionals outside the company at company expense. The Companies Act should be amended to reduce the maximum period of a director's service contract to three years from the present five – a rule that may be circumvented with shareholder approval.

Directors' pay should be determined by a remuneration committee composed wholly or mainly of non-executives. The remuneration of the chairman and the highest-paid director should be fully disclosed and split into their salary and performance-related-pay elements. The basis upon which performance-related pay is measured should be explained.

Boards must establish effective audit committees within the next two years, composed entirely of non-executive directors, a majority of whom are completely independent of the company.

The audit committee should be able to seek external professional advice and consult advisers. They should also meet at least annually with the outside auditors, without any executive board member present.

Fees paid to audit firms for non-audit work conducted worldwide should be fully disclosed and regulations under the Companies Act should be reviewed and amended as necessary.

Interim financial statements should include balance sheet information.

Although it is not necessary for interim statements to be audited, they should be discussed with auditors, and Stock Exchange listing requirements should be amended to include that requirement.

The accountancy profession is urged to draw up guidelines to guarantee a periodic change of partners involved in the preparation of any particular company's audit over a period of years. However, the committee rejected a proposal to change auditors every few years to prevent relationships between management and auditors from becoming too comfortable.

Boards should state that it is a reasonable expectation that their company will continue as a going concern, with supporting assumptions or qualifications as necessary, and auditors should be required to report on that statement. The committee has urged the accountancy profession to develop guidance on the 'going concern' rule. Legislation may be an option if voluntary compliance appears ineffective.

Although detecting fraud remains the responsibility of boards, the committee recommends new legislation allowing auditors to report suspicion of fraud to government authorities without breaching client-confidentiality rules implied by their contracts. Such laws are already in place for auditors for banks and other regulated entities.

The committee also lays out what it believes to be the proper role of shareholders and their relation to boards of directors. In what is likely to be a disappointment to many institutional shareholders, the report said the committee considered, but rejected, a formal role for shareholders in the appointment of directors and auditors.

The report noted that there had been suggestions that shareholders should be allowed to form committees that would have a say in the drawing up of director service contracts and the selection of external auditors.

Mr Michael Sandland, chairman of the Institutional Shareholders committee and a member of the Cadbury Committee, said such committees often did not work because institutional investors were unwilling to turn over their proxies to be exercised by someone else. Other shareholder groups, though, have sought such a mechanism because individual shareholders typically held too few votes to force management changes.

Instead, the Cadbury Committee urges shareholders to back up its recommendations by 'requiring' companies they invest in to implement the code.

The report also acknowledges the disparity in power between institutional and individual shareholders. It stops short of urging any mandatory public disclosure requirements when significant developments occur, although it urges companies to ensure that any 'significant' statements concerning their company are made publicly and are available to all shareholders.

The report also suggests ways to use the annual meeting as a forum for shareholder concerns. It says: 'If too many annual general meetings are at present an opportunity missed, this is either because shareholders do not make the most of them or because boards do not encourage them to do so.' Possible ways forward include providing forms in annual reports on which shareholders could send in written questions before the meeting so that prepared answers could be given at the AGM. After the meeting, the board could circulate a summary of questions and answers to all shareholders.

7 COPING WITH SHORT-TERMISM

INTRODUCTION

Do financial markets put pressure on companies to make decisions with short-term horizons? Or do companies – and, more particularly, their managements – create pressure on themselves which leads them in the same direction?

In the early 1990s this perennial argument gathered renewed pace as the perceived excesses of the 1980s boom gave way to the ravages of recession. The accusations are specifically levelled at UK and US stock markets and investors. Both, it is alleged, make such demands that company managements cannot sustain strategies which seek long-term returns, quite possibly at some short-term expense. Compared with German and Japanese industry the competitiveness of British and American industry is therefore put at risk.

Simon Holberton addresses the arguments in this chapter from a variety of perspectives. He seeks to get at the heart of the debate and examines evidence which sets out to exonerate the markets. He also looks at the constitution of boards of directors and how this might influence the short-term/long-term debate. Industrialists also have their say, putting forward their own evidence which contradicts the apologists for the markets.

One such, Alan Clements, a former finance director of ICI, Britain's biggest chemicals group, sets out an argument which clearly lays some blame for short-termism in industry at the door of the markets and institutional shareholders, but also puts forward suggestions as to how the two sides of the divide might attempt to understand each other better with a more common purpose in mind.

The pro-markets lobby is roundly supported by Paul Marsh, Professor of Management and Finance at London Business School. Simon Holberton cites his research suggesting that all relevant information about a company is contained in its share price and that that price almost invariably reflects a long-term, rather than short-term expectation.

Marsh also weighs in against managers, arguing that they are themselves much to blame for getting themselves stuck in a short-term cycle. This, he suggests, is the result of the reward system, based on profits and return on investment, which encourages short-term results. Such a system inevitably leads management to ignore investment projects which would fundamentally strengthen their company simply because the returns would not come quickly enough.

There is an irony, not unnoticed in both the City of London and industry, that many industrialists who grumble about the short-termism of the markets and investors are the self-same people who have their remuneration evaluated by reference to short-term results.

Suggestions abound as to how the dilemma can be resolved. Legislation is advocated by some, but is deemed undesirable by those, like Marsh at LBS, who feel it would be directed at the wrong target. Others feel that non-executive directors have an important role to play, perhaps by sitting on boards as representatives of institutional shareholders but with a brief of assessing, for example, management's remuneration without reference to the short-term yardsticks now so criticised. Against this is the problem that with Britain's system of unitary boards, no director can represent a special interest.

The predatory instincts which stock markets encourage is an additional bone of contention. No company, goes the argument, will sacrifice short-term gain by investing in long-term research and development since such a step will invariably lead to their share prices becoming depressed – leaving them extremely exposed to an unwanted takeover. This view became the subject of particularly heated argument during the mid- to late-1980s and British companies which sought to find rich pickings in the US found themselves frustrated by State legislation.

Inevitably, as Simon Holberton relates, there is a counter-argument. This rests heavily on studies which point to dissatisfaction with a company's management being much more a factor in the acceptance of takeover bids than the fact that certain long-term decisions have yet to come to fruition.

Alan Clements – basically an advocate of the view that markets think short term – argues that professional institutional investors have changed their view of the capital market's prime purpose. No longer do they see it as the means through which industry and commerce raises capital; rather they see it as a source of income and capital gain.

One thing is clear. For any argument that nails the blame for short-termism to the markets' mast, there is another which counters it with evidence that this is a myth, and that the cause of perceived pressure to perform short-term lies elsewhere. It is an argument that is unlikely to go away.

CUTTING THROUGH THE CONCEPTUAL FOG

By Simon Holberton

First published 7 November 1990

Short-termism is a topic which has generated much sound and fury over the years. The proposition underlying the debate is this: the operation of the UK capital market is inimical to long-term planning and investment because the stock market and investors in it are driven by short-term considerations, such as company profits and dividends statements, and their need to perform.

From this core proposition dangles a number of other subsidiary points, such as that share trading turnovers are too high; that destabilising investors act like speculators not owners; and that investors facilitate predatory takeover behaviour. Other countries, notably Japan and Germany, are eyed enviously, their industries enjoying a lower cost of capital mostly because they have benign and understanding owners.

Paul Marsh thinks almost all of this is bunkum, and, in *Short-termism on Trial*, published by the Institutional Fund Managers Association, he provides a lucid justification for his views.

Marsh is Professor of Management and Finance at the London Business School. He is also a non-executive director of M&G Investment Management, one of the City's avowedly 'long termism' investors, and is no stranger to the issue. He was a member of the 1987 CBI task force on City and industry relations.

Marsh is a believer in the 'efficient market theory' for explaining the behaviour of share prices. This widely accepted theory holds that all available information about a company is contained in its share price. He also believes that self-interest motivates investors and that they tend to act rationally. What does the share price tell one?

Take Imperial Chemical Industries, a company which has just announced a 10 per cent cut in capital expenditure for 1991. At the end of August its share price was 905p, earnings per share were 116p and gross dividend per share 74p.

In theory ICI's share price should reflect the present value of all future dividends. Using a standard model to work out the future dividend growth and discounting it by ICI's cost of equity finance, Marsh finds that the market is expecting ICI's dividends to grow by 13 per cent a year.

'These figures would imply that of ICI's current market capitalisation, only 8 per cent is attributable to the current year's dividend, only 29 per cent can be explained by the present value of the dividends expected over the next 5 years and only 50 per cent by the value of the dividends expected over the next 10 years.' While this does not constitute evidence, it 'does raise an interesting question, namely why anyone should believe that there is a strong prima facie case that stock-market prices place too much weight on the short-term.' He notes that the operation of the market turns fund managers' selfish actions to a socially useful end. To exploit their knowledge, fund managers must deal before others reach a similar conclusion, he says. But such activity alerts their competitors, and the share price is adjusted accordingly. Yet 'by spotting market inefficiencies, ie mispriced shares, the fund managers help to keep the market efficient.' Marsh reports survey findings which show that the influence of quarterly performance measurement of fund managers is less draconian than is often assumed. He also presents evidence to suggest that there has not been a rise in share price volatility or turnover in recent years.

This leads Marsh to suspect that the problem of share prices and investor behaviour is one of 'perception and relationships' rather than of any underlying bias in share prices. 'There is no evidence that shares are priced in a way which emphasises their short-, rather than long-run prospects. Nor is there any evidence that the market penalises long-term investment or expenditure on R & D by awarding the shares of the company in question a lower rating – indeed quite the contrary.' Marsh is good at cutting through the conceptual fog concerning share prices and investor behaviour. He also makes some telling points about managerial behaviour and corporate governance.

He identifies 'managerial short-termism' as a key force behind poor investment in the UK. When it comes to making plans for the future, managers' perception will be influenced by their organisational systems and contexts, including the way they are remunerated and rewarded, their time horizons within their job, the role played by the internal performance measurement and management accounting systems, and the internal capital budgeting and project appraisal systems.

Marsh notes that while executive remuneration packages may motivate executives by focusing on short-term profit performance, they may discourage long-term thinking. If short-term accounting earnings are being rewarded, a potentially profitable investment which could have an adverse impact on earnings in the early years may be rejected.

By contrast, in Japan it is rare for senior executive salaries to be tied to short-term accounting profits. Bonuses are paid company-wide and the structure of rewards is biased towards long-term performance in the organisation, with salaries based on seniority, experience and individual appraisal. Job mobility is also less than in Anglo-Saxon countries.

Marsh reports the findings of an LBS survey of managers involved in making capital investment proposals. It shows that the current level of profitability is a major influence on investment decisions. The measure used is accounting profits and return on investment – both short run measures.

But as Marsh points out, profitable investments ought to be judged on the basis where expected benefits, in terms of discounted cash flows, exceed the costs.

The LBS survey found that two-thirds of its 100 respondents used 'pay-back' as the method for evaluating investment. A failure to meet pay-back requirements was often cited as a reason to reject an investment proposal. Marsh says: 'This is worrying, since pay-back is anyway a potentially short-termist measure, since it ignores cash flows after the pay-back period, and, if used in the manner implied above, can encourage managers throughout the firm to believe that "shorter is better".' On corporate governance, he points out a contradiction. Those concerned with better communication focus on the commonality of interests between owners and managers, yet many concerned with better corporate governance are so because they want companies run in the interest of shareholders rather than managers. Better communication could reveal these differences.

The number of non-executive directors may be increasing but that does not guarantee their independence. Although technically appointed by shareholders, non-execs are in practice appointed by the management and are often selected for their connections with the company and because they conform.

Marsh rejects legislative attempts to cure short-termism. Laws would be directed against the wrong culprits, namely the markets and investors.

He assails the government's short-termism for not making the necessary investment in Britain's infrastructure but he believes the solution to short-termism lies with management.

'The problems which British industry and commerce faces in an increasingly international marketplace – key questions of competitiveness, market orientation, quality and excellence – are all issues which, by definition, have to be addressed by the managers and workforces within companies . . . Any policy prescriptions which ignore this will be fundamentally flawed.'

WHY THE IDEAL BOARD REMAINS SO ELUSIVE

By Simon Holberton

First published 4 July 1990

If there is one thing that was underlined by last week's Department of Trade and Industry conference on short-termism, the City and industrial innovation, it was that the issue will not go away.

Despite the rather muscular dismissal by Nicholas Ridley, the secretary of state at the DTI, of many of the solutions to the perceived excesses of the City, those looking for action know that nothing is forever, especially the tenure of the DTI's highest ministerial job.

But one of the ideas which the secretary of state did embrace – the creation of institutional shareholder committees to nominate non-executive directors – was seen by interested parties as a non-starter. The notion of a committee of institutional shareholders proposing and disposing of directors for Britain's companies appears to find little support among those most interested in improving corporate governance and promoting active investors.

The opposition to Ridley's idea rests on the view that a director of a company is there to represent the interests of all shareholders, not just those who possess superior clout. A further objection is that of information: no single group of investors should have or be seen to have the opportunity of privileged access to a company's plans by way of a director representing their interests.

Yet for some there is a space between what Ridley has proposed and the outright rejection of it. This embraces both improving the structure and membership of boards of directors and provides for the use by large shareholders of their undoubted potential influence on management, but it draws short of dictating who should join the board of a company.

Advocates of a more systematic policy towards corporate governance, such as Jonathan Charkham, adviser to the Bank of England, argue that industry's fear about the commitment of its shareholders could be lessened if companies brought more outsiders on to their boards of directors. Link this to a more active posture by institutions and it would foster trust, understanding and the adoption of a longer-term perspective by shareholders – or so the theory goes.

There is ample evidence that investors are concerned about the state of corporate governance in the UK. Last month the Association of British Insurers published a discussion paper. In it, the ABI expressed concern over the combination of the role of chief executive and chairman, advocated a greater role for non-executive directors, and called for greater transparency in the determination of senior executive remuneration.

A recent survey of executive pay and issues facing British boardrooms, published by Korn/Ferry International, showed that companies moved quickly last year to increase the representation of non-executives on their boards.

During most of the 1980s, the non-executives occupied about a third of board seats; last year it shot up to 44 per cent and, for companies with sales in excess of £500m, the ratio was nearly 50:50.

The claim for non-executive directors is their independence. This is important when it comes to the determination of senior executive salaries and the evaluation of proposed management buy-outs. Equally important is the non-executive director's role in commenting on the company's corporate strategy where, the ABI says, 'they can bring an objectivity and independence of view borne by outside experience'. The list of qualities a director needs are, however, such that some observers are left wondering whether the pool of potential talent is large enough to satisfy the perceived need for them, and why these exemplary persons are not occupied elsewhere actively managing successful companies.

Paul Marsh, professor at the London Business School, says also that people should be realistic about what non-executive directors can achieve. 'I suspect that if we got it right overnight and then looked at British industry 10 years hence we would notice only a small improvement in the performance of industry.'

He says the idea of taking non-executives on to boards is sold as a way of improving British business. In reality, however, non-executive directors are able to do little more than the albeit valuable task of asking questions and acting as watch-dogs over possible management excesses. 'They don't have the detailed knowledge of the business to make informed decisions,' he argues.

But in their role as watch-dogs, the Korn/Ferry study suggests that, on the face of it, boards of directors are working harder and monitoring more closely the activities of management. In 1980 only 13 per cent of UK companies reported having an audit committee, now 45 per cent have; in 1980, 36 per cent of companies had a remuneration committee, now 62 per cent have.

It is not surprising that the biggest area of growth should be remuneration.

The 1980s have seen a huge growth in management literature on the alleged positive relationship between the enrichment of senior management and shareholder wealth, where shareholder wealth is defined as the year-to-year growth in a company's market capitalisation.

Senior executives receive bonuses for exceeding planned growth in a single year's profit before tax, bonuses which can amount to a significant percentage, or multiple, of base salary. Executives are also remunerated for succeeding in increasing a company's earnings per share above a specified threshold over periods of one to three years. Share option schemes encourage senior management to focus on the growth in a company's profits and share price.

Institutional investors have broadly supported senior UK management in these changes to remuneration. As investors, they too benefit from a steady growth in earnings per share. But it does strike many, on both sides of the City/industry divide, as a little inconsistent for industrialists to bemoan the inability to invest for the future yet seek to be evaluated for purposes of remuneration on their success at generating short-term profit increases.

The Korn/Ferry survey also discloses a growing concentration of power in the hands of the executive chairman. Today 32 per cent of companies have the roles of chief executive and chairman combined; a year ago the figure was 25 per cent. Where a company has a non-executive chairman it is more than likely that he was formerly a full-time employee of the company.

The ABI's discussion paper pointed out that combining the roles 'can give rise to conflicts and concentration of power'. James Shillingford, managing director of M&G Investment Trusts, agrees. 'We feel strongly that boards of companies are appropriately structured and constituted with competent directors,' he says. 'We do prefer to see the roles of chairman and chief executive separated. While we are not convinced that the company's performance would necessarily be better, we have seen, with a number of companies that have got into difficulties, that both roles have been combined.' The other leg to bolstering better, long-term relations between management and shareholders is for institutions to adopt a more active role. This is especially talked about in the context of detecting and correcting management failure before the bluntest instrument for correction – a takeover – becomes the only option.

Donald Brydon, managing director of BZW Investment Management and chairman of the Institutional Shareholders Committee, has suggested that institutions, through a formally constituted agency, evaluate an ailing company's business strategy. The analysis and options for change could form an agenda for discussion between shareholders and the company concerned. He envisages this approach being offered to only a handful of the most pressing cases.

It is too soon to determine whether Brydon will be able to generate enough support among his colleagues. Some senior institutional investment managers believe that it is not their job to manage companies they invest in. 'One is not in the business of setting oneself up as alternative management for all and sundry,' says one.

Possibly it is their sheer size and the mystique they are cloaked in, but the power of institutions is often over-estimated. They find it difficult to co-operate – hence their collective power, which could be great, is rarely marshalled – and when they do intervene it is not always welcome.

As a top manager of one of Britain's biggest investors notes: 'Our strength increases the weaker the company's position is. Until the company's strategy has been proved wrong all one is doing is simply exchanging opinions. You do need to be pretty sure of your position before you can push things through.

'The chance of doing something when the situation is quite clear is pretty good. But that means the situation has been deteriorating for some time. It is much more difficult when you express your views at an earlier stage, especially if the non-executive directors are prepared to back their executive colleagues.'

The search for better relations and understanding between owners and managers is unlikely to end with one or more non-executive directors on the board of every British company.

It may be a useful step in that direction but, as Marsh of the LBS notes, the problems of British industry as it faces an increasingly international marketplace – problems of competitiveness, quality and excellence – are ones best addressed by the day-to-day managers. A watch-dog cannot do that, less so a group of investors which tries to prop up a teetering house of cards.

ARE THE FINANCIAL MARKETS AT FAULT?

By Simon Holberton. Additional research by Christopher Lorenz

First published 21 May 1990

The unprecedented takeover boom of the past decade may be petering out, but it has breathed life into the debate about the role of financial markets in promoting economic well-being.

Critics of the recent behaviour of financial markets are beginning to find growing support for their view. This was most succinctly summed up by Keynes: 'When the capital development of a country becomes the by-product of the activities of a casino, the job is likely to be ill-done.' Disparate forces on both sides of the Atlantic are eager to frustrate what they see as the most egregious aspect of modern capitalism: the contested takeover. Research carried out by the Confederation of British Industry and the Department of Trade and Industry has turned up widespread dissatisfaction among industrialists, especially those in technology-intensive industries, about the limits placed on them by financial markets.

Businessmen, such as Ivan Yates, deputy chairman of British Aerospace, maintain that efforts to develop companies through greater emphasis on research and development have been frustrated by the need to watch their companies' share price continuously for signs of vulnerability to hostile takeover. They say that funds which could be put into R & D are being diverted into dividend payments and that management has to concentrate on keeping short-term profits high.

In the US, 36 states have passed legislation which seeks to frustrate hostile takeovers within their territory. The failure of BTR's bid for Norton in Massachusetts is just the most recent case.

In the UK, as the DTI prepares for a conference late next month entitled 'Innovation and Short-termism', its officials are trying once again to interest ministers in ways of curbing what they see as the worst excesses of the City of London. Some DTI officials have taken comfort from the move by the US states to deter hostile takeovers.

They are investigating ways of making hostile takeovers in the UK more difficult and to allow target companies more time to prepare their defences.

They are also looking at ways of penalising institutional investors, pension funds, life companies and the like, which 'churn' their share portfolios for short-term financial gain. One suggestion, which would require the Treasury's agreement, is that a steep rate of capital gains tax be applied to gains made from short-term share dealing.

The title of the DTI's conference is indicative of a stream of thought concerning financial markets, managerial behaviour and economic performance.

This view sees a concrete link between low levels of research, development and economic performance on the one hand and the short-termism of financial markets on the other.

According to this view, short-termism is characterised by companies' perceived need to bolster short-term earnings and dividends at the expense of R & D because of management's concern about hostile takeovers. Investment institutions are preoccupied with their own short-term performance because they have a fiduciary responsibility to achieve the highest return for their clients, and they live in an intensely competitive world where their performance is measured quarterly.

There is a lot that is attractive in the short-termism critique. In the UK, at least, it offers a scapegoat (the City) for British companies – with notable exceptions such as Glaxo, Pilkington and Fisons – neglecting commercially-oriented research and downstream product development.

But attractive as it is, there is little evidence to suggest that those who advance this argument can prove it. Indeed, some studies of investor behaviour suggest that the critics are incorrect and that a company's susceptibility to takeover has more to do with management failure than City or Wall Street cupidity.

According to one such study of 324 companies across 20 US industries by the US Securities and Exchange Commission, the short-termism thesis throws up at least four testable hypotheses:

- that there is an inverse relationship between a company's research and development activity and institutional investment.

    The study found that institutional shareholding rose from 30 per cent in 1980 to 38 per cent in 1983 at the same time that the average ratio of R & D spending to sales rose from 3.38 per cent to 4.03 per cent. In the SEC's sample, 88 companies experienced a fall in institutional ownership while 236 companies experienced an increase. But the average change in the R & D-sales ratio was identical, thus refuting the claim that increased institutional share ownership causes managers to focus more on the short-term.

- that takeover targets exhibit high levels of spending on long-term projects relative to their past experience and that of their competitors.

SEC economists also examined data on R & D spending for 57 companies subject to takeover. This revealed that these companies had an average R & D/sales ratio of 0.77 per cent, less than half of that for an industry control group in the year immediately preceding the takeover offer. 'These data strongly suggest that investment in long-term projects does not increase a firm's vulnerability to a takeover,' the study concluded.

- that institutions should hold a higher percentage of a target company's equity relative to companies not subject to takeover in the same industry.

The average institutional ownership of takeover targets in the quarter immediately preceding an offer for the company was 19.3 per cent compared with 33.7 per cent for companies in an industry control group of non-target companies.

- that public announcements by a company that it is embarking on long-term investment projects should result in a fall in its stock price.

On this question, the SEC study found that there was a statistically significant rise in companies' share prices, net of general movements in the market, after they said they would embark on a new R & D project. This evidence, taken over the period 1973–1983, rebuts 'the argument that the market penalises companies that invest in long-term projects and thereby makes them candidates for hostile takeover'. In the light of the last finding it is curious that British industry resisted until last year the adoption of US accounting practices that require companies to detail what they spend on research and development.

British companies' longstanding resistance to doing this did not assist them in convincing their shareholders of the benefits of R & D.

Adherents of short-termism as an explanation, partial or otherwise, of Britain's industrial malaise also support their views by comparing conditions in Japan and West Germany. In a contribution to a recent pamphlet published by the National Association of Pension Funds, Lord Alexander, chairman of National Westminster Bank, asked a series of rhetorical questions.

'For how long can we ignore the very positive performance of competitors whose systems are not so driven by the need to produce short-term rewards for shareholders? Does our stock market when analysed do less to raise capital than serve as a market for . . . the gaming chip? Has government no role to play in guiding the structure of industry? Have institutional investors, who hold 60 per cent of shares, and financing banks got ultimately to become more involved in allowing and facilitating a long-term strategy?'

The stock market as a 'market for corporate control' is a largely Anglo-Saxon phenomenon. Stock markets on the Continent and Japan are in many ways just as 'short term' in many respects as those in Anglo-Saxon countries. The Tokyo Stock Exchange, for instance, is driven by capricious fashions; on the Frankfurt Stock Exchange prices rose sharply during the Christmas and New Year period on the promise of the super profits German companies might earn from the economic redevelopment of central Europe.

But what the Continental and Japanese stock markets, so far, are not is a market for corporate control. Cross-shareholding among Japanese companies means that only 25 per cent of the equity of listed Japan Inc is available for trading and speculation. In Germany, only a relatively small part of industry is publicly owned. For that part which is owned by the public, the role of banks as shareholders and custodian of proxy votes of other investors (which gives them control over nearly 60 per cent of market equity value), ensures that the ownership of German industry remains stable.

The German and French legal systems also support stability of ownership and management. The two-tier board structure in Germany and the ability of French companies to place restrictions on the transfer of shares and voting rights means that the balance of power between owners and managers is decisively in favour of the latter.

Julian Franks of London Business School, and Colin Mayer, of City University Business School, have questioned whether Europe is moving in the right direction by seeking to make UK company and takeover law the basis for Europe. In the UK, change of ownership is the primary way in which managerial failure is corrected. By contrast, in both the French and West German systems, as they currently operate, the connection between the correction of management failure and change in ownership is diminished.

'This is reflected in a relatively low incidence of hostile takeovers, buy-outs and buy-ins. Furthermore, the overall level of executive dismissal is apparently relatively low in both France and Germany.' They go on to point out that the stability this affords to management on the Continent may provide managers with incentives to engage in long-term investment. In a situation where European law and practice comes to resemble that of the UK, investment in R & D and training may suffer, Franks and Mayer claim.

But, although the evidence used to support the short-termism critique varies, its proponents have drawn blood. Lord Hunt, the chairman of Prudential, Britain's biggest institutional investor, felt the need to respond to such criticisms in the Prudential's latest annual report.

He pointed out that in 1989 there were 84 bids for companies in which the Prudential held shares; it accepted only five of the offers. Furthermore, since 1984 there have been 490 bids for companies in which the Prudential had an interest; it failed to support the incumbent management in only 25 cases.

But just to show that the issue of the long and the short term is here to stay, Lord Hunt reminded the Prudential's shareholders: 'Managements should recognise that their primary obligation is to maximise the value of shareholders' investments in the company in both the short term and the long term.'

DO INDUSTRY AND FINANCE UNDERSTAND EACH OTHER?

By Alan Clements

First published 22 July 1991

The argument between industry and the City over short-termism has not gone away. Indeed, the current wave of criticism of the banks for 'profiteering' on their loans to companies during a recession, and in spite of falling base rates, is just another example of the fact that to many in industry and commerce the City has failed to do what is expected of it.

It is unfortunate that there is a mismatch in both perception and reality between the City and the corporate sector over the roles of both the capital and the money markets.

The City, and especially that part of it concerned with the capital market, seems to think that the corporate attack on it is that it is short term in the sense that it misprices shares. It is perceived to do that because at the heart of its operations are two malfunctions.

First, analysts and fund managers emphasise current earnings and dividends rather than future ones, and apply their price/earnings rates to figures which are too low.

Second, fund managers are under short-term pressures because of the way in which they are evaluated on their quarterly performance.

The fact is, however, that the corporate critique of the City is much broader. Business sees the equity market primarily as a source of capital: that is, the place where, in the first instance, companies become widely owned by the public as a result of initial issues of shares for cash, and then later as the place where additional capital is raised as a result of secondary issues. But unfortunately over the years the City and the capital markets have, to an extent, lost sight of this fundamental purpose and no longer see themselves primarily as company developers, finding finance for industry and commerce via the promotion of new stocks.

The City's counter-attack is that: the stock market's pricing behaviour is not the cause of the problem: shares are not mispriced. The market does not over-emphasise current earnings and dividends; price/earnings ratios do reflect long-term forecasts and growth prospects. Indeed, company announcements about capital expenditure, research and development and new investments often result in price increases. The markets are not, in fact 'short term'.

Management, however, often takes a 'short term' stance in the corporate sector. Current businesses are milked, and R & D is neglected because of short-term pressures to increase the dividend, to increase the share price, to respond to fund managers who are evaluated quarterly, and to ward off the takeover threat.

All this intensifies management's propensity to be short term. This is brought about basically by reward systems, internal measures and capital budgeting, lack of profitable opportunities, and erroneous concepts about the cost of capital.

The solution is not to tinker with systems (the markets, taxation, financing techniques, regulations etc) but for management to 'manage as if tomorrow mattered'.

What is the reply of business to this? It is a three-part answer.

Investment and merchant bankers and brokers used to hold the view that the capital market's prime purpose was as a source of capital for industry and commerce. But over the years most of the operators in the market – market makers, brokers, investment bankers and investors – have come to see the market as something else. They seem to view it now pre-eminently as a place in which stocks are purchased for their income return and for capital gain.

What is more, they are concerned less with stocks newly issued by companies than with stocks which have been in existence for a long while, and which will have changed hands many times before. The results are that buyers and sellers who ought to attempt a fundamental evaluation of their commodity – stocks and shares – often do not, and instead think more of the market as a whole, and what it will do next.

It seems that the equity markets have developed in a way which has placed undue emphasis on secondary or trading markets. This is revealed by their pre-occupation with liquidity, and behind that, by the degree of speculation which has been seen as a necessary concomitant of liquidity. These two, it is argued, are vital for the sustenance of efficient capital markets in equity stocks.

The test of an efficient market does not seem to be its ability to provide new finance for industry and commerce, but rather its capacity to oil the wheels of trading in stocks and derivatives from them, such as futures, options and indices.

The result has been a tendency for equity investors to lose interest in the essential characteristic of an equity investment, namely the fact that it is a purchase of a part-ownership of an enterprise.

The reasons behind this loss of interest have often been stated – ownership of companies has become too fragmented (if you are a small shareholder why bother to interfere if over 99 per cent of any benefit is going to accrue to others), and larger shareholders (the institutions by and large) are more concerned with diversification of their portfolios and performance against an index. The result is dilution of the ownership role, and a distortion of the market's fundamental purpose.

That purpose is the facilitating of long-term investment in the economy via the raising of new finance, and the purchase of a share of ownership in business. Unfortunately, investors have been persuaded that it is only the secondary or trading market, which matters, that by studying and understanding it one can become a successful investor.

Instead, the experts have argued, a study of a stock's short-term fluctuations relative to the market plus a feel for what the market will do next, is all that is required. Liquidity is, of course, a vital feature of the market, but those developments have meant that liquidity has become synonymous with volatility and high turnover.

Why does the equity market need so much liquidity to make it efficient? What is wrong with investors concentrating on long-term fundamentals, while speculators who need liquidity fill in the gaps and smooth out fluctuations? Is it perhaps that the efficiency pursued by the market – aided and abetted by liquidity and speculation – is an efficiency of operations measured by volumes, turnover and commissions? The result is that the capital markets seem either to drown in their own liquidity or to complain because of starvation as a result of drought. Small wonder that the corporate sector asks: what is it all about, especially when after all the activity, and the ups and downs, the big institutions look little different from a year, or two years ago?

The second point is that this whole process has been made worse by developments which the markets have hailed as innovative life savers such as futures and options on indices, and 'portfolio insurance'. They have to be regarded as counter-productive because, although they have represented the markets' attempts to make long-term investment in unstable times easier, they have intensified liquidity and volatility, and in the end they have not really worked – witness the stock market crash of October 1987.

More important, they have widened the already sizeable gaps which existed between investors and the companies whose shares they contemplated buying.

Why? Because now the investor could, in a large way, buy the market and not individual stocks.

The stock market exists, in the eyes of the corporation, as a mechanism which transmits investors' decisions as to which industries and companies are most likely to prosper, into final values, and thus makes it possible for these favoured 'names' to raise new capital and grow. But now, as a result of derivatives and the like, investors commanding huge pools of money can influence the market without exercising this vital judgment. In fact by 1987 a massive amount of money was only 'passively managed' – small wonder that disillusionment with the whole system set in.

The corporate sector is still perplexed that companies can have two values – one the result of the normal interplay between buyers and sellers in the everyday efficient market, and the other the product of a bid. The real point about the difference between the two valuations is that it seems to prove that in the normal course of things the true value of retained earnings is overlooked. The price/earnings multiples which emerge in takeovers are nearer the 'truth', if one can use that term in what is, after all, a game played against a background of almost total uncertainty.

Having restated the industrialists' case, what can be done about it? First of all, the City and the corporate sector should stop blaming each other.

Once again both are in deep trouble.

Both sides need to see whether they can appreciate each other's point of view, agree that there is something in each side's case, and then sort out how to work together to make the economy viable and vibrant again.

POINTS OF VIEW ON SHORT-TERMISM

By Simon Holberton

First published 11 February 1991

The debate about the relationship between the City and industry, which goes under the generic title short-termism, comes and goes. Currently we are in a 'come' phase.

The tempo of the debate will no doubt pick up later this month when the Commons Trade and Industry Committee begins hearing evidence to further its inquiry into mergers and takeovers in Britain.

Fifteen years ago short-termism was the subject of a Stockton lecture given by Professor Harold Rose at the London Business School. Last Thursday, in his peroration to the first of the 1991 series of Stockton lectures, Sir James Ball suggested that it may well reappear on the LBS lecture circuit in 2006. It seems that short-termism is one of the least tractable issues for the UK's industrial society.

Sir James shared the podium with Peter Williams, chief executive and chairman-designate of Oxford Instruments, a high-technology company. It was Williams's job to argue that short-termism was a 'reality' in today's Britain and Sir James's to argue that it is a 'myth'. Both speakers – having 'proved' their opposite points of view – ended their lectures on the theme of corporate governance.

Corporate governance is a far cry from the most pressing issue identified in the mid-1970s – when the short-termism debate was framed almost solely in terms of the City's reluctance to supply industry with enough capital for investment – but it is indicative of the growing importance which it is assuming in management circles. It also suggests that the latest version of the short-termism debate, having started as a slanging match about a year ago, is now beginning to focus on some issues of substance.

Williams, in the context of more communication between City and industry, said that one way of breaking down the barriers would be for companies to appoint more independent directors. (Oxford Instruments has, in fact, a majority of independent directors.) 'But again,' he said, 'it is a two-way street: it is necessary if we are to make progress that greater openness in the boardroom is matched by better informed responses from the financial world to the problems we confront together.' Sir James pointed out that good investor relations could go only some way to ameliorating the conflict between industry and the City. He noted that Legal and General, the insurance company, of which he is chairman, had more than 500 meetings with companies last year, but there was a 'chronic ambivalence' among managers for investor involvement in management.

He suggested that many of the issues associated with short-termism could be settled in 'properly constituted boardrooms'. There, where this is a distinction between direction and executive management, management failure could be corrected without resorting to a change of ownership.

Sir James said the law ought to be invoked. The role and number of independent directors should be specified, and there should be legal requirements placed upon shareholders to participate in the nomination and election of directors. 'Without changes in the legal framework within which the game is played, I foresee the players continuing to engage in a relatively fruitless debate,' he said.

It is in the nature of debates, as with cards, to lead with one's best suit. But surely Sir James found too little fault with investment institutions. They have been singularly ineffective in operating as interested shareholders and acting to correct management failure. Although they may be the last to sell out, they seem to favour the takeover market for the punishment of poor management.

The sorry tale of Chloride, once Britain's premier battery maker, is one of almost culpable institutional neglect in the face of nearly 20 years of management failure. The company has not yet received a takeover bid; perhaps the institutions are waiting for one so they can vote with their feet.

8 RECESSION –
A SURVIVOR'S GUIDE

INTRODUCTION

When the Financial Times 'Managing in recession' series began in late 1990 the likely severity and extent of the UK's economic downturn were uncertain. But even then the economic indicators were clear where recession was going to bite most. As this chapter explains, the auguries for small and medium sized companies were not good. This sector was clearly going to face the greatest challenge in riding out a recession. The debt of these companies was proportionately in worse shape than that of the big corporations, and their ability to raise funds more circumscribed.

This prognosis was proved correct. With the number of companies going out of business reaching record levels, and with personal bankruptcies showing a similar trend, the smaller firms sector was vociferous in its demands for the government to do something to help, most particularly by bringing down interest rates. The means by which some banks and accountants endeavour to mitigate the effects of the financial squeeze on these companies are the subject of an article by Charles Batchelor, who has specialized in the small and medium-sized enterprise sector for the FT for several years.

Outside the UK, bankruptcies and company failures showed a remarkably similar cyclical trend in the US over the decade to 1992, and even in Japan the traditional resilience had come under severe pressure, with the number of failures gently moving up. France also saw a steady rise, though, unusually, its upward trend was constant rather than cyclical. Germany, though, showed a flattish rate after peaking in the mid-1980s.

Other victims of the recession in the UK, this time round, were middle management. Relatively unscathed until around 1992, middle managers suddenly found themselves in the front line when cost savings were being identified and redundancies set in train.

One reaction to the recession, in companies of all sizes, was to circumscribe capital expenditure programmes severely. Authority to sanction spending on capital projects was clawed back right up the management line, and main boards of directors started to insist on running their slide rules over expenditures which only a year or two earlier they would have left to divisional management.

As Simon Holberton discovered, ICI was well under way in 1990 with a review of all its budgets, long before it came under siege from the Hanson conglomerate in 1991. Significantly, the review revealed one of the features many companies have experienced in the past few years – that growth in the good years frequently results in a rise in fixed costs which requires radical attention when the downturn comes.

If recession generally had a savage effect on companies it also uncovered partial exceptions where sound management had already laid the basis for a greater financial resilience. ERF, the UK's last independently-owned truck manufacturer, almost went to the wall in the early 1980s as world demand slumped, hitting the entire truck making industry. But in 1990, John Griffiths found a company that had gritted its teeth, accepted that its manufacturing processes were hopelessly outdated, and had addressed the problem with determination. The outcome was a streamlined, largely debt-free operation that faced up to yet another slump in the market with a degree of equanimity and certainty that it would continue with its essential capital expenditure programme, and would be able to survive an even worse downturn. In the summer of 1992, it still appeared to be doing so.

John Brown similarly learned from the experiences of recession a decade earlier, but had to follow a different route to survive. First, it was taken over by the Trafalgar House industrial conglomerate and, second, it finally said goodbye to its traditions by getting out of shipbuilding and concentrating on its relatively newer business of power engineering.

All recessions, of course, have a human cost, but traditional methods of cutting back workforces have tended to be discarded in recent years. Last in, first out (Lifo) was, historically, deemed the easiest and fairest method of implementing a redundancy programme. A number of factors, including legal ones, changed this – prompting managements to take a more pragmatic line. Not only do decisions on redundancy choices have to be able to stand up to scrutiny at an industrial tribunal, but companies have increasingly found that redundancy programmes can all too easily result in the loss of good, skilled, workers. With skill shortages a worrying trend in British industry, in spite of the recession, managements' choice of who leaves and who stays has more far reaching consequences for the time when recovery finally arrives.

MANAGING IN RECESSION

By Charles Batchelor, John Griffiths, Simon Holberton, Charles Leadbeater and Michael Smith

First published between November 1990 and June 1991

Where the axe will fall

It is no longer a question of whether we are in a recession, but of how deep and prolonged it will be.

The economic indicators have begun to tell us what company results and surveys by the Confederation of British Industry have been saying for months: output is falling in the face of weakening demand and company profits are being squeezed.

Most companies can make money in a boom but recession is the great leveller. It has the habit of exposing the flaws in ambitious growth strategies.

The onset of recession in the UK has laid bare management deficiencies masked by the high-growth, debt-fuelled boom conditions of the mid- to late-1980s. Companies are now engaged in a scramble to repair their overstretched balance sheets by cutting costs.

Stars of the 1980s, such as BET, the international support services company, and APV, the UK engineer which manufactures food-processing equipment, are now finding that their debt-based growth strategies are coming unstuck.

Rising interest payments are eating into profits.

Even companies with sound balance sheets, such as Imperial Chemical Industries and British Steel, have instituted programmes to control costs and cut investment spending, in the case of the former, and payrolls in the case of the latter.

More generally, companies are considering and enacting a broad range of measures to cope with the downturn, all of which are designed to cut expenditure. The two main areas are labour costs and expenditure on investment. Employment policies from the shop-floor to the boardroom and all areas between are being reconsidered.

Boardroom coups, sometimes initiated by shareholder dissatisfaction, sometimes by strong non-executive directors, have resulted in high-level departures, especially where growth strategies associated with a powerful chairman/chief executive have begun to unravel.

The combining of the roles of chairman and chief executive is now decidedly out of fashion. Large institutional shareholders are objecting to it because of issues of concentration of power. It is no coincidence that those chairmen/chief executives who have resigned have been associated with growth strategies that have left their companies with too much debt.

Ralph Halpern resignation from his position as chairman and chief executive of the Burton Group was just the latest in a series of top-level resignations that include those of Michael Henderson of Cookson, John Marvin at Hickson International and James White at Bunzl.

Cookson is now paying the price for nearly £800m of acquisitions it made over the past five years. It has sold its 50 per cent interest in Tioxide to its partner ICI for £171m and Cookson Graphic to International Paper of the US for £147m. The sales should reduce Cookson's debt to around £280m – about half of shareholders' funds – but still the company will have to reduce spending on investment and research and development.

But the men at the top are not the only ones to feel the sharp winds of recession. British Steel, which is facing contracting margins and slack demand, plans 'significant redundancies' in its white-collar workforce of 12,500 to raise efficiency levels. This is consistent with the reviews many companies have been making of their middle management requirements.

According to Ian Gooden, a consultant at OCC, a management consultancy, in the high growth period of the latter part of the 1980s, companies did not look at middle management with the same hard-headedness as they had been forced to look at the shop-floor during the the early 1980s.

Middle management's function is 'two thirds administration – quietly passing information up, down and sideways – and one third decision making,' he says. 'Companies are now trying to replace this tier of middle management with information systems or doing without the middle managers by pushing responsibility deeper into the core of their business.'

British Telecom is a good example of this. The onset of recession has added impetus to plans under way to take a significant number of middle managers out of its organisation. Mike Grabinder, director of quality and organisation, says the delayering of BT will save money but its principal aim is to bring the organisation closer to the customer so as to meet customer needs in a more timely fashion.

Further down the line jobs are also being cut. The Engineering Employers' Federation in September 1990 forecast job losses of up to 80,000 in the ensuing year. ECC Group, formerly English China Clays, plans to cut 750 jobs over the next five months. Howden Group, the Scottish engineer, is closing its Renfrew plant near Glasgow with a loss of 500 jobs and the over-stretched Laura Ashley has plans to close five factories in the UK with a loss of 1,000 jobs.

But the trend towards traditional job cutting as a way of responding to recession concerns some who believe it may prove short-sighted. Says Bridget Litchfield, of Focus, an out-placement consultancy: 'Companies are getting rid of experienced people at a time when we are told there will be labour shortages in the mid-1990s.' Investment is the other area where British industry is cutting back. ICI, which is looking hard at getting its fixed costs down, will cut at least £100m from its previously planned £1bn capital expenditure plans for 1991. In planning the cuts, Alan Clements, the company's finance director, says: 'We did the figures on what we could afford to spend without letting interest cover (how many times pre-tax profits cover interest on borrowings) slip below 5 or 6 times.'

BET – one of the high growth stars of the 1980s – has found it necessary to curtail drastically capital expenditures because of high debt levels. In the first half of the year capital spending fell to £166m – nearly half that of the previous corresponding period – and Nicholas Wills, BET's chief executive, says he is determined capital spending will be cut by a further £100m in the second half.

'We have now severely tightened our controls from the centre,' he says. 'Capital expenditure has been frozen except with my personal sanction.'

But some companies are bucking the trend towards cuts in capital spending. In August, Michael Montague, chairman of Yale and Valor, the security and home products group, initiated 'Operation Hairshirt', a company-wide cost-cutting drive with a difference. Managers were not allowed to recommend cuts in spending on new product development and capital investment.

He says that Operation Hairshirt has been completed. Cost savings resulted in Yale and Valor's workforce being cut by 500 to 7,500. But investment has been preserved.

In an industry where product life-cycles tend to be around five years, 'new products are the seed corn of tomorrow,' Montague says. 'If we neglect that then our competitors would be in a stronger position than they would otherwise be.' The evidence so far is that British industry is on the defensive and its response to the gathering downturn is depressingly similar to industry's reaction to the recession of the early 1980s.

Investment plans are being clawed back, jobs are being cut and management consultants are being called in to advise on 'restructuring'. As with last time, there appears to be a marked reluctance on the part of companies to make savings by cutting dividend payouts, the recent decision by Barratt Developments, the house-builder, to do so notwithstanding.

While all these developments have served to foster a growing sense of gloom, it is by no means clear that the recession of the early 1990s will be as severe as that of the early 1980s, although the signs already are that it will be painful and the prospect of a war in the Gulf remains the joker in the pack.

But whatever happens there is evidence that the financial state of UK industry is significantly different this time round compared with the early 1980s. This is what emerges from research carried out by UBS Phillips & Drew – and it is also possible to conclude from the UK stockbroker's findings that a disproportionate amount of the adjustment is likely to fall on small and medium-sized companies.

Phillips & Drew follow in detail the largest 160 industrial companies listed on the London Stock Exchange. Their research indicates that while the government's data on companies' interest gearing, liquidity and financial deficit shows them at their most precarious for decades, the situation for larger companies is relatively sanguine.

Interest gearing (interest payments as a percentage of pre-tax profits) for all industrial and commercial companies in Britain is estimated by the government to be at around 35 per cent of pre-tax profits – higher than in 1974 and about the level of 1980/81. For the top 160, interest gearing is half that.

Company sector liquidity (short-term assets as a percentage of short-term liabilities) tells a similar story. Officially, estimates indicate that companies' liquid assets are around 70 per cent of their liquid liabilities.

But for large companies, liquid assets are 1 1/2 times their liquid liabilities.

As for the financial deficit (retained earnings less investment and stock appreciation) Phillips & Drew can find little of the estimated £24.7bn shortfall in 1989 accruing to the top 160. For the companies it follows, Phillips & Drew estimates a financial deficit of £3.3bn in 1989.

The message from these observations is clear: the lion's share of the adjustments in this recession will be felt by the small and medium-sized sector of British industry – the sector least able to raise equity finance and, therefore, as the data show, the one most dependent on the banks for finance. The large should escape relatively unscathed the corollary, of course, is that it is a lot worse for the rest.

Drastic measures at ICI

The question of whether the UK is in recession may be a fine technical point for Norman Lamont, the new Chancellor, but for senior managers at Imperial Chemical Industries the issue is not whether the country is in a recession but how severe it will be.

Well before the Gulf crisis and the strengthening of the pound managers had noticed that ICI was being hit at its gross margin costs were rising but the company was unable to raise prices because demand was weak.

The finance men at ICI's headquarters at Millbank in London, alert to this, have spent the past 12 months poring over planned expenditure, both fixed and long-term, and have identified areas of ICI's activities ripe for pruning.

An early result of this work led Sir Denys Henderson, the company's chairman, to announce in Tokyo in early October that ICI planned to lop at least £100m off planned capital spending of £1bn in 1991.

By the end of October when he announced the company's third quarter earnings, Sir Denys also mentioned that a strict control was being kept on other current costs as well. Divisional managers, who presented themselves at Millbank for the company's ritual 'hell fortnight', which ended last Friday, got an even tougher time than usual head office sought real cuts in spending.

ICI earned pre-tax profits of £1.5bn in 1989 this year pre-tax profits look like coming in at around £1bn. With uncertain economic conditions both in the UK and abroad, the reasons for the cuts were not about protecting this year's earnings but next year's and beyond.

'If we continued with planned capital expenditure it could have developed into a worrying situation,' says Alan Clements, ICI's finance director, who notes that ICI's capital spend next year would be in the range of £800m to £900m.

'With profits falling off and internal cash generation affected, if we had allowed capital expenditure to continue growing we would have run into a worrying situation where we spent more than we were generating internally.

'That would have made it difficult for us to take advantage of acquisitions that may come along. So we decided to cut capital expenditure and make sure we were really investing in what was worthwhile.'

Clements says the process by which ICI set about cutting capital expenditure entailed trying to 'get a feel' for what was in the spending pipeline. This meant letting the planners and finance people crawl through the proposed capital expenditure programme.

They then attempted to sort out what were essential expenditures for the growth businesses ICI wanted to be in, in the long term. 'If growth does not look that good, then what will that do to cash generation within the business? Therefore, what cut will get capital expenditure back to a level we can live with?'

These questions were framed with the maintenance of balance sheet strength in mind. In the end they came down to how big could the capital expenditure bill be so that in a year or two the company's gearing and interest cover would still be affordable? 'We did the figures on what we could afford to spend without letting interest cover (how many times pre-tax profits cover interest on borrowings) slip below 5 or 6 times,' says Clements.

He says that cutting investment has not been easy. ICI's capital expenditure budget is split into two components: big ticket investments which require headquarters approval and, 'maintenance and sustenance' expenditures which can be made by divisional chief executives without referral to Millbank. The former account for about 40 per cent of ICI's capital expenditures, the latter the remaining 60 per cent.

In the early 1980s ICI made deep cuts in its capital expenditure programme as part of the cost savings necessary to see it through that recession. Authorised spending was cut from £546m in 1979 to £241m by 1982. Those cuts had two principal consequences for expenditures in the future.

'A lot of equipment needs heavy capital expenditure to keep it going because replacement expenditure was not kept up in the early 1980s,' says Clements. 'On top of that growing problem, a lot more expenditure was needed to satisfy safety, health and environmental requirements.'

The way in which ICI recovered from the last recession has also had consequences for managers today faced with another recession. The company embarked on a growth-through-acquisition strategy – Beatrice Chemical, in 1984, Glidden, the paints company, in 1986 and Stauffer, speciality chemicals, in 1987 – and during this period headquarters agreed with divisional managers 'quite ambitious strategies' which included not only how the strategies would be financed, but possible further takeovers as well.

As ICI hit a period of slowing growth a year ago it became apparent that its fixed costs were rising at a faster rate than inflation. 'We had too many growth strategies,' says Clements. 'Once they were allowed to start they embedded a higher level of fixed cost in the business.' In March 1989 Millbank began to realise that these growth strategies were too ambitious. A review was conducted, the central theme of which was, was the company still on its strategic path? 'No, we were not. We had dropped below the growth path in terms of profits, everything, and managers were not meeting their milestones' – a method of management-by-objective whereby business plans are defined in terms of achievable goals in the future.

'In November 1989 we had quite an exercise in the 1990 budget meetings. We said that we would accept the divisional managers' budgets for 1990, but said that we would agree only if the business units were sure of achieving targets. We thought that their belief in getting higher prices and volumes was not achievable.'

Although some costs were clawed back, ICI allowed its managers to try to achieve the volume and price plans they had made. But, throughout this year, the headquarters view that those goals were too ambitious was validated, and many managers failed to keep to budgeted costs.

Yet, lurking behind the discussion of cuts in investment and fixed costs is ICI's concern about the stock market and the way it evaluates the company.

ICI cut its dividend in 1980 and the market's savage response to that event is seared on the minds of the company's top executives.

It has taken ICI until 1989 to get its dividend to a level which returns it to the path it would have been on (allowing for inflation and some real growth) had it not cut its payout in 1980. It would be highly unlikely for ICI to cut its dividend from the 55p a share level reached last year.

'We have struggled so long to get the shares fully appreciated, to get the appropriate rating,' says Clements. 'The dividend has become an important ingredient in getting the right rating. (The City) is looking at the drop in profits without looking at the spectrum of the whole chemicals business. They are critical and the dividend is important in holding the share price even where it is.'

Tuning ERF

If Peter Foden is a worried man, he shows not the slightest sign of it.

Theoretically, he should be gnawing his fingernails as chairman and chief executive of ERF (Holdings), the UK's last publicly-quoted independent heavy truck-maker.

The UK truck market on which ERF is overwhelmingly dependent has plummeted by nearly one-third this year and by one-half compared with two years ago.

Big truck-makers like the Anglo-Dutch DAF have warned of big financial losses ahead, and job and production cutbacks have spread across most of the industry.

In almost exactly the same market circumstances a decade ago, ERF teetered at the very brink of bankruptcy.

Its product range was chaotic – ERF would meekly fit whatever make and combination of engine/gearbox/axle was demanded by an individual customer's whim.

Its production processes were inefficient. And it was unable to match the big discounts and other marketing support employed by larger rivals desperate, like ERF, to keep assembly lines moving.

Sales plunged. Output came to a virtual standstill. The workforce was more than halved and only particularly understanding bankers allowed ERF sufficient time to pull through the crisis.

Yet ten years later, it is ERF which has survived to retain its independence and thumb its nose at the fates of Bedford – sold off to the entrepreneur David JB Brown by General Motors Leyland Vehicles, now part of DAF and Ford's truck operations, placed into a joint venture with Italy's Iveco.

And Foden, a burly, moustached figure whose well-developed sense of humour belies an appearance which is the archetype of the hard 'muck and brass' North Country businessman, insists that ERF's survival is not in doubt despite the severity of the current recession.

'We've seen it all before. This time round, I'm perfectly comfortable – if you allow for the fact that no one likes having to introduce lay-offs. We've got lots of cash. We're looking three years ahead. We don't believe in "short-termism", and a downturn of 12 months or so is something we can now take in our stride.'

Even before disclosing its 1990 interim results on Wednesday, Foden was making no attempt to disguise the fact that there would be a deepening of the losses into which ERF plunged in the second half of its financial year (ended last March 31), after four years of sustained profitability which saw a record £7.83m, pre-tax, achieved the previous year.

Before the market slumped, analysts had been predicting profits of up to £10m. Instead, the £3.27m for 1989 overall disguised a second half loss of £474,000.

The market was well prepared, therefore, for Wednesday's disclosure of an interim loss, before extraordinary items, of £1.51m and a halving of interim dividend, to 2p per share. The fact that ERF's share price closed that evening up 5p at 80p indicated that the market shares a little, at least, of Foden's confidence, although, like most truck-makers, the closing price was but a shadow of the 500p-plus levels reached in 1988/89.

Despite the recent one per cent cut in base rate, Foden and most others in the industry maintain that further cuts of two or three percentage points will be needed before truck operators even start to regain confidence.

Most in the industry will now be pleased if there are signs of upturn by the second half of next year.

Foden can point to ERF's legacy of the mid- and late-1980s boom years – accounts showing consolidated net assets of £29m and no borrowings – as evidence of the Sandbach, Cheshire-based company's ability to stay on the road, helped by a rights issue last year which raised £6.1m, the recent sale of a plastics subsidiary for £4.5m and £2m from selling a 37.7 per cent stake in a South African truck-assembly subsidiary.

Nor, he declares vehemently, is there the slightest chance of scaling down a recently-launched £6m development and retooling programme, intended mainly for a new generation of cabs to be launched in less than two years' time. 'Short-termism is not practical in an industry where product development needs long-term investment in terms of monetary and management resources.'

The contention that ERF currently is on top of the situation is given some support by deft footwork carried out as far back as August last year, when truck sales overall still seemed to be booming. Nevertheless ERF's board decided to cut 65 of its 1,100 jobs and start reducing production in expectation of a downturn.

There was little time for rivals' rumour-mongering, before they were starting down the same cutbacks road. Since then, ERF has reduced its workforce to just under 800. Partly through natural wastage output is battened down to seven trucks a day from a peak of 21 two years ago and there will be four-day working in January.

Even ERF's loss of market share at a greater rate than the market's own fall appears to be viewed pragmatically.

Rod England, ERF's marketing director, describes some of the deals now being offered by some truck-makers desperate to keep production lines moving as absurd – up to 20 per cent off list prices, with other incentives worth several thousand pounds more, on £50,000 heavy trucks.

Foden stresses two main factors as having changed ERF's viability. The first is the product rationalisation in the early 1980s, which, in Foden's own words, 'stopped us being a fruit salad maker'.

Out went the wide array of engines, gearboxes and axles, from a variety of manufacturers, with which ERF had been willing to make virtually customised trucks for individual operators – at a high, but unrecuperable, cost.

In came a more standardised truck range built around Cummins engines, Eaton transmissions and Rockwell axles on a more modular basis.

Individual truck operators can be as subjective and prejudiced about truck engines and gearboxes as any car enthusiast, and there were plenty in the commercial vehicle world who predicted that ERF would have a customer revolt on its hands. As it turned out, deserters from the marque have been few.

And the simplified production processes also made easier the second key decision: to cut the number of operations undertaken in-house.

It still makes the cabs for its own larger trucks, but buys in those for its smaller ranges from Steyr-Daimler-Puch in Austria. In most respects, it has become just like the majority of North American truck-makers in that it is now essentially an assembler of other manufacturers' parts. As a consequence, says Foden, 'we do not have huge machine shops and foundries – all we have to do is turn off the tap from our suppliers'. The tap is now turned to a relative trickle. By the time this year is out, ERF will have done well to produce and sell 2,000 trucks.

One seemingly obvious counter-measure for ERF is to develop export markets. But ERF currently is much more concerned with conserving resources than committing them to the uncertain success of an export drive. Such caution is understandable. Foden himself readily admits ERF had a 'horrendous' time in the early 1980s truck market collapse. Instead, ERF is endeavouring to maximise revenues from UK operations. To that end it has set up two wholly-owned distributorships – currently it owns two out of a total of 25 – and may set up more provided, says Foden, independent distributors don't feel ERF is 'stepping on their toes'.

Despite such efforts, ERF clearly is going to have its work cut out to keep losses to manageable proportions. Presuming it succeeds, ERF does not rule out an orderly expansion into the Continental European market takes shape – and particularly if the UK's 7.5 tonne breakpoint for operators' licences disappears and there is a substantial market shift from the highly popular 7.5 tonne sector to 10–12 tonnes. 'That's close to what we already make – we could broaden down to 10 tonnes,' says Foden.

Customer pressures could require ERF to set up a continental shop more seriously anyway. 'We know a lot of our customers are looking at Europe. We've already got arrangements with Cummins service points in Europe, and we're looking at ways of improving service availability further.' One solution, he suggests, could be a joint venture, certainly in distribution and finance, and maybe on major future components like cabs.

Foden himself is at something of a loss to explain the tenacious grip ERF has maintained on its market niche. Like any other truck-maker he talks of producing a vehicle 'the customer wants to buy'. 'It's competitive, and not just on price, but to operate. The cost of parts is low and so is downtime.' Another factor, he suggests, is the ability of a small company to respond more quickly to customer needs than a larger.

Not least of its assets, however, he acknowledges, is that there are still a lot of operators who like 'buying British' from a small company determined to retain its independence.

Rescue and recovery

In the 1981 recession the company which looked likely to be unable to meet its commitments to its bankers could expect to be put into the hands of a receiver. In the current recession there is a greater chance that the business in difficulties will be asked – at its own expense – to call in a team of accountants to see whether they can achieve a turnround of its fortunes.

'The philosophy of lenders has changed,' comments Bill Roberts, head of corporate advisory services at accountants Ernst & Young. 'Rather than assume the worst there is a greater tendency to call for an accountant's review.' One reason for this shift has been the passing of the 1986 Insolvency Act which has given troubled companies greater breathing space by allowing them to go into administration rather than receivership.

The result has been a sprouting of turnround or recovery teams alongside the traditional insolvency departments at many of the larger accountancy firms.

Often this is no more than the grouping together under one title of the firm's existing range of investigation and consultancy services. But the accountants' decision to re-package their services in this way reflects a fundamental shift in attitudes by many lending institutions.

The venture capital industry, provider of equity finance to many growing businesses, has also adjusted to the tougher economic climate by devoting greater resources to monitoring its investments. Nick Jolliffe, an accountant with experience of corporate recovery work, joined the 22-strong executive team at Lloyds Development Capital six months ago to provide help to troubled companies in its portfolio.

Venture capitalists have an advantage over banks in that they usually have closer and more frequent contact with the companies in which they are invested and they do not charge for their advice to companies in difficulties. 'We are a free resource and, unlike a team of accountants, we are already known to the management,' says Jolliffe.

This does not mean, however, that the venture capitalists will be any more forgiving in their judgment of management failings. We try to avoid conflicts but that does not mean we are soft, says Jolliffe.

There will also be a financial cost if the venture capitalist is only ready to provide extra funds on more onerous terms than his original investment.

For managers, dealing with investigating accountants is an unnerving experience. 'It is an exhausting and time-consuming process for a company,' says Mark Batten, partner in the corporate reconstruction department at accountants Price Waterhouse.

The directors may not have the financial projections or analyses which the accountants need. Senior managers are often concerned that news of the investigation will unsettle middle managers and shop-floor workers who may fear their jobs are at stake.

'Initially, in most cases there is suspicion,' comments Hew Dalrymple, a consultant in the turnround unit of accountants KPMG Peat Marwick McLintock.

The management's sense of grievance is often fanned by the fact that even though its bankers have called the accountants in, it is the company which foots the bill.

'They face extra fees at a time when they are strapped for cash anyway,' says Dalrymple. 'But if the accountants are any good the managers realise that they can help them.' A common trigger for the bank to call in the accountants occurs when a company reaches its borrowing or overdraft limit and is forced to go back to the bank for more. 'The company may have missed a profits forecast or be providing what the bank regards as unreliable or inadequate information,' says Mark Batten. 'The management may have decided to take the company off in a new direction and the bank becomes nervous.'

So what do the accountants do when they come in? 'We go in for a day to answer the question: "Can anything be done to save this company?",' says Dalrymple. 'If the answer is "Yes, probably", then we go ahead.'

'We start with a reasonably lengthy discussion with the management about their business,' says Bill Roberts. 'We might have seen management accounts but we would not at this stage have done any research of our own.' If the company can be saved, the accountants will move on to a detailed study of the financial numbers. 'We would review the business's current financial position, its prospects and projections,' says Mark Batten. 'We would look at the commercial assumptions and at what could go wrong. We would also review whatever proposals the management had to turn the situation round.'

'The bank wants to know if the management's figures are factually accurate and whether, in our opinion, they are achievable,' comments Dalrymple. 'It wants to establish the business's immediate cash position and its future needs for new money.' Once the accountants have the basic information they would discuss the implications of their findings for the business and attempt to agree with the management a plan to resolve its difficulties. 'We like to get agreement from the directors on the facts, or raise areas of disagreement and to test out our conclusions with them,' says Bill Roberts.

Speed is important to a company facing cash-flow problems and the accountants would expect to complete their work – depending on the size of the company, the efficiency of its information systems and the complexity of the problems – within one to two weeks. Their report would then normally go both to the bank and to the management.

One recent assignment carried out by Bill Roberts at a company with turnover of £16m-£18m began with five to six days of fieldwork to dig out the financial information and a total of 2 1/2 weeks for completion of the report. If the bank agrees to continue to back the business after reading the report, the accountants may continue to monitor the company's progress – by visits or by reviewing its monthly management accounts – for a further three to six months

The cost of this process will depend on the amount of bank finance at stake, the size of the company and the complexity of its problems. If management co-operates and the financial information systems are in reasonable order, costs will be reduced. A £4m turnover company recently faced a bill of £10,000-£15,000 for a turnround review, says Dalrymple.

A team of two to three, often comprising management consultants as well as accountants, should be enough to investigate the affairs of a company with turnover of £10m-£15m but larger companies might involve a team of five to 15 people.

The accountants are keen to point out that if the company under review can be saved the costs may well be recouped by improvements in profitability or the discovery of opportunities to save on tax, for example.

In spite of the rapid leap in the number of business failures the greater willingness of the banks to call in turnround teams has cut the number of receiverships and liquidations, the accountants say.

'In the past we would be able to save 40 per cent of the companies we were called in to help but that figure is now moving to 60 per cent because people realise the merits of getting us in earlier,' comments Hew Dalrymple.

New business ventures at John Brown

Ray McCabe was tired. He had been up at 5 am to continue negotiations in a crucial stage of an overseas deal. Such round-the-clock dealing is not uncommon in the City of London, but McCabe operates from the heart of Clydebank, near Glasgow.

From what used to be one of the foremost civil shipbuilding yards in Britain, McCabe runs the power engineering division of John Brown, the engineering group.

In an office no more than a stone's throw from the dock in which the liner, the Queen Elizabeth II, was built and fitted out, McCabe deals with power engineering contracts throughout the world.

Last year the group managed seven sites in China. He recalls: 'We had to maintain daily contact with sites which started with no toilets, no electricity and no telephones, hundreds of miles apart on the other side of the world.' The international scope of John Brown's activities, and of the Clydebank site in particular, is the secret of one of the great industrial escapology stories of the past 30 years.

It is the story of how a medium-sized company has managed to prosper through a series of radical shifts in strategy, to jettison its heritage and establish new businesses. While the name John Brown has remained an enduring emblem of engineering prowess, what the company does has been completely transformed.

The UK recession is only the latest in a long series of challenges to John Brown. The recession of ten years ago almost claimed it. Thanks to the changes that were forced upon the group it is now in a much better position to weather a worsening economic climate.

John Brown has gone through considerable pain to build up its resilience to a downturn. That is what might lie in store for other groups which enter this recession ill-prepared.

The original John Brown built his company up from a barrow selling iron goods in Sheffield in 1837 into one of the most prestigious vertically-integrated industrial groups in the world encompassing coal, steel and shipbuilding.

In the 20 years following the second world war nationalisation forced the company to dispose of all those businesses. With the proceeds it started to develop three activities – engineering construction, boiler-making and machine tools along with the rump of John Brown's old activities.

In 1965 John Brown signed a deal with General Electric of the US to become a licensed manufacturer of gas turbines using GE's technology. The first turbine to be built at the Clydebank site was wheeled out under the bow of the QEII. It symbolised the shift in John Brown activities which were under way.

By the end of the 1970s it was on the crest of a wave. Armed with a record £28m profit in 1978 it went on an ambitious spending spree in the US: it pumped $150m into engineering construction, machine tools and textile and plastics machinery businesses.

Then several things went wrong at the same time. The recession in the US meant that the recently acquired businesses did not deliver the expected returns, while the UK recession ate into profitable businesses at home. John Brown, for decades a company associated with solidity, was on its uppers. At the bottom of the trough shareholders' funds of just £37m were supporting £150m worth of debt.

The banks grew restless. John Brown was ignominiously placed in the National Westminster bank's lifeboat for companies in danger of going under. Managing Director Allan Gormly says: 'It was a close-run thing. The banks were fairly close to pulling the plug.' The banks insisted on management changes which led to Sir John Cuckney becoming chairman and Gormly's appointment as chief executive.

In an unfavourable climate, they set about refashioning the group – selling off machine tools, its road transport business, underwater systems and its textile machinery concerns.

Sterling was unwinding against the US dollar, pushing up the sterling value of the company's dollar-denominated debt. Just when the company needed high inflation to erode its debts, inflation started falling.

There were also problems at Clydebank. In 1982–83 McCabe was surrounded by stocks of unsold gas turbines worth about £60m. The overstocking was caused by a sudden fall in world energy demand. It came only a year after John Brown was thrust into world politics by its involvement in a Soviet oil pipeline project which became a cause celebre for the Reagan administration in Washington. For several years McCabe's name was among those in the big books which US customs officials leaf through intimidatingly at airports.

Two years into the recovery programme in 1985 John Brown was still earning only very modest profits. The company was not financially stable enough to assure its large customers, groups like BP, Shell and ICI, that it could complete long-term contracts. It desperately needed a partner which would give it some financial support.

Hawker Siddeley, the diversified engineering group, had come close to buying the power engineering business, while the General Electric Company of the UK had looked at it.

However, John Brown's preferred partner was Trafalgar House, the construction and shipping group. In 1985 Trafalgar House took a 29.9 per cent stake in John Brown to refinance it. It converted that into a 100 per cent stake a year later.

From the outset it seemed a promising partnership. Gormly says: 'We needed financial strength to allow us to go for big contracts. Trafalgar House understands big capital projects, the risks they entail and the management they need.' Eric Parker, Trafalgar House's deputy chairman who has become chairman of John Brown, explains the adopted parent's position: 'We always wanted to get into engineering construction because we were at the rough end of the construction industry. John Brown has an international orientation and technical flair while we have been able to add financial and commercial disciplines for handling large contracts.' John Brown now comprises plastic machinery manufacturing, mainly in the US, and an offshore oil industry division which was formerly part of Trafalgar House, as well as a stake in BREL, the former British Rail engineering division which is owned through a joint venture with Asea Brown Boveri, the Swedish-Swiss conglomerate. Gormly does not see this as the foundation of a new division in rail equipment but as a medium-term investment which will be disposed of when the time is ripe.

The largest division, with a turnover last year of £600m, is engineering and construction, which in the 1970s was mainly confined to the UK. It has become a market leader in design in Africa, Europe and North America, running close to ABB.

However, in many ways the most significant success is McCabe's power engineering division in Clydebank. It does two things. It makes gas turbines using General Electric's designs and its key components, the rotor blades. That manufacturing activity, carried out in the lofty halls facing the river Clyde in which ships used to be fabricated, is surrounded by the design and project management teams which work on power plants around the world.

As Parker puts it: 'It is amazing how a small business in Scotland can come through with no home market.' John Brown's success shows that even if a company does not have its own technology it can compete with companies which dwarf it, such as ABB, Siemens, Hitachi and GEC-Alsthom.

McCabe says: 'We have to be very quick on our feet. Our strength is our ingenuity.' Recently it sold a portable power station to the Philippines which is built on barges which can be towed around tiny islands.

The power engineering division has never fallen foul of a penalty clause for late delivery. Its turnover has grown five fold since 1980 to £250m last year. It accounts for about 10 per cent of sales of gas turbines made to GE's designs.

There are several ingredients in Clydebank's success.

The foundation is its relationship with General Electric. John Brown hangs on the so-called 'string of pearls' which GE created to license its gas turbine technology around the world. The partners have a well developed web of contacts to maintain their relationship, stretching from an annual technology meeting to regular contact with a GE manager who deals full-time with John Brown. In 1983 when Clydebank was faced with its overstocking crisis GE helped it out by providing it with sub-contract work – a relationship which continues.

John Brown's policy of licensing the best gas turbine technology from overseas is being extended to provide the foundations for a new business in environmental engineering. John Brown is licensing technology from GE for flue gas desulphurisation in power stations, and European technology to launch into the UK water-treatment industry. This market should grow significantly in the next few years thanks to investments to be made by the privatised water authorities.

Alongside this carefully managed co-operation GE and John Brown compete fiercely for orders, although John Brown concentrates on smaller turbines.

The company is thoroughly internationalised. From the outset it has had to seek out export markets. Electricity privatisation in the UK and the growing interest in combined cycle gas turbine power plants is opening up a significant UK market for the first time since John Brown entered the business.

Working from buildings designed to build ships, the company has nevertheless significantly improved manufacturing efficiency.

In 1986 it introduced a flexibility agreement among blue-collar workers which has cut unproductive time by more than 50 per cent and reduced lead times on a gas turbine by thousands of hours. After the overstocking crisis of the early 1980s it has moved towards a just-in-time production system with suppliers and established a core and periphery workforce.

In the fabrication shop 80 workers are permanent employees, while the other 70 are temporary staff, often recruited on contracts lasting several months.

They have come from among workers made redundant at other engineering groups in Glasgow such as the Howden group and Yarrow shipbuilders.

Even more important than improvements in manufacturing technology has been the development of the service side. A decade ago half Clydebank's turnover came from manufacturing with the remainder from services; last year only one-eighth came from manufacturing. 'We have to concentrate on knowledge, technology and service rather than manufacturing. That is where we can make money,' says Gormly.

The group has moved up-market into more complex sophisticated projects. A decade ago it was supplying basic power plants almost like a box within a power station, leaving a lot of the other tasks to be completed by other contractors. Now it aims to offer a complete service, from design through to construction management.

Trafalgar House's backing has been essential to give John Brown the financial muscle to back large projects for which it needs to provide non-performance bonds worth upwards of £200m.

However, apart from this financial interdependence the two companies have been slow to exploit other areas of common interest between John Brown and Trafalgar House's civil construction divisions such as Cementation. This is partly because large contracts often stipulate that the main contractor cannot award work to a subsidiary.

Gormly says: 'There has been less synergy than we expected. These things take some time to develop. We have done more in the last 12 months than we have in the last three years. We are developing a better understanding between people and Trafalgar House is becoming more decentralised.' The lesson of how John Brown has had to change is simple, according to Gormly: it bred a will to survive. 'In 1983 it would have been easy to have ended it, to throw several thousand people out of work and end a tradition of engineering that goes back 150 years. We could not just let that history, knowledge and experience go down the drain.'

Reassessing Lifo

Norman Lamont, Britain's chancellor of the exchequer, may see signs of economic recovery, but in companies up and down the country cutting staff numbers is in full swing.

If industry's experience after the 1980–81 recession is any guide, companies will continue to cut the size of their workforces well after the recovery Lamont now predicts becomes a reality.

But no two recessions are the same and there appears to be a significant change this time around in the way companies are selecting people to be made redundant.

Traditionally British companies have chosen workers for enforced redundancy on the principle that the shortest serving employees go first.

Trade unions like the last in, first out (Lifo) principle, partly because it is seen as fair. Employers, however, are growing increasingly dissatisfied with it and growing numbers in the current recession are turning to alternative methods. None the less, the path out of Lifo can be fraught with difficulties.

Alternatives can cause conflict with unions, lead to claims of unfair dismissal and, most damaging of all, take up large amounts of managers' time and energy when they are needed to help their company fight for survival.

What, then, are the alternatives and why is Lifo declining in popularity? The most common complaint is that 'last in first out' is too blunt an instrument. It gives managers little control over who goes and thus runs the risk of creating an unbalanced workforce which is ill equipped to meet the company's demands when recession ends.

Victor Gauntlett, managing director of Aston Martin, the car manufacturer, says his company abandoned Lifo in 1984 because 'we were looking to get the best out of the people who were left. Seven years ago there were some people made redundant who we would not wish to re-employ. A measure of our selection success then is that when we embarked on another job-cutting exercise this year, there was no-one we wanted to lose.'

A second complaint is that Lifo can add to pay pressures. Paul Foden, management services director at truck maker ERF, recently negotiated a pay freeze for white-collar staff which he says would be difficult to achieve among blue-collar workers. He believes the Lifo system, which is operated among blue-collar workers but not their staff colleagues, can fuel wage expectations.

Under the Lifo system, the majority of workers know they will not be in in line for redundancy and so are likely to press for high wage increases even though they may lead to job losses, says Foden.

For those managers who have abandoned Lifo there are pitfalls aplenty. One, when asked recently how he would choose among his staff for redundancy, replied that he would go for the people he did not know. Decisions based on that principle would be unlikely to stand up in an industrial tribunal.

Nor would a company which chose redundancy candidates on gender grounds stand much chance of successfully defending a legal challenge. One employer in the south-east recently dusted down its redundancy agreement procedure to find that it specified women should go first in any job cuts programme. Acas, the conciliation service, advised a speedy change of policy.

It pointed out to that company, as it does to all employers, that they are required by law to select redundancy candidates fairly and not, for example, discriminate against them for their race, sex or for their trade union activities.

Companies which want to abandon Lifo are well placed to do so if they have performance appraisal schemes. 'They minimise the challenge,' says David Russell, director of Acas in the south-east of England (excluding London). 'The trouble is that, in spite of all the talk, few employers have them in place, particularly for manual workers.' None the less, growing numbers of companies are adopting policies for redundancy selection which assess workers for skills or qualifications, their standard of work and aptitude for it, and their attendance and disciplinary records.

Aston Martin, which earlier this year made 85 employees redundant from a 540 workforce, judges workers on performance, attendance, reliability, adaptability, time-keeping, enthusiasm and perception.

Line managers are asked to rate workers from one to four in each of the categories. On attendance, for example, the top mark would be for no absences, the second would be for two days or less, the third for under six and the fourth for above that.

Only when employers end up with an equal number of points does the Lifo principle come into operation.

Like many companies, Aston Martin asked for volunteers for retirement and severance before implementing its points system. Only eight people came forward.

Some companies, particularly those cutting jobs among large numbers of managers, have used voluntary severance and early retirement in all cases, although unions sometimes question how voluntary the schemes are.

BT, formerly British Telecom, is just completing a programme which has cut over 6,000 managers from a total in 1990 of about 43,000. No-one has been forced to go against their will, it says.

Howard Marchant, deputy general secretary of the Society of Telecom Executives, says some were less willing than others. 'By and large it was well handled and fair, but an awful lot of pressure was put on people who would have preferred to stay.' BT implemented the job losses in two stages: first through a programme of 'targeted volunteers' and then through a scheme by which management jobs were redefined or eliminated. Existing staff went through an appointment process as if they were applying for new jobs.

Paul Newman, director of personnel policy, says the company rejected an open volunteer scheme in favour of one in which the company approached individuals.

He says an open scheme would have meant handing over control of the process and the company would have risked losing its most able managers, who could find jobs most easily elsewhere. 'It can also lead to a disaffected workforce because you raise expectations of people when perhaps you find you cannot let them go after all.'

In the second stage of job losses, managers not appointed were sent through a clearing house for vacancies elsewhere in the company. If that failed to match them to a job, negotiations for voluntary severance or early retirement were offered.

BT's ability to get through the programme without the need for enforced redundancies was helped considerably because it was able to offer generous redundancy or early retirement packages. It is, after all, enjoying record profits. Problems arise when companies are having to cut jobs to survive and so can offer little, if anything, more than the statutory minimum. Kevin Curran, southern region organiser for the GMB general workers' union, says the problems are compounded further if the companies offering poor redundancy terms are abandoning Lifo because the alternative systems are more likely to aggrieve workers. 'Many companies panic and as a result introduce unfair selection methods. There was one in my region that applied solely subjective criteria and as a result we supported eight cases of unfair dismissal against it. We won out of court settlements and the next time the company implemented redundancies it returned to Lifo.'

There are other arguments in favour of Lifo, which in spite of its decline remains the most usual form of redundancy selection, according to Russell at Acas.

In spite of his reservations, Foden at ERF says Lifo can provide stability because it retains older, more experienced workers. It is also relatively cheap to implement because short-serving employees are entitled to less redundancy pay.

Nor does Lifo have to be quite as blunt an instrument as its opponents suggest. Many companies, including ERF, are able to effect redundancies in particular areas of their factories, thus minimising the chances of producing an unbalanced workforce.

But perhaps the main reason why Lifo remains is the unwillingness among managers to take on unions at a time when the potential for conflict is already high. 'We already have our work cut out trying to get union agreement for abandoning skill demarcations,' says one manager.

Another is more blunt. 'It would always be preferable if we could be more selective but we have good relations with our workers here and we do not want a confrontation. Times are difficult enough.'

9 EASTERN EUROPE – OPPORTUNITY OR RISK?

INTRODUCTION

In the euphoria that accompanied the opening up of the former Eastern bloc, there was much speculation about the potential that it presented to Western industry and commerce. Much of this was overstated, and bore little relation to the realities that existed in a region where economic and political systems had for decades been ruthlessly divorced from the concept of a free market system in a democratic society. Equally, acknowledgement of the sheer scale of the economic problems in the former USSR and other communist states tended to be obscured by a general belief that, somehow, enormous opportunities were there for the taking.

However, as this chapter illustrates, when the economic and structural problems began to be analysed it became clear that, whatever the theory, the practice of Western companies moving into and expanding in Eastern bloc countries was going to be hazardous, hard work and long term.

There were no easy answers and no quick fixes. As one industrialist remarked: 'Some of the investments we are making in these countries are not going to pay off. I have no doubt we will see economic catastrophes in one or more of these ventures in the next decade.'

Companies seeking to operate in Eastern markets face dealing with a system that, historically, operated on the basis of centralised demand. Nor has the concept of profit existed – a problem attested to by each of the articles. There has also been an abundance of costly practices which had more to do with a welfare state (e.g. supply of housing) than with free-market commerce. Moreover, valuing assets in a way understandable in the West has been fraught with the difficulty of Eastern accounting practices being either virtually non-existent or so different as to create an enormous gulf of understanding (for example, in many instances there was no concept of bad debts).

Added to all these problems is the fact that the concept of management was virtually non-existent. There was no need to question what had to be done and how. Central demand meant targets were merely handed down and the organisation, such as it was, set out to meet it without any real thought to cost effectiveness.

The result has been a series of unknowns for Western companies. Many of them are epitomised by the article on the exploratory moves by ICI, Britain's biggest chemicals and pharmaceuticals group. ICI realised that the Eastern states were a market to which it had to offer commitment – but tempered with caution. It was not a newcomer to the region, but the breaking down of barriers offered considerable opportunities to set up various joint ventures. All of these would have to fit in with the group's overall strategy, but precisely how that would be achieved was something of an unknown because of the underdeveloped state of the Eastern economies.

Another of the unknowns was related by David Waller in an assessment of the Eastern bloc's lack of accounting discipline and its weakness in other aspects of financial management. With no notion of profit, and none of productivity, bad debts and so on, any Western company wishing to acquire an Eastern bloc company was going to find putting a value on assets an uphill task.

As one UK accountant put it: 'It's difficult to tell from the reported figures whether a company is on the verge of insolvency or grotesquely undervalued at the price offered by a Western concern.' But some companies were taking the plunge. Andrew Baxter found Otis Elevator had bought majority holdings in two East Berlin lift manufacturers. To Otis it was a revelation to see the antiquated plants and processes of the East – even the West Germans had thought that East Germany was one of the more advanced of the Eastern bloc countries.

Redland, the UK building products group, was another that ventured into the East. Through its West German Braas subsidiary, it bought four state-owned tile-making plants. It realised as it did so that it would not only have totally to up-date them, but also among many other things, to inculcate the concepts of profitability, cost effectiveness, quality, delivery times, and marketing – another almost unrecognised concept.

For many companies buying plants in the East, there was also the dilemma of how quickly modernisation could be achieved and whether in the meantime competitors would fill the void with imports from efficient plants in the West. That is, in a sense, where the real competition for Eastern plants lay in the early 1990s.

WHY ICI IS REAPPRAISING ITS LOGISTICS

By Charles Leadbeater

First published 29 June 1990

You will not find many chairmen of international companies with a turnover of more than £13bn touring a small, dishevelled chemical plant at 8am on a Saturday morning.

But early in June 1990 Sir Denys Henderson, the chairman of ICI, the large UK chemicals group, was sampling the delights of the polymer plant, set amidst the tower blocks in Kiev's sprawling suburbs.

After a swift survey of the plant, which is one of ICI's leading Ukrainian customers and a discussion with its energetic director, the Soviet managers offered their British counterparts traditional hospitality. As the clock struck 9am they were cautiously lifting glasses of Georgian wine to their lips.

Sir Denys's trip to Kiev was designed to symbolise to ICI's management and staff its determination to explore and expand its Eastern markets. Next month the company's board will consider a report prepared by John Mitchell, head of its East European operations, which will recommend that each division include plans for Eastern Europe as part of its global strategy.

Although none of the East European economies has yet created a fully-fledged market economy, competition between Western chemical manufacturers is intensifying. The West German companies BASF, Bayer and Hoechst are strongly represented in many countries and US groups are showing mounting interest.

ICI will be committed to these markets, but its commitment will be tempered with caution. Sir Denys says of the Soviet Union: 'This is an enormous market, with huge potential. The standard of living is well below the West, but people have Western ambitions which will have to be satisfied. But it will take a long long time until the political and economic framework is of a kind which we can understand and do business within.' ICI will pursue an evolutionary approach. Its long-standing trade with the country has made it Britain's largest exporter to the Soviet Union with sales of between £50m and £60m this year.

ICI opened a Moscow office in 1979 and has become adept at dealing with a centralised democracy. It has agreed orders through negotiation with a foreign trade organisation in Moscow which in turn would distribute the product to final customers.

That system is starting to break down, as republics, city councils and enterprises claim more power. Increasingly, the company will have to start selling in the way it does in other countries, dealing directly with thousands of customers, haggling over prices, bidding and re-bidding for business.

'We were very good at playing the old system. It used to be a very cost effective way of selling. Now we have to get out of Moscow to deal directly with customers,' Mitchell says.

ICI believes the Soviet market offers considerable opportunities for many of its divisions.

The shortage of many staple foods will create strong demand for agro-chemicals to raise crop yields. Through a series of recent acquisitions ICI has built up a strong seeds business, which includes the unlikely jewel of Garst seeds at Coon Rapids in Iowa, in the US.

Garst, which mainly produces maize seeds, has strong links with the Soviet Union stretching back to a visit Nikita Kruschev made to Coon Rapids' maize fields when he was general secretary of the Soviet Communist Party.

Polyurethanes will be in demand from the expanding car industry and shoe manufacturers. The parlous state of Soviet health care will make investment in pharmaceuticals a priority. The huge unmet appetite for higher quality consumer durables should feed through into demand for better paints and coatings.

ICI plans to exploit these opportunities gradually to build up a sustainable business base.

After six months of negotiations it is on the verge of opening an office in Kiev, in the Ukraine, and has plans for another in Vladivostock to complement its other Far Eastern activities.

Beyond spreading its expanding salesforce across more of the territory, ICI will pursue selected joint-ventures, designed to build up a customer base and form the foundations for eventual manufacturing.

Its first joint venture in Leningrad, to create a marketing and engineering centre for powder paints used to coat consumer goods, will test not just the size of the market, but its sophistication as well.

ICI wants to educate its potential partners in the importance of quality and service as well as price. It also wants to establish which customers are most likely to prosper and thus which it should concentrate on. Only then will it move into paint manufacture.

A similar strategy in polyurethanes means that the first step will be to establish a systems house to mix polyurethanes to meet particular customer demands. If that is successful, there may well be a case for a Soviet polyurethane manufacturing plant, Sir Denys says.

In agrochemicals ICI is attempting to build on the success of its experimental farm just outside Kiev, where wheat and fodder pea yields have been increased dramatically. It is working on a further five farm projects and demonstrating its products at another nine.

It hopes to encourage collective farms to form large associations which will bulk-buy agrochemicals and technical support. As centralised state buying comes to an end it will be a handy alternative to sending a salesman tramping around thousands of collective farms.

However, even a judicious approach will not allow ICI completely to escape some troubling dilemmas.

Any expansion into Eastern Europe will have to fit with the rest of ICI's strategy whether in product development or on the environment. Yet that will be difficult because the Eastern economies are so underdeveloped.

ICI wants steadily to move away from bulk commodity chemicals towards higher value added products tailored more to the needs to final consumers.

'We will not be putting in huge investments into vast plants. We may not be in that scene anywhere,' Sir Denys says.

Yet there is still a lot of unsatiated demand for fairly standard products which simply trade on price. Most Soviet producers are just starting to think about setting their own prices and haggling over input costs. Customer service and attention to quality is still on the far horizons.

So it may be difficult for ICI to maintain the integrity of its international strategy to trade on quality and service as much as price, while also building up its Soviet presence.

Environmental issues will present a similar dilemma. ICI does not want to be associated with plants spewing out fumes over industrialised cities. Yet it will cost billions of dollars to clean up the Soviet chemical industry to current Western standards, which themselves are under attack from environmentalists for being too lax.

It wants to pursue the sort of strategy it has adopted elsewhere to forge close links with customers which will prosper in the long term. It is possible to assess the differences in the quality of Soviet managers, but most plants look shoddy by Western standards after underinvestment and neglect. Picking out the customers most likely to be successful in the long run will be difficult. The most successful may turn out to be those which received a lot of Western investment and management at an early stage.

The centralised selling system based in Moscow was a much more cost effective way of doing business than the more decentralised system which is emerging.

Selling in the Soviet Union will require more Russian linguists prepared to tramp from Kiev to Kharkov and back again selling their wares. The costs of doing business in the Soviet Union will rise quite significantly.

But in the long run cost will probably not be as important as politics. For it is the course of political reform which will determine the balance of risk and return.

'If there is a high political risk you want to be able to get your money back fast. The more stable the regime the happier you are to take a patient approach. This market will require a patient approach, but without much political stability for some time,' says Sir Denys.

The demands for investment in the East will have to be set against the needs of other parts of the world where customers are affluent and sophisticated, such as Western Europe and the Far East. Sir Denys says the Ukraine's roads, hotels, clothes and cars most reminded him of India, which he estimates is ahead of the Soviet Union in the international competitiveness of its industry.

In a good year ICI gets about a 12 per cent return on sales and a 24 per cent return on assets that is the standard Eastern Europe will have to match to claim investment funds as it becomes more integrated into global business strategies.

So significant manufacturing joint ventures, demanding large capital sums are unlikely before the second half of the decade.

As Sir Denys remarks: 'If it has taken us some time simply to negotiate our way to opening an office in Kiev it is interesting to think how long it would take to build a plant.'

INSTILLING ACCOUNTANCY INTO EASTERN EUROPE

By David Waller

First published 1 June 1990

Bored with your accountancy job? Tired of the 'tick and bash' business of auditing, and fluent in Hungarian, Russian or Czech as well as the language of business – double entry book-keeping? Then there is bound to be an opening for you in one of the rapidly expanding East European offices of the big international accountancy firms.

Accountants are in the vanguard of Western capitalism's advance into the Eastern bloc, and their offices are now to be found in virtually every capital City in Eastern Europe. Their job is two-fold: to advise Western investors interested in buying up Eastern European assets, and to help East European businesses interested in expanding into the West, preferably with an injection of capital and management know-how from a Western joint venture partner.

However, the process of inward investment to those countries deemed attractive to Western investors is much hampered by the somewhat rudimentary state of financial management in Eastern bloc countries it is virtually impossible to look at a set of accounts for a Hungarian ball-bearing company, for example, and decide what it is worth.

'It is difficult to find a company in Eastern Europe which doesn't need a major overhaul,' observes Michael Gibbins, head of the East European department at KPMG Peat Marwick McLintock. 'What is needed is rehabilitation followed by privatisation.' The problem can be stated simply: East European companies have hitherto had no notion of profit. The purpose of business activity has not been to produce profits for shareholders, but to meet output targets set by central governments. As Duleep Aluwihare at Arthur Andersen explains: 'They are geared up to meet production targets but they have no notion of productivity. They will move heaven and earth to make one extra unit, without thinking to ask whether it's worth it financially.' As a Price Waterhouse guide to doing business in the Soviet Union puts it: 'Both Western and Soviet accounting systems have as their aim the collection of information to facilitate economic decision-taking. Unlike their Western counterparts, however, Soviet accounting procedures were designed to collect the types of information required by a centralised hierarchical planning system.

'Much of the information that the Soviets collect on their numerous accounting forms would be conveyed by prices and sales performance in a market economy.' The aggregated information for each factory is sent up to a higher planning authority in the USSR. This is Gosplan, the state planning agency where information is lumped together with similar data from other factories.

Gosplan – or its equivalent in other Eastern bloc countries – reviews the data and formulates the stage of the plan. 'Despite recent Soviet economic reforms aimed at increasing the role of market factors in Soviet planning, this hierarchical form of interaction still predominates,' PW relates.

According to Aluwihare, who worked last autumn as part of a team of Western accountants advising Barbara Piasecka-Johnson, the Polish-American heiress, on her potential purchase of the Gdansk shipyard, the basic information-gathering process is unwieldy, but the information produced is accurate. There is elementary computerisation, but the records are prepared in the main by squadrons of under-employed blue-collar workers. There are technical differences between Eastern bloc and Western accounting for example. East European accounts are prepared on the basis of cash transactions completed rather than on the Western 'accruals' model (which takes account of monies owed or due at the accounting date). Business conditions dictated that there were no bad debt write-offs, because state-owned companies simply did not go into liquidation.

Another technical difference is that balance sheets look bizarre by Western standards since they are loaded with vast agglomerations of stock. The stock is not valued in line with the common Western principle that inventory should be in the accounts at the lower of cost or market value, and there is no attribution of overheads to the stock valuation, either.

The size of stock-holdings reflects the reality of business in a command economy: 'You don't buy things when you want to buy them but when you can get hold of them,' observes Les Bonnay, general manager of PW's 60-strong office in Budapest. The practical difficulty for financial managers trying to move to Western standards lies not in the quantity of information, but in the quality. 'It is difficult to get the information required to manage a business on a day-to-day basis for maximum profitability,' reflects David Harrison, the finance director of Tungsram, the Hungarian light-bulb manufacturer which was acquired by General Electric of the US last November.

Earlier in 1990, he went over to Budapest as part of a 'hit-squad' of US executives whose task it is to make the company competitive by world standards.

'There is as yet no financial consolidation of the company's numerous subsidiaries, and very little mechanisation in terms of basic accounting or financial analysis,' Harrison says.

'We are working hard to make our production more market-driven,' he continues, 'but we want to be competitive in the finance function as well. Our aim is to get a handle on working capital to bring stock levels down in line with sales and get to the point where we can make detailed cash flow forecasts. There's lots of data, but it's not decision-making data. The financial controls are good and the people bright and eager to learn, but there's a need for frequent reports giving detailed and accurate information on sales, pricing, costs and outstanding receivables.

'Once we can predict our cash flow requirements for both the short and long term, we will be able to improve productivity and ultimately profitability.'

There is a practical difficulty, too, for Western businesses wishing to invest in the Eastern bloc on the basis of old-style accounting information; it is very difficult to come to a valuation of the assets being acquired.

This is true in a capitalist economy too, when a valuation can be made on a multitude of different bases – on cash flow forecasts, on the record of profits over recent years or on assets – but the problems are accentuated in the Eastern bloc because of a lack of reliable financial information.

'It's difficult to tell from the reported figures whether a company is on the verge of insolvency or grotesquely undervalued at the price offered by a Western concern,' observes Michael Boyd of Ernst & Young. The Western investor has to weigh up the past – which if restated in line with Western accounting standards would invariably suggest that the company made little or no money – against the potential for the future. After all, one may not be buying profits, but one may be buying a sizeable share of a fast-expanding market.

The question of valuations has already led to tensions in Hungary, where there is a legal requirement that a valuation be made when a company is being privatised. Earlier this year, the state intervened to unscramble a deal between Hungar Hotels and Quintus, a Swedish company. Central to the government's case was that the valuation prepared by Ernst & Young Bonitas was too low.

Robert Bellia, senior partner at EY's Budapest office, counters by saying that the asset valuation was not designed to reflect the market price for the hotel company, and in any case, the price offered by Quintus was higher than that valuation in any case. In the event the charter for the joint venture was revoked by the Budapest Supreme Court.

According to Bellia, one of the problems was the inability of government officials to understand Western-style accounting. There is bound to be more such misunderstanding as the privatisation process accelerates.

HOW OTIS ELEVATOR HAS BOUGHT ITS WAY IN

By Andrew Baxter

First published 1 March 1991

It takes just a three-stop ride on the Berlin subway to cross from the Otis Elevator factory in the old Western sector of the city to one of its two new half-sisters in the East, but for Pierre Fougeron it is a journey back in time.

'We used to believe in the West that East Germany was among the most developed of the socialist countries, but this is not true,' says Fougeron, who heads European operations for the world's biggest lift-maker. 'In our case they were 30, 40, even 50 years behind. They were using twice as much material as they needed to make their lifts, and the culture and working methods were very poor.' The butt of Fougeron's comments is Berliner Aufzug – und Fahrtreppenbau (BAF) – an East Berlin liftmaker in which Otis Germany bought a majority interest last September. One of BAF's two plants is a rambling, 95-year-old building in a drab district near the old Berlin Wall, where employees used to assemble wooden lift cars. The manager would ride to his office in a lift with buttons numbered for 10 floors – although the building has only four – because using standard button panels helped BAF cut costs.

Otis plans to change all this over the next two or three years, introducing Western production machinery and manufacturing methods, reviving dormant technical skills, and instilling new attitudes towards customers as BAF is nudged away from the strait-jacket of a command economy. In the communist era BAF was even obliged to devote 5 per cent of its production to consumer products such as garden hose reels and trailers, much to the chagrin of its executives.

The BAF project is an important element in a long-term plan for Otis to hoist Eastern Europe and the Soviet Union into the last decade of the 20th century. 'A third of the world is up for grabs. And if you're a global company you might as well start grabbing,' says George David, Otis chairman and chief executive.

The initiative is also a rare example of US manufacturing industry taking the plunge beyond the old Iron Curtain, where German industrial groups have been blazing a trail in the past two years of political and economic upheaval. The most eye-catching US deal was the $150m acquisition by General Electric of a majority stake in Tungsram, but the transformation of the Hungarian lighting company since the takeover in 1989 is making slow progress.

In the heavy equipment sector, most US groups have been content to rely on export sales, although Westinghouse did announce in December a co-operation agreement with Skoda, the Czechoslovak engineering group, in power systems.

Otis, part of Connecticut-based United Technologies (UTC), has gone further, and over the past few months has announced a string of acquisitions and manufacturing joint ventures in Eastern Germany, Hungary and the Soviet Union.

Last month, Otis announced its second Soviet manufacturing joint venture, and there may be more in the pipeline. David also predicts a smaller transaction in Poland this year, and says 'we will do something in Czechoslovakia pretty soon'.

'We are going to be decisively ahead of our competitors in Eastern Europe and in fact ahead of most Western investors,' claims David, who has been closely involved in the Otis foray from its inception early in 1989.

But the US company's two big rivals, Schindler of Switzerland and Kone of Finland, are not far behind and as one seasoned US observer of the industry's competitive battles says: 'If one goes in, the others have to keep up whether it makes sense or not.' All three companies are attracted to Eastern Europe by the size of the market, and demographic trends that underpin its potential for further growth. David gives a 'ballpark number' of $3bn for the market in the former Socialist countries, against $15bn-$16bn for the rest of the world.

The Soviet Union, the world's largest national market for new lifts, accounts for the lion's share of the total, due mainly to housing trends.

The ugly apartment blocks that are home for most Soviet citizens all need lifts, and much of the installed base is fit only to be ripped out and replaced, says one analyst. Much of the housing stock, in any case, is substandard, and rebuilding will add to the demand for new lifts.

This humdrum context is a powerful attraction for Otis. The average electro-mechanical lift does not have the electronic sophistication that would fall foul of Cocom rules on technology transfer, and, says Fougeron, the US company will continue to import its larger, more complex models for hotels and skyscrapers into Eastern Europe. This market has historically been dominated by Kone of Finland, but has opened up considerably over the past two years with the weakening of trade ties between Finland and its large neighbour.

Consequently, Otis is much further ahead of other UTC businesses in establishing a foothold in Eastern Europe. Lifts, after all, are intrinsically less politically sensitive than Pratt Whitney's aero-engines, for example.

For David and Otis, Eastern Europe holds another strong attraction which is rooted in the company's decentralised culture and diverse character. With 43,000 non-US employees out of 50,000, he says, 'It's natural and normal that we're in every market in the world. When Eastern Europe opened up in the latter part of 1989, our company just made a right-hand turn and headed East.' The reality was a little trickier, and David acknowledges Otis has had its share of luck. The company's top six executives spent a week in Moscow and Leningrad in early 1989 assessing whether there might be any opportunities.

David admits that this was to prove 'amazingly fortuitous' as it enabled Otis to make plans well ahead of the upheaval in the Eastern bloc later in the year.

But, in common with many US companies, Otis had difficulty picking its way through the complexities of East European bureaucracy until it realised that the key to success was making contacts at factory level with managers who had 'elevators in their blood'.

'You find the factory manager, get him started and organised, and let him worry about the issue of Finance Ministry approvals and all the rest of that stuff,' says David. 'We nudge, nurture and support, but they make it happen.' In East Germany, says Fougeron, Otis was able to move fairly quickly because the company's exports of high-class lifts for big city hotels had opened doors in the industry. Even so, it had a stroke of luck late in 1989 when a retired East German official walked into Otis Germany's West Berlin office out of curiosity and wrote down all the lift company addresses he knew, from memory.

As Otis moves to build on its foothold in Eastern Europe, it faces four clear challenges:

● Political risk: David admits he is worried about recent events in the

Soviet Union, but says his own local contacts there have given him a very different perspective compared with what appears in the Western press. 'There are lots of national events – legislation, politics and regional conflict – but meanwhile people eat, sleep, and ride in elevators. And the people that do all those things will continue.'

- Economic risk: Despite Eastern Europe's long-term housing needs, analysts wonder where the money will come from to finance them. David is keeping his feet firmly on the ground: 'Some of the investments we are making in these countries are not going to pay off. I have no doubt we will see economic catastrophe in one or more of these ventures in the next decade.'

- Manufacturing and product development: Buying manufacturing assets in East Europe is less risky for Otis than for other capital goods producers because so much of its work is done away from the factory, in the customer's premises.

  Even so, the company faces an uphill task transforming BAF, which would almost certainly have collapsed had it not been taken over. Nobody – least of all in Western Germany – wants to buy lifts made in Eastern Germany. So Otis will move the manufacturing and technology base mainly towards making Western-designed lift parts. Executives estimate it will take two years to get things right.

  The situation is different in the Soviet Union, says Fougeron, where 'you do not wittingly take over old factories, they are such a mess'. But in both countries the manufacturing equipment will be purely Western-made – no East European machine tool would do as good a job, says Fougeron.

- The people challenge: This looks like being the least of Otis' problems. It is buying workforces with strong electro-mechanical skills, especially in Eastern Germany, and observers say David is justified in his confidence that the workforce quality can be lifted fast with decentralisation, incentives and training.

As for adapting to the demands of capitalism, Otis thinks this will be easier in Eastern Germany and Hungary than in the Soviet Union. Jean-Pierre van Rooy, an engaging Belgian who is Otis' chief operating officer, says: 'East Germans were capitalists until 1945. They have not forgotten everything.' Van Rooy recalls asking the manager of a Soviet lift factory how much profit he made. 'He said 20 per cent. Now I am sure he was going to answer me 20 per cent on anything I was asking. He had found out that it was a nice round figure. I am quite sure he did not have a clue what he was talking about because that is not their system there.' So far only the Hungarian joint venture is operating, but the two Soviet ventures, which come on stream next year, are expected to be producing about 5,000 lifts annually by 1996/97. Fougeron believes that, eventually, production could reach 15,000 lifts a year, giving Otis 25–30 per cent of the Soviet market.

That would also enable Otis comfortably to achieve its cherished double-digit market share in the Soviet Union, which it alone of the lift companies has achieved in every other big market.

For David the potential rewards justify the effort involved in taking Otis eastwards. 'We are buying market position and establishing relationships, and our time horizons are very long.' They may well have to be.

RADICAL EXPANSION AT REDLAND

By Andrew Taylor

First published 16 January 1991

On an average day it takes about four hours to drive from the modern headquarters in Frankfurt of Braas, West Germany's biggest roof tile manufacturer, to the run-down and melancholy tile factory at Voigtstedt in Eastern Germany.

To Erich Gerlach, chairman of Braas, which has paid DM 25m to acquire four out of the five former state-owned East German tile plants, the journey is like travelling back 40 years in time.

According to Gerlach, the empty shelves in the nation's shops, the general inefficiency and dilapidation and the worries about the future as new and existing businesses struggle to survive are all too reminiscent of the 1950s to many West Germans.

Braas itself was started in Frankfurt in 1953 with virtually nothing more than a brave idea and a large potential market in repairing and rebuilding war-damaged homes. The machinery and technical expertise with which the group started were provided by Redland, the British building materials group and the world's largest roof-tile maker.

Now it is the turn of Braas to play godfather. It will provide the investment in machinery and the technical, financial and management skills needed by its Eastern German factories as they get to grips with a commercial environment completely different from the one to which they have been accustomed.

Redland still holds a 51 per cent stake in Braas – which has grown to become one of its most important subsidiaries. The former West Germany accounted for more than a quarter of Redland's profits in the first half of 1990.

Profits from Braas increased by more than 50 per cent, compared with Redland's overall profits increase of just 3.7 per cent to £108m.

Eastern Germany provides another large potential market for Braas which it cannot afford to ignore. Much of the housing in the former Deutsche Demokratische Republik is in a very bad state of repair.

The roofs are in particularly poor shape. In Leipzig, one of the biggest cities, just under half the city's 250,000 dwellings are at least 120 years old. Of these, 30,000 are classed as no longer habitable even by Eastern German standards.

Improving the quality of the housing stock is likely to become a priority as the East starts to catch up with living standards in the West. Braas, however, is aware that it has taken on a large job in attempting to turn round its new businesses.

'Eastern Germany has operated in a centrally controlled economy for more than half a century – if the years under Hitler are included,' says Gerlach.

'It is not going to be easy to adapt. There will be a lot of pain and redundancies. Many companies will not survive.' During September four fifths of the working population was laid off in Voigtstedt.

The four plants now under Braas management control are at Voigtstedt, Jatznick, Magdeburg and Rostock. They previously employed 690 workers working 42 hours a week, three shifts a day, to produce 60m tiles a year.

Braas plans eventually to produce up to 100m tiles a year with just 320 workers working 39 hours a week in two shifts. As part of the takeover deal the group has had to convince the authorities that it will provide satisfactory redundancy payments to workers losing their jobs.

The speed with which wages rise will to some extent determine the pace of redundancies. At the moment Braas is moulding some roofing components by hand. If salaries rise too quickly this process will become uneconomic it will have to become mechanised, thus causing more jobs to be lost.

The profile of the workforce of its Eastern German plants at the time of its acquisition illustrates the scale of the problem facing Braas.

Of the 690 workers, about 150 were bureaucrats – 'they were not managers in the sense that Western companies would understand,' says Braas. 'There were no salesmen. Cash-flow and other financial controls were virtually non-existent. Output was determined by how many houses the state had decided to build or repair and upon the ability of raw material producers to keep the company supplied and the availability of transport to deliver the finished products.' Of the remaining 540 employees only about half were involved in production.

The bulk of these were involved simply in keeping the plant running. East German law required hot meals to be served for each of the three shifts.

Buses had to be available to ferry employees to and from the plant even if there was only one worker in a village. Party members were employed to organise political lectures.

Large numbers of staff were employed to keep worn-out and inefficient machinery operating. 'It was usually not possible to send for manufacturers to come and fix their machines when they broke down or failed to work properly. Shop-floor workers just tried to keep them running as best they could. They had to be very resourceful,' says Gerlach.

Braas discovered one machine at a former East German brick manufacturer which was dropping bricks in a heap on a conveyor belt rather than in neat lines. For some reason it had not been repaired and a worker was employed to straighten the bricks by hand before they were moved off to the next process.

The group has been quick to make changes in the way in which the plants are managed. Bonus payments have been introduced for meeting targets. New equipment has been installed in some of the plants to replace 25 year-old British machinery and up to 15 year-old East German machinery.

Two separate stacks of tiles outside the Voigtstedt plant illustrate how simple changes can quickly produce improvements. One of the piles manufactured before Braas took over the plant's management were in a light shade of purple and broke easily when handled. The second pile, a traditional orange colour and produced recently, were much tougher.

The reason for this, says Braas, is that iron oxide used in the manufacture of tiles was previously produced from poor-quality scrap metal. Braas now 'imports' iron oxide from Western Germany and the quality of the product has improved dramatically.

In a move to improve efficiency it has installed an IBM computer to process sales invoices and accounts at its head office at Halle which looks after the East German operations. Staff who previously dealt with accounts manually were trained during the summer to use the equipment and cope with new financial procedures.

At present it is impossible to link computers at all four plants as there are insufficient telephone lines in Eastern Germany to transmit financial data electronically. On average there are just 7 lines for every 100 people.

The postal system is also poor. Mail can take seven days to travel just 21 km, says one Braas manager. A money order from Frankfurt to Halle took the best part of a month to be processed.

During the summer the company took groups of its Eastern German employees to work at its plants in Western Germany to enable them to be trained.

Braas has twinned certain of its Western German plants with Eastern German factories to assist with re-education and to act as a first port of call for assistance if problems emerge this means that difficulties do not always have to be referred upwards to an overstretched head office.

As part of this programme, East German managers have been shadowing executives at their twinned factories in the West in order to learn new management, technical and financial skills.

Braas says its biggest problem has been to find salesmen. 'Factories never had to try to sell their produce. Lorries just came and took it away. There was no concept of marketing,' says Gerlach.

The company will need to overcome all of these problems if it is to compete with other West German roofing specialists which have already begun to export to the East.

Half of all roofing sales this year have been supplied by Western German manufacturers, sales from Eastern German factories, therefore, are 20 per cent of what they were a year ago.

Redland says Eastern Germany eventually could contribute about 30 per cent of Braas' sales and profits. It argues that an entry cost of just DM 25m has provided a platform for a business with the potential to make twice that amount in annual profits.

NOTES ON CONTRIBUTORS

The contributors to The *Financial Times* on Management are:

JAMES BUXTON, Scottish Correspondent
STEVEN BUTLER, Tokyo Correspondent
ALAN CANE, Computer Industry Correspondent
CHARLES BATCHELOR, Growing Business Correspondent
ALAN CLEMENTS, former finance director of ICI and presently non-executive chairman of David S Smith plc
NORMA COHEN, Investments Correspondent
CLIVE COOKSON, Science Editor
MARTIN DICKSON, Head of New York office
JOHN GAPPER, former Labour Editor, now member of Financial staff
JOHN GRIFFITHS, Motor Industry Writer
SIMON HOLBERTON, former Management Correspondent, now Hong Kong Correspondent
GUY DE JONQUIERES, Consumer Affairs Editor
LOUISE KEHOE, Technology Correspondent, San Francisco
DAVID LASCELLES, Natural Resources Editor
CHARLES LEADBEATER, former Industrial Editor, now Head of Tokyo office
RODERICK ORAM, Company News Editor
IAN RODGER, former Head of Tokyo office, now Zurich Correspondent
MICHAEL SMITH, Labour Correspondent
ANDREW TAYLOR, Construction Correspondent
MAGGIE URRY, Senior Companies Correspondent
DAVID WALLER, Frankfurt Correspondent
RICHARD WATERS, Securities Industry Correspondent
LISA WOOD, Labour Staff

INDEX